Praise for *Miracle Brew*

'Entertaining, engaging, and simply fun, *Miracle Brew* offers a kaleidoscopic portrait of beer through the prisms of hops, barley, water, and yeast. Pete Brown takes us on an experiential romp through the world of beer, full of topsy-turvy adventures. Put down your scientific journals and remind yourself what beer is really all about.'

— **Charlie Papazian**, author of *The Complete Joy of Homebrewing*; founder, Great American Beer Festival

'When Pete Brown describes something, you feel you've explored it yourself. Whether it is an investigation of Maris Otter barley or a visit to Carnivale Brettanomyces, he conveys the feel, the facts, and the findings in a way that's concise yet satisfyingly complete. *Miracle Brew* enlivens the exploration of beer's foundational ingredients with colorful details drawn from diverse experiences. Brown's take will certainly nurture fascination among those new to the territory, but veteran beer fans will also find plenty of new information and insights. For both, Brown's thoughtful writing makes any dip into this work rewarding.'

— **Ray Daniels**, founder and director, Cicerone Certification Program

'Pete has an enthusiasm for his subject matter that is both hugely entertaining and highly infectious, particularly when — true story! — he climbs behind the wheel of a combine to harvest a field of malting barley! You may think that you "get" beer, all its ingredients and processes, but by the end of *Miracle Brew* he will have you marveling at how little you fully understood.'

— **Stephen Beaumont**, coauthor with Tim Webb of *Best Beers* and *The World Atlas of Beer*

'In a spirited, engaging romp through the confines of the *Reinheitsgebot,* the German Beer Purity Law of 1516, Pete Brown pulls apart and examines the four essential ingredients of late-medieval Bavarian lager beer: barley, water, hops, and yeast, which was first observed in the seventeenth century. Earlier European medieval ales, flavored with *gruit* herbs such as bog myrtle, yarrow, and meadowsweet, stepped aside to make way for the hop invasion. To the delight of modern craft brewers, Pete then deftly puts these seemingly simple constituents back together again to produce a thirst-quenching finished product.'

— **Patrick E. McGovern**, author of *Ancient Brews* and *Uncorking the Past*

'Pete Brown is my favorite kind of person — an intellectual hedonist. In this exceptionally engaging and informative book, he lays bare his gleeful pursuit of knowledge into what makes us humans vigorously pursue our passions for the good things in life. I've read a lot of beer books; this one tops them all for the sheer thoroughness in which the art, history, science, and plain old enjoyment of this most complex of beverages is explored.'

— **Jereme Zimmerman**, author of *Make Mead Like a Viking*

Other Books by Pete Brown

Man Walks into a Pub:
A Sociable History of Beer

Three Sheets to the Wind:
One Man's Quest for the Meaning of Beer

Hops and Glory:
One Man's Search for the Beer
that Built the British Empire

Shakespeare's Local:
Six Centuries of Everyday Life
Seen Through One Extraordinary Pub

World's Best Cider:
Taste, Tradition and Terroir,
from Somerset to Seattle

The Pub:
A Cultural Institution —
from Country Inns to Craft Beer Bars
and Corner Locals

The Apple Orchard:
The Story of Our Most English Fruit

PETE BROWN
MIRACLE BREW

Hops, Barley, Water, Yeast and the Nature of Beer

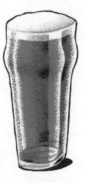

Chelsea Green Publishing
White River Junction, Vermont

Originally published in the United Kingdom
by Unbound in 2017.

This edition published by
Chelsea Green Publishing in 2017.

Project Manager: Alexander Bullett
Project Editor: Michael Metivier
Proofreader: Angela Boyle
Indexer: Linda Hallinger
Designer: Melissa Jacobson

Printed in the United States of America.
First printing September 2017.
10 9 8 7 6 5 4 3 2 1   17 18 19 20 21

Chelsea Green Publishing is committed to preserving
ancient forests and natural resources. We elected to
print this title on 100-percent postconsumer recycled
paper, processed chlorine-free. As a result, for this
printing, we have saved:

62 Trees (40' tall and 6-8" diameter)
28 Million BTUs of Total Energy
5,314 Pounds of Greenhouse Gases
28,821 Gallons of Wastewater
1,929 Pounds of Solid Waste

Chelsea Green Publishing made this paper choice
because we and our printer, Thomson-Shore,
Inc., are members of the Green Press Initiative,
a nonprofit program dedicated to supporting
authors, publishers, and suppliers in their efforts
to reduce their use of fiber obtained from
endangered forests. For more information, visit:
www.greenpressinitiative.org.

Environmental impact estimates were made using the Environmental Defense Paper
Calculator. For more information visit: www.papercalculator.org.

Our Commitment to Green Publishing
Chelsea Green sees publishing as a tool for cultural change and ecological stewardship. We strive to
align our book manufacturing practices with our editorial mission and to reduce the impact of our
business enterprise in the environment. We print our books and catalogs on chlorine-free recycled
paper, using vegetable-based inks whenever possible. This book may cost slightly more because it
was printed on paper that contains recycled fiber, and we hope you'll agree that it's worth it. Chelsea
Green is a member of the Green Press Initiative (www.greenpressinitiative.org), a nonprofit coalition of
publishers, manufacturers, and authors working to protect the world's endangered forests and conserve
natural resources. *Miracle Brew* was printed on paper supplied by Thomson-Shore that contains 100%
postconsumer recycled fiber.

Library of Congress Cataloging-in-Publication Data
Names: Brown, Pete, 1968– author.
Title: Miracle brew : hops, barley, water, yeast and the nature of beer / Pete Brown.
Description: White River Junction, Vermont : Chelsea Green Publishing, 2017.
  | Includes bibliographical references and index.
Identifiers: LCCN 2017031092| ISBN 9781603587693 (pbk.) | ISBN 9781603587709 (ebook)
  | ISBN 9781603587822 (audiobook)
Subjects: LCSH: Beer.
Classification: LCC TP577 .B755 2017 | DDC 663/.42 – dc23
LC record available at https://lccn.loc.gov/2017031092

Chelsea Green Publishing
85 North Main Street, Suite 120
White River Junction, VT 05001
(802) 295-6300
www.chelseagreen.com

MIX
Paper from
responsible sources
FSC® C013483

To Liz,
who now drinks beer
even when I'm not there.

CONTENTS

ONE

The Nature of Beer

'Miracles are a retelling in small letters of the very
same story which is written across the whole world
in letters too large for some of us to see.'

C. S. LEWIS, *MIRACLES*, 1947

1. Keeping Up with the Lads

A friend of mine works for one of the UK's biggest brewers. They make some very nice beers, and one or two really special ones, but their main product – the one that pays everyone's wages and pension contributions – is one of the biggest standard lager brands in the UK. It's adored by those who drink it, but regarded with disdain both by people who see themselves as knowledgeable and passionate about beer and by those who don't care for beer at all. It's the kind of beer that's often referred to as 'cooking lager', synonymous with the British 'lad' culture that peaked in the mid-1990s, and was characterised by men enjoying a prolonged or even revived adolescence characterized by beer, football and having a good time with their mates.

In those days, this beer and its competitors were seen (by the lads if no one else) as smart and funny, with great ads on the telly that were all about the good times, big logos at Premiership football matches, and pictures of bad–boy rock stars in the newspapers with their arms round each other at some festival, peace sign on one hand, tin of lager in the other.

But these days, laddism has lost its golden lustre, and the beers that were associated with it have started to seem a little too crude for our metrosexual modern world. Don't get me wrong, they're still the biggest sellers in the UK and are still enjoyed by groups of men watching football down at the local pub (or increasingly, at home on their plasma screen TVs), but for the twenty-first-century lad, who doesn't really think of himself as a lad any more anyway, come to think of it, it's not necessarily the drink you want to be brandishing on your first date with Emma from the accounts department, or the quiet pint with your boss to discuss your first serious promotion.

So this lager, along with most others like it, has been looking for a change of image. It wants people to see it now as more of a quality, premium product. If it saw itself in the mid-nineties as a party animal with a Britpop, pudding-bowl haircut and simian gait, by the second decade of the twenty-first century it wanted drinkers to see it as some combination of George Clooney and Professor Brian Cox.

Which is why my friend found himself behind the two-way mirror familiar to anyone who has worked in marketing, watching a focus group of young beer drinkers respond to ideas for new ads that were being shown to them by a moderator.

This new campaign was designed to appeal to people who rejected the lager, to persuade them that maybe it was better than they'd always thought. As a precaution, they were also showing the ideas to people who already drank it, just to make sure nothing changed their mind about the beer they loved. So here were the lads, preening and jockeying for position in the emerging dynamics of the group, being shown posters that focused on the ingredients of the beer in question. The lead poster was very simple: a background of clear blue sky and golden fields shining in the sun, and in the foreground a strong, manly hand gripping a dew-frosted pint, hoisting it from the field into the sky, a gender-reimagined Lady of the Lake brandishing a modern Excalibur, illuminated by a very simple line, no gag, no clever wordplay, just a statement of fact:

MADE WITH 100% BRITISH BARLEY.

'Ugh,' said the lads, 'I don't want *plants* in my beer. Can't you go back to making it with chemicals like you always used to?'

2. Chemical Fizz

This story, which is true, illustrates how most of us have looked at beer – whether we drink it or not – over the last forty years or so. Beer is honest, down-to-earth, democratic and approachable, and that's what makes it so appealing. Sit down over a beer and it removes hierarchies, uncomplicates situations and liberates us from reserve. But that can easily flip over into regarding beer as common and unsophisticated, a simple commodity that's less important than the great times that happen around the drinking of it. Beer itself is often an afterthought, taken for granted even by the people who love it. The oddest thing about beer – and there's much that's odd about beer – is that even some of its most ardent drinkers are not only unaware of what it's made of, they don't actually seem to care.

The 'chemicals' line is one that's often thrown at industrial beer as an accusation, but it can also be part of beer's perceived appeal. In *The Football Factory*, the frequently misunderstood* author John King writes, 'the lager tastes like heaven. Cold and sharp against the throat. Chemical bubbles brewed quickly for lager louts', which manages to make it sound appealing – in context, and to my ears at least. That moment King describes is referred to more diplomatically by the beer industry as 'first-pint refreshment', and for the lager drinker nothing else quite beats it. The anticipation of that prickly hit, a sensation that comes close to delicious pain if you drink quickly enough, is what keeps you going through a day of hard toil, and beer as reward remains one of the fundamental tropes of lager advertising around the world.†

Sometimes you can destroy the magic of a thing by taking it apart to see how it works. Part of the appeal of beer is its straightforward simplicity. Would it spoil that first-pint perfection to be thinking about what's actually in the glass? Does the simple dismissal of 'chemicals' actually help preserve some magic?

Maybe. For some of us, some of the time. But I still think the extent of our collective ignorance about beer is strange. The '100% British barley' campaign ended up running on the sides of bus shelters. The brewer received complaints from loyal fans saying the beer no longer tasted as good now they were brewing it with barley. But it has always been brewed with barley – it's just that people didn't know until they saw the posters.

Unless I'm talking to a fellow beer geek, it's very unusual to find someone who knows the main ingredients of the beer they're drinking. Pretty much anyone who has been in contact with them knows that bread is made from wheat, wine is made from pressed grapes, cheese is made from milk and

---

* Misunderstood – usually by people who haven't read him – as part of the English football hooliganism glorification/exploitation scene of the nineties, King's books are actually powerful studies of working-class male relationships and the disaffected alienation that informs them.

† Even now, after years of beer exploration and with a cellar and two refrigerators full of luscious, aromatic IPAs, barrel-aged stouts, Belgian Trappist ales and sharp, sour red ales, and with an informed appreciation of what makes them so special, and in the certain knowledge that drinking straight from the bottle rather than a glass means I lose the aroma and therefore a good deal of the character of a beer, if I've been doing physical work, an ice-cold lager downed from the bottle neck is still the only thing that will do.

cider is made – in theory at least – from crushed apples. But ask someone what beer is made out of – and I've done this a lot – and the most popular answer is 'Um . . . hops?'

OK, but what are hops?

'I haven't a clue.'

Anything else?

'What, you mean as well as hops?'

Yes.

And a much smaller group of people will say, 'Blimey, er . . . *wheat?*'

Well, sometimes, but it's not one of the main ingredients.

Then, with recovering certainty, the third and final guess will invariably be, 'Chemicals.'

I spend most of my professional life persuading people to drink beer, and to drink better beer. I do this because I'm passionate about beer myself, about its history, its cultural significance, its power to bring people together and make things better, and also about the incredible variety and complexity of flavours and sensations you can get in the glass. Increasingly, I'm not alone. Beer is undergoing a renaissance, and even people who never drank it before are realising that there's more to beer than John King's chemical bubbles brewed for lager louts. Beer is capable of outstanding beauty, grace and elegance. There are beers that belong in champagne flutes or brandy balloons rather than pint glasses. The right beer can feel comfortable on the fine dining table as well as in the pub snug. At a time when many people are increasingly concerned or just curious about where their food and drink comes from and what's in it, the ignorance around beer seemed increasingly odd. And then, a few years ago, I found myself in a hop garden where I realised that my own knowledge was limited, and that this had to change.

3. Of Sovereigns and Challengers

'What makes English hops so special is that their flavours are distinct – there are fruity and woody notes present – but no one note is predominant. The effect is that you want to have another drink of the same beer. There's no need to change to another brand.'

Dr Peter Darby loves hops. I thought I loved hops. But no one loves hops as much as Dr Peter Darby does.

'English flavour is like a chamber orchestra, the hops giving simultaneously the high notes and the bass notes. In comparison, a Czech beer is more like a full orchestra with much more breadth to the sound, and an American hop gives more of a dance band with more emphasis on volume and brass. The recent New Zealand hops, such as Nelson Sauvin, are like adding a voice to the instrumental music.'

See? I told you.

Peter Darby is one of the world's leading hop breeders and one of the public faces of the British Hop Association. Among his many duties he's the curator of the British National Hop Collection in Kent, where old varieties are preserved and new ones raised. Peter is a short, slight man with thick, wavy grey hair and a full moustache. When he talks about hops, his face lights up and his body fizzes with enthusiasm. He's not only excited about his subject; he's thrilled with any opportunity to share his passion.

The National Hop Collection is spread across two farms near Canterbury and Faversham. This one, at Queen Court Farm, takes up an acre of land and is paid for by local brewer Shepherd Neame. There are 250 different hop varieties planted here – the earliest dating back to the 1700s; the latest, Sovereign, named in 2010. The tufty, springy grass is soft beneath our feet. The hops grow on bines – long, vegetal ropes that twist around coconut strings and rise in curtains either side of us – growing in thick columns up towards taut wires running along the field about twenty feet above the ground. Stand between two of these rows and look down the tunnel they form, and it's like nature has tried to create an ornate passageway to some sun king's palace, a green Versailles. I half expect a faerie trumpet blast to summon me from the other end. Has a production of *A Midsummer Night's Dream* ever been staged in a hop garden? It should be.

It's not just the way they look; the smell of a hop garden creates a heady atmosphere. 'All the aromas of the field come into the beer,' Peter is saying, as if reading my mind. I drift away, enraptured by the hops themselves. The varieties here were chosen to help 'understand the heritage of the British hop industry', and I'm immediately fascinated by the range. A hop flower is bright green, shining against the darker leaves of the plant. It's fat at its base, where it hangs upside down by a stalk, and on the bine it tapers down to a point in layers of overlapping, scaly leaves. Some varieties are short and heart-shaped. Others are long fingers, almost like okra. The Fuggle – one of the two most famous British aroma hops – has a long, square cone, and takes its name from the man who allegedly discovered it (but quite possibly didn't) growing as a chance seedling in 1861, before it was cultivated and released commercially in 1875.

At Peter Darby's urging, we crush hop cones in our hands, rubbing them with the heels of our palms to release their essential oils, cupping our hands and breathing in deeply. The Fuggle is distinctly peppery, with notes of herbs and wild garlic. Sovereign is fresh and grassy. A new, experimental hop has vivid lemon and white pepper aromas.

Because this is a museum garden rather than a commercial farm, the hops have remained on the bine long past the time they should ideally have been picked. They're overripe, browner and yellower than they should be, but still impressive enough to quieten a group of brewers and journalists who've had a boozy lunch and were quite jocular on the bus on the way over here. The more Peter talks, the more reverential we become, standing amid the green cloisters. When these hops are finally harvested, the entire plant will be cut at the base and dragged down off the wires that support it. Now, the plants are top-heavy. Having climbed through late spring and early summer, twisting their way around coconut string to reach the wires, over the past two months they've bunched out and swelled in size. The bases of the bines, totally unable to support the weight of the plant without this elaborate structure of poles, string and wire, trail uselessly above the ground, so individual plants look like green ghosts floating through the air.

'Hops make beer uplifting,' Peter is saying. 'They interact with alcohol dehydrogenase in the body to give more of an effect. So for example if you compare Challenger and Admiral hops, you'll feel the alcohol more with Challenger.' And then he jumps straight from this to an explanation of how the surname 'Hopkins' came to be.

Like a ship's captain, I get the impression that Peter Darby is not quite happy unless he's here, in his element, at his station. He holds forth like a father presenting his talented children. And maybe the nautical analogy is not entirely random. Surrounded as I am by Challenger, Sovereign, Target and Admiral, it strikes me that hops are often named in the same spirit as ships of the Royal Navy, with as much heart-swelling pride and unconditional love.

I wonder why this is. Even now, enraptured by a hop field, I find it curious that hops came to be the poster ingredient for beer, the only ingredient most beer drinkers can name. It's not the first time I've thought this, and it's not the first time I've been around people who are admiring or even out-and-out *worshipping* hops.

There's been a change in my non-beery friends, too, as the craft beer revolution gathers pace. I get sent quite a lot of beer, more than I can drink, especially as I do most of my drinking away from home. Every year, we have a summer barbecue and a Christmas party where we ask people to bring anything they want except beer, and we try to clear my cellar. Ten years ago I would have to grudgingly go out and buy some mainstream lager because most people wouldn't touch the range of golden ales, best bitters, pale ales, porters and stouts I put out. Seven years ago, they were happily drinking those beers, even asking questions about them. For the past five years, those same drinkers have looked at the range of beers I've been sent, sniffed, and said, 'Haven't you got anything with Citra hops? Or Nelson Sauvin?'

Hops are working for beer in the same way a focus on grape varieties helped Britain and other traditionally beery countries fall in love with wine over the last thirty years. We may not know much, but we know our favourites. And I realise there's a story to be told about hops – about their cultivation, characteristics, varieties and flavours, and about people like Peter Darby who raise them and nurture them. Threads of different experiences I've had over the years – an insane hop festival in the Czech Republic, a hop expedition to Slovenia that turned into a horrible *Man v. Food* moment, a session rubbing and sniffing different hops with a brewer until my front was coated in green and yellow dust – suddenly tie together in my head.

And then I realise it's happening again: I'm being seduced by the glamour of the hop. It's one of four main ingredients in beer. Historically it's the most recent addition, and is, arguably, the only one of the four that you don't technically need in order to make beer. I want to praise the magic of hops. But I also want to put them in context, and shine a light on beer's other ingredients – the ones even my craft-beer drinking, Citra-loving party guests struggle to name. Because while hops possess all the glamour in both the modern and ancient sense of the word, there's magic in beer's other three primary ingredients, too.

4. Making Water More Interesting

Our ignorance about beer doesn't seem to be much of a barrier to most people who drink it, and there are an awful lot of them. But that's precisely why I find the lack of knowledge to be particularly bizarre – because beer is, by some distance, the most popular alcoholic beverage in the world.

As a species we drink more water than anything else. Between 60 and 65 per cent of an adult human's body weight is accounted for by water. We're losing it all the time, and if we don't replenish it we'll probably die within three to four days. But there are two problems with water. One is that to drink the required amount of two to three litres (three and a half to five pints) a day to remain fully hydrated can become a little monotonous. Second is that you can't always be sure your water supply is perfectly clean.

To solve the first issue, humans add things to water to make it taste more interesting. To solve the second, for thousands of years we've been in the habit of boiling water to sterilise it. Do both, and you can make tea and coffee – the two most popular drinks in the world after water itself. But for far longer than we've been making these hot beverages, we've been mixing water with an assortment of grasses, weeds and fungi to make beer.

We know and accept that tea is made by picking leaves from small bushes and steeping them in water, and coffee is made by picking beans that grow on shrubs, fermenting, roasting and grinding them and steeping them in water. But it probably comes as quite a shock to most drinkers to think of beer as grass, weeds, fungus and water.

I'll concede that 'grass, weeds, fungus and water' is perhaps not the most appealing description of beer you've ever encountered, and I could understand if, given that as an option, you felt more comfortable with the 'chemicals' narrative. But these are pretty special types of grass, weeds and fungus. And even the water is more than it seems.

The industrial aspect of brewing helps prevent the average drinker from associating beer with the same romance or exoticism as wine. Think of wine and you think of vineyards in Provence or Tuscany. Think of beer and the best you'll conjure up is a redbrick Victorian factory in an old industrial town. The process of beer making – the diagram laid out in every book and chalked up on every craft beer bar and tap room wall – doesn't lend itself to fascination and wonder. But the ingredients – the seemingly ordinary, natural substances that make beer – are each miraculous, individually and collectively.

5. Miracle Brew

Grass, yeast, fungus and water are brought together by what is, to many, the greatest miracle of all: fermentation. Yeast loves to eat sugar. When it does, it reproduces at a rapid rate, and produces alcohol and carbon dioxide as by-products. Sugar occurs naturally in nature, and, wherever it does, yeast will be there, trying to eat it.

This is a process that is carried out by organisms invisible to the human eye, was inexplicable until recently, and caused great arguments between the world's leading minds in biology and their opposite numbers in chemistry. The transformation of water into wine (or possibly beer if you examine the original language of the gospels) was the first miracle Jesus performed. For centuries, brewers referred to the mysterious catalyst of fermentation as 'godisgoode'.

Yeast needs sugar to produce alcohol. In grapes and other fruit, this sugar is relatively accessible from a microscopic predator's point of view, and their orgy of consumption and reproduction gives us wine, or cider. But beer is made from grain – usually barley – which is wise to the schemes of yeast and has built elaborate defences against it. Brewing beer starts with the collusion between man and microbe to trick barley into surrendering its sweet stash, and that process seems almost as miraculous as fermentation itself.

Brewing and fermentation – and the process of malting that precedes it – can't happen without the barley being submerged in water, and there's far more to this clear, seemingly pure substance than it merely being the medium that allows everything else to happen. While we might think of beer styles as being determined by the nature of the hops and barley that give it its flavour, water in any given region is shaped by the land it falls on and runs through, and has been instrumental in evolving our most important beer styles in the places where they emerged. Hops gain their allure by doing things no other plant can, but they can only do them for a brief time – their glamour begins to fade almost as soon as it appears. And finally the catalyst, yeast itself, doesn't just perform a miraculous feat: everything about its existence is awe-inspiring to both a microbiology novice such as myself and to people who have spent their lives studying it.

At the start of my journey through the ingredients of beer, I set aside everything I'd learned so far and approached it as if I knew nothing. I was right to do so. 'Raw materials' is what brewers call the stuff they make their beer from. That's understandable, but it does an injustice to the extraordinary amount of work and expertise involved in bringing each of these materials to the brewery door. All four of beer's basic ingredients are perfectly natural, but each one has been carefully modified, each subjected to a long history of scientific exploration. On a day-to-day basis, malted barley (grass), hops (weeds), yeast (fungus) and brewing liquor (yes, they even have a fancy word for water) are all subject to painstaking care and analysis, each kept in specialised, carefully controlled conditions.

There are miracles in each of beer's four key ingredients, and when you string these miracles together, the straightforward, supposedly simple drink that emerges is in fact an extraordinary cocktail of natural wonders and human ingenuity that is underrated even by its most ardent fans. And perhaps the greatest miracle of all is that we've been doing most of this for thousands of years longer than we've actually known what we're doing or why. We need to explore the origins of brewing and the processes that surround it in order to figure out how we harnessed the power of enzymes and microorganisms millennia before we knew they existed, and how we learned to influence genetics before we had the slightest idea what they were.

This book is split into four main sections, one for each of the primary raw ingredients. I've made it very easy for you to dip in and read first about the ingredient that interests you most, which is probably hops. But I wouldn't recommend that.

The order of the book follows the introduction of each ingredient to the brewing process. I'm not going to talk a great deal about that process, because this is not a book about how to brew beer. If you want to know more about that process, there's no substitute for seeing it in action.* This may well be a book about *why* we brew beer, in part, possibly. But it's mostly about the elements of beer, the processes and ingredients that come before the brewhouse. If you're a fan of superhero movies or comics, think of it as beer's origin story. If you cook at all, think of it like building a recipe in a saucepan. It wouldn't make much sense to think about adding the seasoning before you've even chopped your onions and garlic. In beer, as in any other form of cooking, we start from the base and build up. Each ingredient that's added works in relation to what's already there. And so we really have to start at the beginning: not just the beginning of the brewing process, but the beginning of brewing, and even the beginning of civilisation itself.

---

* Big breweries offer scheduled guided tours, but while these are interesting, you don't often get to see beer actually being made. If you know your local microbrewer you could always offer to 'help' at a brew day, which will mainly involve you digging out the mash tun. Some brewers and brewpubs offer brew days where you and your mates can be guided through the brewing process and make your own beer, which you can then collect and take home once fermentation and conditioning have been completed.

– TWO –

Barley

'Tradition is not the worship of ashes, but the preservation of fire.'

GUSTAV MAHLER, quoted on the website of Schlenkerla, the Bamberg brewer of smoked beer

1. Science and Magic

I'm a firm believer in magic. But rather than it being the action of super-natural beings, I just think there's stuff that obeys laws of science and nature that we haven't yet discovered. And while in some cases such laws may have been worked out by certain rather clever members of the human race, if you're not aware of their work, or you don't understand it, the phenomena they describe can still seem magical. To explore the miracles of brewing, I need to address my relative ignorance of science.

At school I passed my O levels in chemistry, biology and (eventually) physics, but I always saw these subjects as quite dull compared to the arts. I was one of those bedroom-bound teenagers who saw in literature, music and black-and-white films with subtitles something deeper and more profound than my mundane existence, whereas science – the way we were taught it at any rate – reduced the world to elements and equations, hard and incontrovertible, with no room for dreaming or escape. Until now, my interest in beer has always focused around its cultural and social roles, its history, the way it brings us together, how we use it to help define who we are. I really wasn't as interested in how it was put together or what it was made from. And that was my loss.

I was completely wrong about science, as anyone who has thought properly about it for more than ten minutes knows perfectly well. If you want to see wonder, if you want to contemplate the miracle and meaning of existence, the stuff that lies behind those seemingly dull equations and observations offers as much beauty, as much emotion, as much awe, as the first Smiths album playing on a tinny stereo system in a smelly teenage bedroom. Some would argue even more.

The benefit of my ignorance is that, as a middle-aged adult, I'm enjoy-ing learning about science with such a naïve, childlike amazement that I'm almost glad I left it so late. It's making me feel young again. Obviously, I have a lot of catching up to do.

It starts with biochemistry. Our eventual unravelling of the magic of alcohol was delayed by the fact that biology and chemistry look at the world in quite different ways. It was only by looking at both that people were finally able to explain the process of fermentation, by which yeast ingests sugar and excretes alcohol and carbon dioxide.

This is one of the simplest and oldest biochemical processes on the planet. It's possibly the most miraculous fact in this or any other book about drink, and we'll be raising a glass or three to it later on.

But before that transformation is possible, you need the sugar itself. Sugar is one of the most important substances in nature. The competition for it, the complex interplay of plants, animals and microscopic fungi, ultimately gives us alcohol. So to fully understand fermentation we have to start with the source of that sugar. The kind of plant it comes from is the basis of the distinction between beer and other drinks.

Plants absorb water and carbon dioxide, and with the helping hand of sunlight and a few enzymes* convert these into oxygen and sugar, via the process of photosynthesis. The basic, high school version of this process is summarised as follows:

$$\text{Carbon dioxide + water} \xrightarrow{\text{light energy}} \text{glucose + oxygen}$$

When you express this in the chemical symbols for each:

$$CO_2 + H_2O \xrightarrow{\text{light energy}} C_6H_{12}O_6 + O_2$$

the miraculous notion of being able to create sugar out of water and thin air makes a bit more sense because you can see photosynthesis is merely reconfiguring a collection of carbon, hydrogen and oxygen atoms. But there's nothing 'mere' about it. This simple equation is the source of all the sugar in the world. It's how plants live, and it starts the food chain that keeps animals alive. Run the programme for long enough, and the plants that don't get eaten ultimately become the source of all our fossil fuels, too.

This means the demand for sugar in nature often exceeds supply. This may be hard to believe when you look at the ever-expanding waistlines of

---

* We'll get to enzymes and explore them in more detail on page 20, but for now think of enzymes as biological agents of change, the catalysts that make stuff happen in nature.

the developed world, but sugar in nature is a scarce resource and, historically, the most sugary foods are the hardest to obtain and the most difficult
to make. The domestication and refining of sugar goes back thousands of
years, but in the West we've only been adding refined sugar to everything
since the eighteenth century.

Plants create sugar so that they can grow, and, at certain stages, so they
can make fruit or seeds to give birth to new plants that ensure the survival
of the species. A new seed cannot photosynthesise and create its own energy
until it has grown leaves or shoots, and, usually, roots to anchor it in place
and draw other nutrients from the soil. So the parent packs up its seed with
an abundant source of sugar to help the baby plant survive and grow until
it's big and strong enough to create its own sugar.

There's an important difference in how grain and fruit do this.
Sometimes, the fruit or kernel surrounding the plant embryo has a cleverly
customised role. If you're a tree, you don't want your kids settling too close
or else you'll soon be competing for nutrients and sunlight. So, many fruits
have evolved a symbiotic relationship with animals. They attract wandering beasts or insects with sugary, aromatic flavour compounds. Animals
find the fruit nutritious to eat, then carry the indigestible seeds away from
the tree and deposit them in a fertile pile of manure some distance away.

If this doesn't happen quickly enough, microorganisms will swoop in,
and, when the fruit starts to rot, they'll claim the sugar for themselves.
Yeast is everywhere, especially in hot summers when fruit is ripening, and
it's always ready to claim vulnerable parcels of fermentable sugars. When it
digests sugar it creates carbon dioxide and alcohol as by-products, a process
which we refer to as fermentation. This is a wonderful result for humans
and other higher order mammals, but not so great for the seeds that are left
on the floor to die without their food parcels.

Grain is, in some ways, much cleverer than fruit, and has built sophisticated defences against yeast. Because it's smaller and lighter, it can be blown
by the wind and doesn't need as much distance from the parent plant, so
it doesn't have to put itself on show the same way apples or cherries do.
And that means it can be smarter about how it packages the sugar for its
offspring. Grains such as barley are like armour-plated, souped-up alternatives to fruit. A grain kernel, when it is ready to leave the plant, has a
skin so hard no microbe or insect can get through it – even humans have

to employ stone or metal mills if we want to crush the outer shell of a grain efficiently. And even if we succeed in doing that, the fuel within has further levels of protection: it's stored not as simple sugar, but as long-chain starch molecules that are too big for microorganisms to attack. If a sugar molecule is a brick, starch is a wall. When the unstoppable force of yeast meets the immovable object of mature barley grains, nothing happens.

And so, some of the simplest and some of the most complicated organisms on Earth form an unholy alliance to separate the barley embryo for its sugary stash. Humans harvest and modify the grains to allow yeast to attack the sugars, and in return the yeasts create the alcohol humans love. Of course, the yeast can't even know of or comprehend the existence or role of its human partners in crime. And for most of the time we've been doing this we've had no idea we were collaborating with yeasts either. We were in an alliance in which neither party knew the other existed. While on the human side we sort of knew what we were doing, we had no idea how, or why, it worked. We've been converting barley by 'malting' it before brewing for thousands of years. We've known why we're doing so for less than two hundred.

2. Modification

This is the basic difference between wine (or cider), made from fruit, and beer, made from grain. Mash up some grapes or apples and, in the crudest way, wine and cider will make themselves. To make beer, grain needs to be 'modified', and to make that happen we influence the behaviour of the enzymes in the grain.

When I announced that I was writing a book about the four ingredients of beer, one brewer told me he felt that enzymes were the fifth. Enzymes are biological catalysts that help convert certain molecules into different molecules, thereby allowing cells to metabolise at a rate fast enough to support life. They don't really change the result; they just make it happen much, much faster. There are thousands of different types – the human body contains at least 2,700 – and we'd be dead without them. We use them to digest food (and alcohol), to replicate our DNA, to regulate the body, even to make our muscles move. Outside the body, we use them in everything from biofuel manufacture to laundry detergent. And in barley grains, when the time is right, they dismantle the sugary bricks from their starchy wall.

Although scientists began to work out that some kind of secretions helped break down food in the late seventeenth and early eighteenth centuries, it wasn't until 1833 that French chemist Anselme Payen discovered the enzyme diastase, by analysing a solution of brewing malt. Diastase (now more commonly known as a range of amylases) breaks down starch into smaller, simpler sugars like fructose and, in barley's case, maltose.

When a barley grain is ready to germinate, it releases amylases to convert stored starch into the simple sugars the embryo needs to grow. That hard shell softens so that the seed can sprout rootlets, and if some bastard were to intervene at this point, taking the germinating seed out of its cosy, natural environment, they could manipulate the process and trick the enzymes into converting all that sugar so yeast could finally have its way. Beer is born in savage conflict. There are casualties.

I've just explained the relationship between fermentable sugar in nature, the basic biochemistry of fermentation by microorganisms, the storing of energy as starch molecules in barley, the conversion of starch to sugar during germination, and the hijacking of that process as the basis of beer fermentation. It's pretty complex stuff. And yet we've been doing it for over ten thousand years. And for over 98 per cent of this time we've known absolutely nothing about enzymes, starch or yeast. So how on earth did early brewers figure out what to do?

3. Beer and the Dawn of Civilisation

When you get down to it, the basis of our civilisation is grass. Crop grass down to the ground and it will grow back more vigorously than before, so if you're farming cattle, so long as the rains come, you have an infinite food supply for them that you need do little to replenish. But the basis of organised farming – the trigger for the transition from a subsistence-based, nomadic existence to one where only a small number of us need to work to provide food, so the rest of us can get on with creating art, philosophy, poetry, football, Facebook, warfare and beer – is the noble grasses we call cereals: wheat, millet, oats, maize, rice and barley. One or more of these grasses is at the base of every civilisation in the world.

Before we cultivated any plants, we gathered them in the wild. Human beings tens of thousands of years ago were just as smart as we are now, but learning about how the world worked was painstakingly slow and took thousands of generations.

We have no idea when our ancestors figured out that gathered grain, if not eaten straight away, could start to sprout in the right conditions. In his book *Plants in the Service of Man*, written in 1971, Edward Hyams reckoned it was around 6000 BCE, because, at the time of writing, early tools such as sickles had been found that dated back to that period. Since then, carbon-dating techniques and new excavations have been able to push that back by at least another 6,000 years. Whenever it was, it seems to have been thousands of years earlier than the propagation of vines or fruit trees by primitive grafting techniques.

There is, of course, a big difference between cultivating grains as seeds to eat and processing those grains to make them into something else. Understanding the nutritional value of grasses is not the same thing as switching from a nomadic to a settled existence. Even after we understood the principles of agriculture, we could (and probably did) plant cereal fields in different locations, knowing we had stashes of food ready all across the routes of our nomadic peregrinations. The first towns – and the first farms that supplied them – emerged as the result of a desire to make grain into something else rather than just eat it straight away.

A constant, steady supply of food and drink is at the very heart of most early mythologies and religions, from the Garden of Eden planted with every tree that bore fruit that was good to eat, to the ancient Greek notion of the Happy Isles, where fruit trees were heavily laden all year round.

If gathered and stored, plants will eventually either rot away as micro-organisms break them down, or sprout into new plants. Pretty much every significant innovation in food – cooking, baking, drying, salting, pickling and fermenting – arose in large part as a way of preserving food beyond its natural shelf life. Agriculture didn't develop in isolation: in the lands known as 'the Fertile Crescent', which stretched across the Middle East and had a climate quite different from that of today, humans were able to graze and hunt just fine without it, gathering grain, lentils and chickpeas as they grew wild. Agriculture developed because we wanted to transform and store foods, to ensure a steady supply, as a labour-saving exercise – and ultimately, to improve upon and refine the flavours nature offered.

Barley

The earliest domesticated grains were wheat and barley. The earliest transformations of those grains were into bread and beer. The question that pre-
occupies many archaeologists is, which came first? At the moment, there are
strong arguments either way. Of course I *want* to believe that beer came before
bread – and I argued as much in my first book, *Man Walks into a Pub*. Bread is
often assumed to be far more nutritious than beer, but beer is a good source of
carbohydrates and vitamins. And, of course, alcohol also intoxicates and that's
a very pleasant feeling, and an aspect of history that's often overlooked because
it seems less serious than staying alive, inevitably frivolous in a profound debate
about our survival and development as a species. And yet alcohol and intoxication were central to many ancient religious ceremonies, and remain so in many
cultures around the world – not least the Catholic Holy Communion.

But brewing requires a great deal more than simply a source of fermentable grain. You need pottery in order to store the grain, to mix it with water
and to allow it to ferment. You need a mill, or at least a mortar and pestle, to
grind the grain. And you need the right temperatures for yeast to be happy to
work. When you take all these into account, they appear in the archaeological record at roughly the same time, around 7000 BCE. It would have been far
easier to make flat, unleavened bread from wheat than beer from barley. The
difficulties of modifying barley and getting it to ferment mean that some
crude forms of wine and mead were almost certainly made before beer.

Any attempt to account for the origin of brewing is, at best, informed
speculation. The standard hypothesis among beer historians is that someone
probably gathered some grain in a clay pot and accidentally left it in the rain
to get wet. The grain got mushy, yeast descended and the pot began to bubble.
Someone tasted it, liked it, and subsequently enjoyed a rather wonderful buzz.
But there's a huge flaw in this theory: without malting, the grain wouldn't
have converted starch to sugar, and no fermentation would have taken
place. That hypothetical accident may have produced a tasty, nutritious
gruel, but it would not have been alcoholic. It would not have been beer.*

---

* In 1993, Canadian palaeontologist and brewer Ed Hitchcock attempted to recreate the 'happy
accident' that might have given birth to beer. His plan was to soak some grain until it sprouted, then
pound it to a pulp, leave it to dry in the sun and then attract wild yeasts to ferment it. After no more
than a day of soaking, however, wild bacteria had infected the pot, which bubbled, grew mould and
gave off foul gases. So that's almost certainly not how beer first happened.

If the grains had been encouraged to sprout before going into this hypo-thetical pot, they would have become a 'green malt' that could have been fermented by wild yeasts. But for that to happen, the grain would have had to have been harvested and then given the right conditions to germinate, which would have involved it first being wet, then dry enough to sprout, and then for the sprouted grain to be immersed in water again. It sounds unlikely that all of this could have been purely accidental.

But there is another way. Amylases aren't just present in barley: they're the enzymes in human saliva that helps begin the digestion of food before it reaches the stomach. If you were to chew a mouthful of barley grains, you'd soften them and introduce the enzyme that begins the starch conver-sion without malting having to take place. In parts of Central and South America, *chicha* beer is still made by chewing mouthfuls of corn and spit-ting them out, forming them into slimy balls that are allowed to dry out while the enzymes go to work. Thrown into a traditional maize brew, these balls will then convert the starches to sugar ready for fermentation. In the early days of sake brewing, people did something similar with rice.

A few years ago, Sam Calagione of Dogfish Head Brewery in Delaware, along with Professor Patrick McGovern, the world's leading expert on ancient fermentation, and Dr Clark Erickson, an associate professor of anthropology at the University of Pennsylvania, attempted to make *chicha* the traditional way. They very quickly discovered that it helped if you ground the corn with a mortar and pestle before chewing. Even then, they found it labour-intensive and deeply unpleasant. If this really was the origin of fermentable cereals, the first brewers must have been looking for an alternative pretty much from day one.

That alternative was traditional floor malting. It's quite an involved pro-cess and requires careful attention to understand even today. How the first city-dwellers managed to figure it out 10,000 years ago is miraculous in itself.

Traditional floor malting consists of three stages. First, the grain is soaked in water to bring its moisture content up. Second, it's arranged in a bed on a flat floor to germinate and sprout. This malting floor is the defining characteristic of the traditional process and needs to be smooth and well ventilated. This is where the enzymes activate, ready to convert – or 'modify' – the starch to sugar, and break down the cellular walls of the starch into smaller bits. Finally, the germination of the grain has to be arrested, otherwise the modification will complete and the plant will use the sugar itself to grow. This is prevented by drying the malt, which now happens in a kiln, but could have been done – in the right climate – on hot rocks in the sun.

The success of the germination process depends on getting an even temperature spread, and keeping the rootlets from getting tangled into a big lump that would eventually rot. Both of these imperatives mean the bed of grain has to be turned at regular intervals on the malting floor – that's why this floor must be smooth and firm.

Smooth floors, often made of stamped earth or clay and sometimes using lime plaster – a labour-intensive and complex technology – have been discovered at various archaeological sites across the Fertile Crescent. These floors show signs of having been repaired multiple times, and appear to have served some specialised function. They're often accompanied by evidence of fire pits, hearths, sickles and grinding equipment and frequently have impressions of grains embedded in them. The oldest of these finds recently discovered have been dated to between 10,000 and 12,000 years old. This means we have strong circumstantial evidence of barley malting in some of the earliest permanent human settlements yet discovered. If we settled down not just to cultivate grain but also to modify it, as seems likely, then it's quite possible that malting barley was a key impetus in the establishment of permanent settlements.

4. The T-Word

As we're going to be talking about raw ingredients, we need to have a little chat about the T-word, so it's best that we do it now and get it out of the way.

Terroir is a French word that refers to soil in particular, but also climate, rainfall and the average sunlight a place gets, and how the combination of all of these factors affects the final flavour of food or drink made from ingredients grown in a particular place. The best English translation I've ever come across is 'land taste', which in many ways I prefer.

Terroir is linked with wine more closely than anything else, but it's also discussed very seriously in tea-plant growing. French winemakers use it to add value to their products, arguing that the character of grapes from a certain region, a certain vineyard, or even a certain slope within a given vineyard is determined by that specific location and can't be replicated anywhere else. It's such an important concept in winemaking that when Hugh Johnson wrote the first ever comprehensive overview of wine around the world in the early 1970s, he didn't call it a 'guide' or an 'encyclopaedia' of wine – as later beer guides were named – instead, he called it an *Atlas* of wine. He'd always liked maps, and this was a chance to combine two passions. Johnson found it impossible to write about the character of wine without also writing about the land it came from.

It's a romantic idea, and as such it has to endure close, and often cynical, scrutiny. It's been dismissed as marketing bollocks, part of the French propaganda machine that insists no other country can make wine so well. Then, when growers of other plants or makers of other drinks have tried to co-opt it, they've been regarded with scorn. For some winemakers, nothing else could be so noble as the grape, and exhibit the same land taste – after all, the whole concept is designed to elevate French wine above all else, so it's irksome for inferior drinks to jump on the bandwagon. And from the other side, *terroir* is a poncey French wine concept that doesn't sit well with honest, unpretentious beer or full-blooded, rustic cider.

It's difficult to argue specifically for *terroir* in beer because, unlike wine or properly made cider, beer is a collection of different ingredients, usually from different locations – the soil types and climates that grow hops well are not necessarily great for barley. Whereas a winemaker is stuck with a vineyard wherever that may be, a brewer has the choice of sourcing hops and barley from all over the world. She might brew one beer with hops from the Pacific Northwest of the United States and barley from Germany, and the next with barley from Norfolk and hops from Tasmania, and can still call herself a 'local' brewer whether she's based in Gloucestershire or Vermont.

But if we look at those ingredients in isolation, the concept of 'land taste' is as true for each of them as it is for French grapes. How could it not be? If the amount of sunlight and water, the temperature and the nutrients in the soil affect one type of fruit or grain, how could they not affect all of them? It's a matter of agricultural fact that crops grow better in conditions they prefer: that barley likes a certain type of soil, and that hops are remarkably sensitive to the amount of sunlight they get during the growing season, to name but two examples. The same variety of hops grown in Kent and

Washington State will produce dramatically different flavours. If that's not land taste, I don't know what is.

I suppose the question really being asked by those who populate the Venn diagram intersection between people who are sceptical about land taste and people who know anything at all about agriculture is not whether or not variations exist, but whether or not they're significant enough to have a profound effect on the finished product, especially with something mass-produced like beer, which often just 'tastes like beer' in the eyes (or rather the mouths) of many who drink it.

I think a brewer of any size would tell you, yes, it does. Big brewers go to great lengths *to get rid of* the effects of regional and year-on-year variation by blending ingredients to get the consistent delivery many drinkers expect. But as craft beer continues to redefine how the world perceives beer, those who believe in and champion land taste are now being heard.

5. The Way to Warminster

The Icknield Way is a perfect example of the conflict between two different approaches to history: on one side are the storytellers who seek to present a romantic version, full of great tales, deep meanings and grand narratives, and on the other stand those who insist on constantly questioning the evidence, sticking to known facts and discouraging speculation.

For the first group, the Icknield Way is the most ancient road in Britain. Already old by the time the Romans arrived, it was then used by the Anglo-Saxons to settle England, linking the ancient settlements of Salisbury and Bury St Edmunds on its route from the Wash in north Norfolk down to Dorset's Jurassic Coast, and was probably named by the Iceni tribe. For the latter, its antiquity was the invention of medieval revivalists confecting a history of England through which King Arthur and his knights rode. It wasn't mentioned in records before the tenth century, and, while parts of it are older, there's nothing to suggest a road running its whole length until the Middle Ages.

Either way, it's still incredibly old. It connects the otherworldly location of Seahenge in Norfolk with towns including Oxford, Cambridge and Swindon as well as the aforementioned Bury St Edmunds and Salisbury.

And however old it is, the defining characteristic of its entire length is that it follows a ridge of chalky soil that just happens to be the best terrain in Britain for growing barley.

The Icknield Series is a soil type that took its name from the path. It crops up on the East Yorkshire and Lincolnshire coast, sweeps across Norfolk and Suffolk and heads down through Hertfordshire into the Thames Valley. A tributary splits off and heads east, running across Surrey and Kent, but the main vein runs south-west across Hampshire and Wiltshire to the Dorset coast.

The topsoil is light and airy, while the alkaline, chalky subsoil stays cool through spring. This isn't great for some crops, but it's perfect for barley – especially varieties that are low in nitrogen, which is what brewers want. It's no coincidence that much of Britain's malting industry grew up near the farms along the Icknield Way.

Historically, it seems academics just don't like beer. As with so much in the history of brewing, the significance of barley farming and malting in broader British history has gone largely unrecorded. The possibility that ancient, smooth floors pitted with grain impressions might just have been evidence of prehistoric malting was mostly ignored by those who made the finds until others challenged them. While researching previous books, I was astonished to discover that brewing was second only to cotton in Victorian British industry, because this is scarcely mentioned in histories of the Industrial Revolution. When I spoke to Professor Steven Earnshaw, head of English Literature at Sheffield Hallam University, he told me he was mocked by his peers when he began writing a history of the pub in English literature, despite English literature having been born in a pub when Geoffrey Chaucer decided to begin the first great work written in the English language in a Southwark tavern. Beer is jolly and informal, seemingly unworthy of serious study.

When we think about arable farming and its importance to the economy, not to mention to the table, we invariably focus on wheat and bread. But for most of our history barley was by far the more important crop. In 1688, Gregory King created one of the first attempts to calculate crop yields across England and Wales, and estimated that 12 million bushels of wheat had been harvested, with a value of £2.1 million (approximately 327,000 tonnes, worth over £340 million today) while the barley harvest was 25 million bushels, with a value of £2.5 million (around 544,310 tonnes, worth

£405 million today). Across 11 million acres of viable arable land, barley was sown on 3.2 million acres, or 29 per cent of the total. While some barley was used for baking bread, the vast majority was used for malting and brewing, which we know because it was carefully measured as a source of excise duty. In 1776, Charles Smith estimated that the barley harvest had increased to 37 million bushels (805,579 tonnes) of which 8 million bushels were made into bread and 26 million were malted for beer. The barley harvest was bigger than all other cereal crops put together.* In his exhaustive *The Brewing Industry in England, 1700–1830*, Peter Mathias observes, 'John Bull, pewter pot in his hand and barley ears in his hat, stood for all the shires in England, whereas Hop Queens were crowned only in the most gentle of them.'

Maltings used to be an essential part of many breweries, given that brewing was small-scale and you can't make beer without malting barley. But malting is a labour-intensive and highly skilled process. While some large breweries maintained their own maltings well into the twentieth century, specialised maltings grew up alongside them. There's barely a town in Britain that doesn't have a shopping centre, dockside office-cum-artist studio space or residential cul-de-sac called 'The Maltings'.†

I learn about the Icknield Way at one of the few surviving maltings along its path. The small town of Warminster, west Wiltshire, nestles between Salisbury and Bath in the south-west of England, next to the sweeping chalk downland of Salisbury Plain. In 1720, there were thirty-six maltings here, and the quality of the malt they were producing had widespread fame; the Warminster market was the largest for barley in the south of England. In 1855, William Morgan designed and built a lean, efficient malting complex in Pound Street. As there are now no other competitors left from the thirty-six that preceded it, the Pound Street business is now known simply as Warminster Maltings. It's survived by luck and the dedication of a few individuals, who were inspired by its crucial role in the development of modern malting barley.

---

* More recently, wheat became more popular, and the yields from all crops have grown due to technology and the intensification of agriculture. In 2014, the UK (as opposed to England and Wales) grew 16.6 million tonnes of wheat and 7 million tonnes of barley.

† Yet another cliché in beer history is that even where we get rid of brewing, pubs and their associated crafts, we cling to their names, imagery and associations.

William Morgan passed on the Pound Street maltings to his son, who redesigned the place in 1879 and then in turn bequeathed the business to his younger brother-in-law, Edward Sloper Beaven.

Beaven took over the maltings at a time when scientific research in brewing was newly fashionable. The 1870s represent a technological revolution that changed the face (and taste) of beer forever. Beaven was clearly inspired by this age of discovery, and around the turn of the century he made his own contribution to it.

Barley breeding up to this point had been a refined process of 'unnatural selection'. These grasses were originally wild, but early farmers would take seeds from the best specimens and sow them in fields. They'd take the best seeds and sow them again, and so on, until strains of barley emerged that had been domesticated and showed desirable traits such as large seeds, good yield and resistance to disease. These trial-and-error named strains were known as 'landrace' varieties.

In 1826, a Suffolk labourer named Andrews planted some grains from a field in his garden, and cultivated a small patch of barley. His landlord, the Reverend John Chevallier, an amateur agriculturalist, noticed that they were unusually fine specimens and cultivated them further. Chevallier barley became the most famous variety in England, loved for its thin skin and plump grains.

The problem with Chevallier was that it was a product of its *terroir*. It was perfect in the soil in which it was raised, but behaved erratically when sown in different parts of the country. A good commercial barley isn't just about the size of the grains. It needs to be robust and resistant to pests and the vicissitudes of the British climate. The grains should have a good grip on the ear until harvest, and the straw has to be strong enough to stand up to a stiff wind. As well as the individual grains being high quality, you want a lot of them, to maximise the yield from a given plot. Chevallier was a malting barley of excellent quality, but the straw was weak and became brittle – you could lose the whole harvest in a heavy rain. Writing in 1936, Beaven recalled that bad harvests 'were more frequent in the eighties and nineties of last century than since ... [In 1879] much barley was lying in the fields in November, fit only for pig food.' And while Chevallier may have been the star, you didn't always know what you were getting. Different farmers in different regions would give different names to landrace varieties, and there was no overall classification.

Traditionally, malting was a winter activity carried out between October and May. During the summer, most of the men who worked in a maltings would work on farms, thatching and, later, gathering the harvest. Beaven spent his summers deep in research. He wrote to growers around the world to collect samples of barley from as far afield as he could. Initially in his garden and then in a four-acre plot at Boreham just outside Warminster, Beaven taught himself plant breeding and trialled the samples that looked most interesting.* He also began experiments in crossing the best varieties, carefully pollinating plants by brushing the pollen from one variety onto the stamen of another, then covering it to make sure no other pollination took place. He worked closely with William Gosset, a statistician and chemist with the Guinness brewery – a big customer of Warminster's – for ten years, breeding and trialling, searching for good, stable malting barley that gave brewers what they wanted but was also strong enough to grow consistently well.

In 1905, Beaven combined the strong, stiff straw of Archer with the high grain quality of Plumage to create Plumage Archer, the first ever genetically 'true' barley variety. Beaven tested Plumage Archer for a further ten years just to be sure. When he finally released it commercially in 1914, it transformed British barley farming. Plumage Archer provided more consistent quality, and the average yield was 20 per cent higher than the varieties it replaced. Plumage Archer instantly became the standard for British barley farmers, and remained so for the next forty years.

Beaven, the father of modern brewing barley, lived into his eighties, and his summation of his life's work was published posthumously, after he died in 1941. He left no heir, and Warminster Maltings was absorbed by Guinness, who used it as a research facility. As malting technology progressed, the traditional set-up at Warminster became increasingly outmoded, and in 1994 Guinness announced their intention to close it.

Chris Garratt, who had worked at Warminster since going for an interview in his school uniform in 1976, was one of a group of employees who engineered a management buyout. But the newly independent Warminster Maltings continued to struggle. In 2001, Robin Appel, a successful grain merchant who also owned the rights to a legendary barley variety, saw the

---

* Beaven's seeds still form the basis of the British national collection.

beginnings of a resurgence in interesting, flavourful beer and thought there was a future for the old ways of doing things. He bought Warminster, and, fifteen years later, he invited me for a tour.

6. Floor Malting

Robin Appel is a tall, expansive man with a big laugh and the easy-going confidence of someone who has been very successful but also has a genuine passion for his work. He wasn't expecting to discover such a rich heritage when he bought Warminster, and has written a book on the history of the place and Beaven's contribution to modern malting barley. Ever since he bought Warminster, he's been a man on a mission.

'The perception among brewers is that all malting barleys taste the same. Well they don't!' he booms as we climb into his Jaguar for the short drive from the train station to the brewery. To prove this, in 2007 Robin commissioned research on different varieties of barley. 'If winemakers could demonstrate the differences between Chardonnay and Pinot Grigio, and hop growers could define the peculiarities of Fuggles and Boadicea – then wasn't it about time that we should do the same for barley as well?' he says. A selection of eight barleys were made into porridges and tasted blind, and there was a clear difference between them. Maris Otter, the variety Robin now co-owns the rights to, was outstanding, but Tipple – a variety that was popular for pale ale malt at the time – had a harsh astringency to it. Sure, the malting process is key to what beer tastes like, but the quality of the raw ingredient makes a big difference, too. 'Mouthfeel and the shape of the beer on the palate are glorious attributes of beers, and this is affected by barley variety,' says Robin. 'To suggest, as many commentators do, that all barley varieties taste the same is utter nonsense.'

Warminster is now the oldest working maltings in the country. It's a long, low complex of chunky stone buildings with heavy bars across the windows (I soon find out why). And what beer lovers adore about it is that it still makes malt the traditional way, using the three-stage floor-malting process. It's still presided over on a day-to-day basis by Chris Garratt, the former schoolboy job applicant who helped secure the future of Warminster Maltings when Guinness called time on it.

Barley

Barley has a natural dormancy, and it's stored for six to eight weeks after harvest. When it arrives from the farm it's checked rigorously for impurities, disease and pests in Chris's laboratory, which is filled with a range of apparatus that seems to date from the present day back to the 1970s. 'You can't forget the non-technical assessment as well,' says Chris. 'The first test is smell. It should have no mould, and it should be sweet smelling. And it has to look right.'

At this stage the barley is rock-hard, its defences against predators intact. If you press it between thumb and forefinger as hard as you can, or try to slice into it with your thumbnail, you get nothing except a deep impression in your own skin. The seed embryo is dormant at one end, with a stock of energy many times its size held behind it, like the fuel tanks on an Apollo rocket.

The basic principles of steeping, germination and kilning the way it's done at Warminster have hardly changed in centuries. Robin takes me to the steeping room to see the first part. Here, in an airy space of whitewashed stone, the barley is loaded into deep, open tanks that can hold as much as 10 tonnes of grain at a time. The grain is then completely covered with water. One of the tanks is full, and I can immediately see that part of what's happening here is a cleaning of the grain. The top of the tank has a thin layer of dust, flecks of straw and tiny, useless grains that give it a soupy appearance. But that's simply a by-product of the process. At the farm it will have been dried to around 14.5 per cent moisture. This is perfect for storage, but for germination the water content must be much higher. The 'first wet' lasts for up to twelve hours, and gets the moisture up to around 30 per cent. But being completely submerged in water deprives the grain of oxygen, which it also needs, so it's then drained and allowed to have an 'air rest' of twelve hours before being submerged again. The process is repeated three times and takes two to three days in total, by which time the moisture level should be up to 43–46 per cent and the grains will have 'chitted', meaning the rock-hard skin has softened and a rootlet has appeared.

Here, the maltster is playing a delicate game of cat-and-mouse with moisture and oxygen, because the process the grain wants to follow in order to grow is at odds with what we want for brewing. In a perfect world, the maltster and brewer would love to get the enzymes going, ready to break down the starches, without the seed germinating. But the plant didn't survive in nature this long by being stupid: it wants to modify the sugar only after the grain has sprouted, converting it only when the embryo needs it.

So the maltster allows the grain to get just enough oxygen to survive and germinate, but not enough for it to throw out its rootlets effectively.

After its repeated dunking and rest, the grain is transferred to the malting floors. This is what Warminster is famous for, and here the building has a curious design. The traditional method of getting barley to germinate is to spread it out in a bed three to four inches deep and pass warm air through it. The malting floors at Warminster are stacked on top of each other with very low ceilings. This allows workers to shovel malt from one floor up to the next, for it to be spread out, and for different floors to benefit from the same heat source at gradually lowering temperatures. The heat transfers through a network of holes in heavy floor tiles. The ones at Warminster are very carefully and beautifully designed, with patterns of seven dots orbiting one central dot, like petals around the heart of a flower. These holes need to be cleaned of dust and seeds at regular intervals, which I can only imagine must be a job that's reserved as punishment for anyone who doesn't rake the beds of malt properly. The long, low rooms are illuminated by small windows guarded by iron bars. This is a quirk that dates back to a time when beer was taxed not just on the finished product, but on its raw ingredients, too. At its peak, the tax on malt accounted for 11.6 per cent of all government revenue, and Customs and Excise men were regular visitors to the maltings. Maltsters would try anything to pay less tax, including shovelling malt out of the windows when the Excise men were in the building, and the windows were barred to prevent such nefarious practices.

The first floor we come to is carpeted in a deep bed of grain that's only been out for a few hours. 'People often refer to these floors as drying floors, but that's fundamentally incorrect,' says Robin. 'If you took moisture away at this stage, the grain would stop germinating. The moisture doesn't evaporate off here; it gets absorbed by the grain. You need to keep the moisture, with just enough oxygen to keep the germination going until all the starch has been modified.' The grains are damp and soft now to the touch, but when I squeeze one at Robin's bidding, while I can split the skin the starch is still rubbery and comes out in a thick, solid blob.

Now the enzymes get to work on breaking down the protein walls to release the starch. But they don't convert the starch to sugar just yet.

In its deep bed, with warm air passing up through holes in the floor below, the process of germination is producing carbon dioxide and heat, and the grain isn't getting quite enough oxygen to germinate fully. Because of the heat build-up, the grain on the floor has to be turned four times a day to ensure an even germination.

This part takes four to five days, and it's down to the skill of the maltsters to know when it's finished. Robin takes me up through floors of malt at different stages of germination. When we reach a floor where germination has almost finished, the malt has developed a soft cloud of hazy shoots. Robin urges me to once again take a grain and squeeze it between finger and thumb. Now, the starch bursts out and Robin shows me how to do one of the most important and widely used tests in the malting industry: if you can spread the starch across your thumb in a thin white smear, like corn flour, it's just about done.

Now we have 'green malt', which could in theory be used for brewing. But if we leave it like this, the embryo will still continue to sprout, use up the sugar and become useless to the brewer. Until now, it was essential to keep the embryo alive because all the changes in the grain were responding to its needs. Now, though, the starch has been fully modified. The seed embryo has outlived its usefulness, and must be taken out of the picture. We do this by kilning it.

The kiln room at Warminster is at the top of the building. Here, the malted barley is subjected to a carefully controlled temperature regime. We want to stop the seed from germinating, and to do that we need to kill the embryo. But if we heat it too aggressively we'll also kill the enzymes that we still need to convert the starch to sugar, and everything up to now will have been for nothing. We also want to dry the malt out, getting rid of the moisture we just spent days putting into it, so it can be stored. And finally, by carefully adjusting the temperature and flow of the hot air, and the time the malt spends in the kiln, we can dramatically alter the flavour it will eventually bestow on beer. In that respect, kilning malt is similar in some ways to the roasting of coffee beans for flavour. But in all but a few exceptional cases, it's a much gentler and more complicated process, because we want to keep those enzymes alive. The grains are dried and baked, but in most cases not quite roasted.

As the air moves through the room, it cools, and the cooling can be influenced by ventilation. The art of kilning is the knack of controlling the temperature at which the air enters the room, and the temperature at which it leaves. 'The air goes in at 70 degrees Celsius and comes off at 31 degrees,' says Robin (158 and 88 degrees Fahrenheit, respectively). 'The difference between those two temperatures is the profile that dictates the colour and flavour of the malt.' He invites me to stick my head in the kiln room. The air feels like a monsoon breeze, and is bearable only for a short time. But the cereal smell is wonderful and inviting.

Here at the end of the process we've pulled off one of the greatest heists in nature: tricking a plant with a seemingly invulnerable system for hanging on to its sugars into giving them up to us, and then killing it. But the kilning of the malt that gets rid of the embryo also changes the grain that's left behind, giving us not just fermentable sugar, but also the fundamental flavours of beer.

7. From Blonde to Black

Today, the colour of malt is measured using internationally agreed scales, the first of which was created by Joseph Williams Lovibond in 1883. Lovibond was the son of John Locke Lovibond, who started a brewery in the West Country of England in 1834 before moving to Greenwich, London, in 1847. Joseph initially tried his luck as a gold miner in South Africa while still a teenager, but accidentally lost his earnings by dropping them while leaning over the rail of the ship bringing him back to Britain – or that's his story anyway. On his return home, he joined his three brothers as partners in the family business.

Brewing at a time when clear glass had recently become readily available, he passionately believed that colour was a good indicator of the quality of beer, and was inspired after a visit to Salisbury Cathedral in 1880 to use coloured glass to measure it. In 1885, he founded a company, The Tintometer Limited, to manufacture his colorimeter, which he called the Lovibond Comparator. The company still exists and still makes an updated version of the Lovibond Comparator, which remains for me the most Victorian-sounding name for any scientific instrument.* Lovibond's coloured slides

---

* The Lovibond Comparator outlived the Lovibonds Brewery, which in 1959 ceased brewing and focused on being a wine merchant. In 1968, it was bought by a subsidiary of the London Rubber Co., manufacturers of Durex condoms. Happily, the name lives once more: in 2005 American brewer Jeff Rosenmeier opened the new Lovibonds Brewery in Henley-on-Thames. Jeff is a respected craft brewer and was one of the early British pioneers in the rediscovery of 'sour' beers.

could be held up next to each beer, so everyone agreed which slide was the closest and the colour could be tightly defined. There are limitations to this – not least the variations in vision among those looking at the slides – and while the Lovibond Scale is still commonly used, it's now more often measured by something called light spectrophotometer technology, which evaluates colour more objectively by measuring the composition of a substance relative to the wavelength of light that passes through it. Before Lovibond, colour was subjective. When brewing records and drinkers mention light beer, pale ale, dark beer or brown beer, these terms are relative and not really specific. Among nerdier beer historians, this has provided heated and at times hugely entertaining debates over such questions as what colour 'pale ale' really was in its heyday.

The colour (and a large amount of the flavour) in beer is dictated by what happens during the kilning process at the end of malting. If you expose the grain to enough heat, it doesn't just dry – it cooks. The Maillard reaction causes the amino acids to brown the sugars in the malt and create more complex and highly desirable (to the human palate) flavour compounds. At higher temperatures, caramelisation burns the sugars in the barley to give another layer of deeper, sweeter flavours. We're all familiar from coffee ads with the concept of 'a longer roast for a richer flavour', and the principles of kilning malt are very similar. In modern-day malting, a pale malt, once fully dried, is pleasant to crunch in the mouth. It has a slightly grainy character and a flavour that's reminiscent of breakfast cereal or digestive biscuits. Take it a bit further and you get crystal malt: the texture is chewier and the flavours are sweeter, richer, like granola bars. Take it the whole way to dark malt and the grains become crumbly, and taste distinctly of chocolate and coffee – which, after all, acquire their distinctive characters from similar processes.

There are many different varieties of malt at every stage on the scale: there are pilsner pale malts and pale ale malts. There are Vienna and Munich malts, slightly darker, and after Gold and Ruby, down at the far end, there are fine distinctions between Black and Chocolate. Their production relies on the talent of the maltster, who today can fine-tune the kilning process to consistently create the desired nuance.

The maltster's tools are a controllable, measurable energy source for heating the air that passes through the kiln, vents and extractor fans to

control it, and a sophisticated understanding of how the starting temperature, the finishing temperature, the length of time in the kiln and even the
pitch of the roof all affect the heating and drying process. Malting is an
extraordinary skill – the ability to create a rich and varied array of flavours
from one basic grain. And the tools and techniques on which it depends are
all remarkably recent innovations in the long history of beer.

For years I gave talks about the miracle of malting in which I said that if
you had a pale beer it was made from pale malt, a brown beer from brown
malt and a dark beer from dark malt. I was wrong. The problem with
cooking malt beyond a certain point is that the heat kills off the enzymes
that convert the starch to sugar in the brewing process. Brewers refer to
the sugar they eventually get from malt as 'extract': if you don't have any
enzymes, you don't get any extract. If you tried to make a dark beer using
100 per cent dark malt, you might get something tasty (although it would
probably be too astringent) but you wouldn't get fermentation. So even a
beer like Guinness is around 90 per cent pale malt. I was shocked the first
time I helped brew a stout because on a pile of pale, golden malt there were
mere flecks of dark malt, and yet the beer was deep, dark brown, almost
black, when we finished. Talk to any good brewer today and they'll probably say that you can only get fermentable extract from pale malt. One
maltster I spoke to insisted that Munich and Vienna malts, which create
lager that's slightly darker than pilsner, were the darkest you could use if
you still wanted good extract. So brewers use a cocktail of different malts
to get the right combination of flavour and fermentable extract, and in any
beer, over 90 per cent of the malt bill (the bit in the recipe that describes the
malts used) will be pale malt. But talk to a typical beer historian and they'll
tell you pale malt has only been around since the seventeenth century. So
here's my confusion: you can only get good, fermentable extract from pale
malt, which has only been around for 400 years. But we've been brewing
beer for 10,000 years, and getting successful fermentation all that time.
These are both solid facts, but they contradict each other: either we must be
able to get extract from darker malts, or pale malts have existed for longer
than many of us think.

Experiments brewing with brown malt today, on modern kit, fail to get
extract. The enzymes are dead. But history tells us that beers were once
made with dark malts. Perhaps enzymes could have been introduced from

elsewhere: there's a commercial business today supplying enzymes to brewers so they can ferment with unmalted grains. This is a new development, although in a faint way it does follow the same principle as the saliva and grain balls of traditional *chicha* brewing. Another possibility, going back to Lovibond and the subjectivity that existed before he created his scale, is that perhaps 'pale' and 'brown' today don't mean the same thing as they did historically – perhaps brown malt back then was paler than we think. But even if that were the case, we'd still have needed the technology to make malt that was dried gently rather than aggressively roasted.

In warmer climates, it's possible to air-dry malt. In the Fertile Crescent, grain could have been spread out on hot rocks or even smooth floors exposed to the sun, and dried that way. Any malt produced like this would have been pale, and used on its own would have made a pale beer. But in northern Europe, and especially in winter, when malting was traditionally carried out, a heat source – and therefore a rich energy source – is needed to dry the grain.

So to understand the development of malting, and the evolution of what beer would have looked and tasted like, we have to look at the sources of heat and the ability to control it that were available at any given stage in history. Contrary to the claims of some standard histories of brewing, there were ways of drying malt gently enough so that workable enzymes weren't obliterated; they just weren't ideal. Wood was used to dry malt, and there are early records of patents to draw the smoke away from the kiln. Before devices such as flues and vents, there were raised floors to get the malt further away from the heat source – maybe earlier people even attempted to blow the smoke away manually. Old brewing records talk of the need to dry pale malt for hours if not days, while darker malts were roasted much more quickly. So it's inaccurate to suggest that pale malt didn't exist before the invention of coke smelting (as I did in my book *Hops and Glory*). Early pale malts must just have been inconsistent and probably contained lots of off-flavours.

The invention of coke in the late sixteenth century is intrinsically tied up with the history of modern pale malt. As early as 1693, J. Houghton wrote that malts from Derby owed their superiority and clean taste to the use of 'coaks', and urged the spread of the practice. But he also reminds us that, before coke arrived, other options were available, even if they weren't ideal:

Tis not above half a century of years since they dried their malt with straw (as other places now do,) before they used cowkes, which has made that alteration since that all England admires.

The joy that greeted the arrival of coke, which allowed far greater control of temperature and gave an unprecedented combination of precision and clean flavour, shows what a huge improvement it must have been over what had gone before. I had a small insight into what old-fashioned malt must have been like on a recent trip to South Africa. When you go on a brewery tour, they're often fond of giving you samples of hops to sniff and malt to taste. The Visitors' Centre for South African Breweries in Johannesburg was a little worn around the edges. The brewing coppers hadn't been polished in a long time. There was an animatronic exhibit of the set-up of an old gold mine, in which one of the dummies mechanically hoisting up the cart of gold had one of his arms hanging off. The hops were so old they were brown rather than green, prompting the hop merchant on the tour to take the poor tour guide to task. The pale malt was pale malt, but they also offered us some Crystal malt. This is my favourite malt to chew – I love its sweet, treacly flavour – and I'm used to seeing it as having a uniform golden-brown colour. But this sample of 'Crystal' tasted harsh and astringent, and contained grains of every hue from pale to black. It was either the sweepings from around a malting floor, or malt that had been dried with a woeful lack of precision. It made me think about the rigour of turning the malt and the control of temperature. Before we had modern drying techniques, when you couldn't guarantee an even and regular distribution of heat, all malt must have been closer to this than modern-day malt.

The control offered by coke allowed malting to happen on a larger scale and produced malt of a much better consistency. 'Pale malt' as we understand it today may not pre-date the invention of coke, but malt that was pale enough to keep enzymes alive, and sugars uncaramelised, must have done.

By the eighteenth century, maltsters and brewers were dealing in pale, amber and brown malts. Records show that brown malt gave greater stability to beer but not as much extract as pale – which suggests that what was then known as 'brown malt' still offered some fermentability. Because of its greater extract, pale malt always had a price premium. *The London & Country Brewer*, published anonymously in 1736, tells us: 'It is a common saying that there is brought to London the worst of Brown malt and the best of Pale.' Pale malt 'produced the best wort', because brown 'had its strength destroyed by the heat'.

The proportion of pale malt used in any beer began to increase. But in beer styles such as porter, people wanted the richer flavours of darker malts, so brown malts were roasted more aggressively to restore the balance. By the late eighteenth century, brewers were relying on pale malt for extract, and a mixture of burnt malt, roasted barley and sugar for flavour. In 1802, Matthew Wood patented a process of evaporating the sugary wort to create something with the colour and consistency of treacle, which brewers began adding to their beers to get a richer layer of flavour. Then, in 1817, Daniel Wheeler used an iron cylinder similar to a coffee roaster to roast malt to a point where a small amount could make a beer dark without imparting burnt flavours. Such malts would have had little if any usable extract, but added a great deal of flavour even in small amounts. So when brewers and maltsters today say they can't get extract from brown malt, they're almost certainly talking about malts that are browner now than they were in, say, the early eighteenth century. As pale malt became a more consistent source of extract, brown malt went darker, giving up on usable extract altogether and focusing on flavour.

8. Malt and Modern Brewing

The Crisp Malting Group is the biggest privately owned maltsters in the UK, with sites in Alloa and Speyside (mainly serving whisky distillers), Sussex, Essex and Norfolk. The original site was built at Great Ryburgh in north Norfolk in 1870, replacing an older facility, and today provides a visual history of the malting process. Things weren't replaced here; they were added to, bit by bit. The giant rust-coloured silos, fifty metres tall, each one capable of holding 360 tonnes of malt, dwarf the original red-brick buildings on one side, while on the other looms a bulky grey metal shed. It's a bewildering and exciting place. As I arrive, a lorry parks beneath one of the silos and the malt pours into the back, filling the trailer in seconds.

Crisp supplies malt to everyone from the smallest craft brewers to the biggest multinational brewing corporations, and exports across the world.

The original floor maltings is still in use, but examples of the technologies that have largely replaced floor malting have been added steadily over the last fifty years.

I'm greeted by Dr Dave Griggs, Group Technical Director, and Rob Moody, Logistics Director and also the man who looks after the burgeoning craft beer business that's once more changing the way Crisp does business. Both are dressed casually in regulation Crisp Malting blue polo shirts. And like Robin Appel, both seem relaxed and in love with their work.

'So is this the first time you've been to a maltings?' asks Rob.

I explain that I was at Warminster a few weeks ago, but that this is one of those things where, if you're a novice, you need it all explained several times before you really get it.

Rob smiles and nods. 'So what else do you need explained?'

'Well, I've been thinking a lot about the basic malting process. So, you've got the steeping part, where you're submerging the grain for hours, and then giving it an air rest so it doesn't drown, and then submerging it again. I mean, that's basically waterboarding, isn't it? And then, when you do the kilning, you've tricked the grain into thinking it's safe so it can sprout, and then as soon as the enzymes have been released, the kilning kills the embryo, doesn't it?

Rob nods.

'So malting is essentially the torture and genocide of baby plants, isn't it?'

Now he frowns, and looks at me oddly. 'Well, technically yes, but that's not really the kind of publicity we're looking for.'

After tea and biscuits and another run-through the malting process that secures my understanding more firmly and makes no mention of torture or genocide, we don high-vis jackets and rather cool hard hats disguised as baseball caps and go on a tour of the site. We start at the beginning, where the barley arrives from the farm. Before it's accepted, it goes through a battery of tests similar to that at Warminster, but the scale of this place makes it so much more dramatic.

There's a checkpoint where every lorry has to stop on its way in, and here in the first week of August, with the harvest of winter barley in full swing, it's a busy place. A building resembling a railway signal box stands by the checkpoint, tall enough for anyone inside to look down on the contents of the lorry parked outside. Next to it, a crane arm with a big metal spear on the end swoops down and stabs deep into the trailer full of malt, vacuums up a sample and sucks it into the signal box, which is actually a state-of-the-art laboratory. It does this several times with each trailer, moving and stabbing like a Martian war machine designed by Francis Begbie, and is one of those processes you could watch all day from this high vantage point.

The lorry then has to wait for twenty minutes while its contents are put through a battery of tests. Every load has to be evaluated for its grade and nitrogen content, and identified as the variety the farmer claims it to be. It's also tested for bugs, mould, damaged grains and extraneous matter such as stones and chaff. Crucially, it's tested for its ability to germinate. The seed embryo needs to be alive, but dormant. If it's dead it won't malt, and if it's already started germinating, it's too late to malt. If it's rejected for malting, it goes off to be mere food instead.

'Every brewer has their own spec,' says Dave, 'and the big brewers have far more rigorous specs, some of them with up to thirty-six different parameters. Some are very similar to each other, but they're all tailored to their own production set-up, which it has to go through in the right way and in the right time. There are some quirky specs – things that have been on there for years and are probably not relevant any more – but no one dares change them, just in case, so they just get added to over the years rather than being properly revised.'

This confirms a quirk of the malting industry that I initially found surprising, but makes a lot of sense. A few weeks before coming to Crisp I had lunch with Jerry Dyson, who sources all the malt for Molson Coors in the UK and Canada. If you think about a mass-produced beer like Carling and a lovingly crafted IPA from a microbrewer, you'd imagine the microbrewer would be by far the most stringent in terms of the specification for the malted barley they buy. In fact, the opposite is true.

Jerry is less concerned with the variety of barley he buys than he is the technical quality of it. He agrees that the quality of the barley affects the final product just as the malting process does, but rather than celebrating *terroir*, he buys from all across the country so long as the barley meets his exacting standards, so he can painstakingly blend it for consistency. 'If we were to use poor quality malt, it would slow us up later on,' he says. 'It would lead to things like flavour differences and issues with shelf life. Take nitrogen for instance. Malting barley for lager needs to have low nitrogen. If we have high nitrogen, we'll get hazy beer. Yes, we're always looking for a good price, but if we hammered our growers on price the best barley would go somewhere else. Now, if you're brewing craft beer you can get away with a bit of haze, and variations in flavour are often celebrated. But for a brand like Carling, that would be catastrophic. Craft brewers sometimes end up buying the barley we reject.'

Back at Crisp, once the barley is finally approved it's dried and placed in a holding bin, where it can sit for as long as a year, but rarely does so because there's so much volume going through.

'We buy our malt from around two hundred and fifty farmers, all Red Tractor assured, which means they're guaranteed to be good quality,' says Dave. 'We like to work with local farmers in Norfolk. Malting barley competes on a farm with wheat, oil seed and fuel crops these days, and barley is a high-risk crop because of the demanding quality specifications. It's almost a niche crop. But up here in north Norfolk, the only crops that grow well are malting barley and sugar beet. Working with farmers directly, we can do interesting things with varieties. You're always looking for a new variety that has higher yield and better processability.'

'What about better flavour?' I ask.

'Well, yes that, too,' he concedes, 'but there are a lot of people in this industry and they all have different priorities.'

After Ernest Beaven bred the first true malting barley variety, barley breeding became an industry in its own right. The breeder is responding to the needs of the farmer, who is always looking for better yield so he can get a higher price per acre. The maltster is looking for consistency and usability, a malt that can regularly pass its battery of tests. At the end of the process, the brewer is looking for flavour, and is in some ways last in the queue. And the market is dynamic and ever changing, because at the start of the process the breeder is actively seeking new commercial varieties. When they develop a new variety they are paid a royalty on it for a given period of time, but when the royalty runs out they're out of business unless they have another one to replace it. So being a farmer of malting barley is like being the owner of an iPhone, with your supplier constantly saying, 'You know that barley variety you're using? It's shit.'

'But you sold it to me five years ago telling me it was the best one ever!'

'Did I? Oh, well never mind, because I was wrong. This new one is even better. Seriously, it's the best one ever.'

And so on.

Because of this, barley varieties come and go. Five years ago every microbrewer I spoke to wanted malt made from Tipple barley – it was the standard for pale malt used to make pale ales and IPAs. But as Robin Appel showed with his barley porridge experiment, it contributed a more astringent flavour compared to other varieties. Now, Rob and Dave show me a chart of barley varieties over time. Around 2010, Tipple accounted for about half of the entire barley crop in England and Scotland. By 2014, it was down to less than 10 per cent. A new variety called Concerto, which didn't exist before 2009, now dominates, with 53 per cent market share. Venture appears for the first time in 2011 and Odyssey in 2012, and while both were still small in 2015, they seem to be growing exponentially. The Maltsters' Association of Great Britain meets every spring to compile a list of varieties that it approves for use. Each year, varieties are granted provisional approval, upgraded to full approval, or removed from the approved list.

Crisp's Great Ryburgh Malting, along with Warminster, Tuckers Maltings in Devon and Thomas Fawcett in West Yorkshire, is one of the four last remaining floor maltings in England. 'There's just not enough malting space to supply the needs of the modern brewing industry,' says Dave. 'An old floor maltings used to do 10,000 tonnes in a year. Now we do that in a week.'

The malting floor, like the one at Warminster, is in a long, low room, punctuated along its length with white metal pillars. A four-inch-deep malt bed lies on the floor, with neat grooves running off into the distance from where it was last turned. Rob gestures at a large wooden rake that has three metal prongs curving over at their ends. 'On you go, Pete,' he says.

It's one of those initiation rituals you get in so many industries and crafts. The professional maltster makes turning the malt look easy, like simply dragging a rake along the ground. But if you've never done it before, it's not easy at all. Those metal prongs dig deep into the bottom of the malt layer, and four inches of grain throws up a surprising amount of resistance. My action is jerky rather than smooth. Each time I think I've got some momentum, I shudder to a halt again and have to give it another hard yank.

After one pass up and down the floor, sweat is pouring from me. 'Not bad,' smirks Rob. I look back at my work. If you can picture one of those neat, freshly cut lawns with perfect stripes up and down it, and then imagine how different it would look if it had instead been cut by a giant spider smoking crack, you've got a pretty good idea of the mess I've just made to the previously immaculate malting floor.

I'm not sorry to leave my handiwork behind as we head up to the kiln. Again, it's much bigger than Warminster, and the network of air management that allows control of the drying process is topped off by a pagoda-style roof. 'When you see this style of roof on a Scottish whisky distillery, everyone assumes it's something to do with the distillation process,' says Dave. 'It's not – it's the malting.' For some distilleries, this is a historical feature, but a few still have their own floor maltings.*

We're inside the main building now, which, having been added to over the years, seems to be an endless procession of stairwells and short passages. In the 1960s, Crisp added a Saladin Box, the invention that displaced floor maltings as the norm. Demand for beer peaked in the 1880s, at the same point technology was transforming the brewing process. Floor maltings couldn't cope with demand, and a range of new techniques was developed. The most successful of these was created by the Frenchman Jules Saladin, who was struck by inspiration as he sat bored at the dinner table one night, idly turning a corkscrew through a container of salt. His invention comprises a series of large screws operated mechanically that move along a bed of malt. The power of the screws means the bed can be much deeper and therefore more compact, so it's contained in a large box. Some of these are still in use in older maltings today.

It makes sense to mechanise such a hard, slow, labour-intensive process, at least from a business point of view, and especially to me after my pathetic attempt at turning the malt. In the 1960s, larger, automated drum maltings were developed and Great Ryburgh acquired its first one in 1973.

---

* Just as brandy is distilled wine, so whisky is essentially distilled beer (albeit without the hops). Whisky distillers brew their own beer, which they refer to as 'wash', which I've always thought of as quite a pointed name, denigrating the base beer as something that has little value at this stage. They don't hop it, but they do have to allow it a full fermentation before they have the base alcoholic drink they can distil.

These massive stainless steel tanks have slotted floors through which air can be blown to control the temperature precisely. Large mechanical arms, descended and elaborated upon from Saladin's original idea, sweep round in circles through beds that can be up to several feet deep. These tanks combine both germination and kilning, making malting a much more compact and speedier operation.

As soon as machinery entered the malting picture in the 1880s, those who invested quickly benefited from economies of scale and those who didn't soon found it impossible to compete on a commercial basis. There are thirty-one working maltings in total in the UK now, compared to 1,200 in the 1820s. But the old ways are still hanging on – and possibly even doing more than that.

'This is such an exciting time to be in malt, thanks to the growth of craft beer,' says Dave.

What makes it exciting particularly for the bottom line of companies like Crisp is that, on average, one tonne of malt will make forty-five barrels of craft beer compared to sixty barrels of a global lager. Craft may still account for a relatively small share of all the beer brewed in the world, but craft brewers buy disproportionately more malt than their bigger competitors because they put much more into their beers than the more cost-conscious giant players do. Also, craft brewers want different kinds of malt, and those brewing beers based on traditional English styles such as pale ale and IPA often want to use traditional English malt – 14 per cent of the 1.6 million tonnes of malt grown in Britain every year is now exported.* And as craft brewers engage with where their malt comes from, they're increasingly asking specifically for floor-malted barley. Floor malting is a sign of craft, a story and a slice of heritage and tradition. But if modern malting drums are more efficient and produce a product with a greater consistency, is there any tangible advantage to floor malt?

Dave smiles. 'When you do the technical analysis between the two, they're absolutely identical. But if you give it to people in blind taste tests, they can pick up a real difference. Three days in the kiln as opposed to twenty-four

---

* When you consider that half the malt grown in Britain is used for distilling, this means almost a third of *brewing* malt is exported – sometimes to countries with far bigger barley harvests than the UK.

hours might have something to do with it, as might the difference in air movement - volatile aroma compounds won't get blown off if the air movement is gentle. Maybe with a bigger drum, we drive off those volatiles.'

Robin Appel insisted there was an advantage to floor malting when I met him at Warminster. He argued that small batches received greater care and attention, and that the slow turning of shallower beds means the grain gets to germinate at its own pace. Of course, he would say that. But here at Crisp they have a choice of old and new. The new way is cheaper, quicker and much easier on the back, yet they're saying the old methods produce better tasting malt. There's now such a demand for good-quality floor malt that Crisp are considering reopening another old floor maltings at their plant down the road in Dereham.

Almost as if it had been staged, as we're talking about craft and the revival of tradition, a colleague of Tony and Dave bursts into the room. 'I've got it!' he says. 'It's in!' The other two men leap up and crowd around him to see. 'It' is a small polythene bag of barley grains. 'It's Chevallier!' says Tony.

The popular nineteenth-century malting barley variety that was eclipsed by Beaven's breeding innovation is back. There were just five seeds of Chevallier, stored in the Genetic Resources Unit at the John Innes Centre – an independent plant science and microbiology research organisation. A few years ago, the centre received £250,000 of new funding from the Biotechnology and Biological Sciences Research Council to explore whether there was any commercial viability in Chevallier and other heritage varieties. This is a trend in plant breeding now: in all crops, specialisation has narrowed the genetic variety in the field. By artificial breeding, we keep our apples, barley, wheat, hops and other crops stable and consistent, but all the time pests and diseases are evolving. We face a constant danger that prized varieties may have a fatal weakness to some new threat. The last five years has seen a breakthrough in plant research as genome mapping has become commercially viable, and agricultural and horticultural researchers are going through their archives exploring long-discarded varieties to see if they are harbouring any secrets.

It turns out that Chevallier was. Compared to many modern varieties, it's particularly resistant to mycotoxins, chemicals produced by fungus that can contaminate crops, particularly grasses. Chevallier is especially hardy against Fusarium ear blight, or scab, a common infection in wheat and barley that ruins crops and costs the farming industry billions.* But never mind all that: 'We wanted to find out what the malt was like and how the beer tasted,' said Dr Chris Ridout, the beer-loving scientist who led the project.

In 2012, the John Innes Centre grew half an acre of Chevallier, which was then floor-malted here at Crisp in Great Ryburgh and used by north Norfolk's Stumptail Brewery to create a Victorian-style nut-brown ale. Apparently it was very good.

Local farmers grew twenty tonnes of Chevallier in 2014, and from those twenty tonnes they've been able to grow 200 tonnes in 2015. Chevallier is now commercially available once more.

The possibility that traits in Chevallier that were undetectable a century ago may now be crossbred back into other varieties is truly exciting from a scientific point of view. But reading the press release from the John Innes Centre, and watching the Crisp guys now, that's not really what they're interested in. They're thrilled by the simple achievement of bringing Chevallier back to life after almost a century's absence, and by the flavours it might impart to beer. They know craft brewers will be queuing up to try it, too. Despite all the science, all the screenings and detailed specs, the conversations about yield and nitrogen, the malting industry in its heart is driven by curiosity, romance – and an eternal hankering for good beer.

9. For the Love of the Otter

On the sales charts that show the rise and fall of different barley varieties as they come in and out of fashion, there's one curious exception to the pattern. In any given year, it's one of the smallest varieties on the chart. But unlike the others it's absolutely consistent year after year, although recently it's showing signs of steady, marginal growth. Given its size relative to its

---

* If scab makes it into the human food chain, it induces nausea, fever, headaches and vomiting. Another mycotoxin, ergot, is of even greater concern for crops intended for human consumption and is one of the key dangers maltsters test for when the grain arrives. Ergot poisoning – which used to happen through the consumption of infected bread – was known as St Anthony's Fire, and caused gangrene, spasms, damage to the central nervous system, headaches, nausea, diarrhoea and psychotic effects such as mania and psychosis. When it was first diagnosed, it explained phenomena which had previously been blamed on witchcraft. That's even worse than the effects of ten pints of Stella Artois.

siblings, it's remarkable how much it is talked about. If we were measuring the amount of discussion over a barley variety rather than its volume sales, Maris Otter would dominate the chart.

In 1912, the Plant Breeding Institute (PBI) was founded at the University of Cambridge with the aim of reviving Britain's sagging rural economy by breeding better crops. Over the next seventy-five years it was extraordinarily successful, breeding over 1,300 new crop varieties and allowing Britain to become self-sufficient in wheat and barley. E. S. Beaven's cultivation of Plumage Archer was the start of modern barley breeding, and other varieties soon followed. The next was a cross between Spratt and Archer, bred by Dr Herbert Hunter in Cambridge in 1908. By 1940 Plumage Archer and Spratt Archer together held an 80 per cent share of the total barley acreage in the UK. At the Plant Breeding Institute, George Douglas Hutton Bell was relentlessly looking for varieties that had even better yields. In 1943, he introduced a new variety called Pioneer. Then in 1952, he crossed Plumage Archer with a Danish variety called Kenia, which had great yield but was of poor malting quality, and got Proctor, which has the advantages of both its parents.

By now the development of new varieties was happening in roughly a twelve-year cycle, and in 1965 Bell introduced a cross of Proctor and Pioneer, which he named Maris Otter.* Pioneer was Britain's first real 'winter barley,' and Maris Otter inherited this trait from its parent. Genetically, winter and spring barleys are quite different. Winter barley is sown in the autumn, and requires a period of 'vernalisation' – a spell at cold temperatures that activates its ability to produce seeds later in the year. Spring barley can't survive the winter, so is sown, as the name suggests, in spring. Winter barley is harvested in the early summer, spring barley a few weeks later. So winter barley has a longer growing period but rewards the farmer

---

* The Plant Breeding Institute stood on Maris Lane in a real place that is actually called Trumpington, a suburb of Cambridge. So if you were going to name it after the place of its birth, unless you had a particularly excellent sense of humour, you were always going to go for the street name rather than anything else. Maris Otter shares its birthplace with Maris Widgeon, an organic wheat variety, and Maris Piper potatoes. 'Otter', 'Widgeon' and 'Piper' are all signs of a fondness for wildlife at the PBI, and it's believed (by some fans, at least) that Otter's competitors in trials went by names such as Maris Mink, Maris Puma, Maris Badger, Maris Dingo and Maris Yak. I think those last two may have been added to the legend at a later date.

with a higher yield, while spring barley doesn't yield as well but is quicker and therefore cheaper to grow. Also, given the vagaries of English weather, those few weeks' difference in harvest time mean the winter barley harvest usually happens in better weather than the later spring barley harvest. Winter barley is therefore a useful insurance policy for farmers who are drawn to the economics of spring barley.

Maris Otter soon found fame and devotion among Britain's ale brewers, competing strongly with spring barley varieties. But in 1964, a year before Otter's launch, the Plant Varieties and Seeds Act was passed, introducing the system of royalties for plant breeders. By the 1970s there was a range of new barley varieties that all had higher yield than Maris Otter, which started to look like it would become the first high-profile victim of the planned obsolescence that has defined malting barley ever since. In the brutal world of plant breeding, it was being killed off by its children – many of the new varieties were crosses of Maris Otter with other, better yielding varieties.

But even though Otter was being beaten on yield, which meant farmers no longer favoured it, some brewers stuck stubbornly with it in the belief that it made better beer. A modern variety such as Venture yields 3 tonnes of barley per acre, whereas Maris Otter only gives you 2. So if you want a farmer to grow Maris Otter, you have to be prepared to pay a premium for it. Proving that the barley market is very different from a simple commodities market, brewers such as Wolverhampton & Dudley, who at this stage still operated their own in-house maltings, were prepared to pay this premium. But the economics of spring varieties still meant that farmers reverted back to them, and by the end of the eighties plantings of Maris Otter had grown worryingly scarce for its band of loyal supporters. Even where it survived, it was neglected in favour of newer varieties, and cross-contamination with other plants diluted its quality and reliability. In 1989, the National Institute of Agricultural Botany removed it from their list of approved barleys.

That should have been Maris Otter's death knell. It wouldn't have been the first to die like this: by the end of the eighties, no one really expected any barley variety to last longer than six or seven years. But as I've now witnessed, certain barley varieties can inspire great passion.

Robin Appel founded his barley merchant business in 1980, and by 1990 Wolverhampton & Dudley were one of his regular customers. W&D

loved Maris Otter, and bought a lot of barley. Robin Appel knew how to talk to farmers. So together they created an alliance, along with Norfolk barley merchants H. Banham, to negotiate new Maris Otter contracts and persuade farmers to grow it.

By this time the Plant Breeding Institute had been privatised and sold to Unilever. In 1998, Unilever sold it on to Monsanto, who gradually ran it down and transferred its functions elsewhere. The place where Maris Otter, Maris Piper and all the rest were born is now a Waitrose. This meant that in 2004 the Maris Otter Consortium was able to buy the Plant Breeders' Rights, which meant Robin Appel and Roger Banham now owned the object of their passion outright.

Since its rescue, Maris Otter has become a byword for quality ale brewing, an article of faith for many brewers. The rescue and revitalisation of Otter coincided with the popular surge of craft brewing, and Otter's reputation as the perfect malt for brewing pale ale and IPA is so strong that in the United States it's considered to be a speciality (or over there, 'specialty') malt, even though its distinctive identity comes from the barley itself rather that the malting process. It may have a tiny share of British malt production (just 3.4 per cent in 2015) but over the last sixteen years ten of the beers judged to be Champion Beer of Britain at the annual Great British Beer Festival were brewed with Maris Otter. As I'm researching and writing about malt, and as Maris Otter gears up to celebrate its fiftieth birthday, the Champion Beer of Britain at the 2015 Great British Beer Festival is a red ale called Cwtch, brewed by Welsh craft brewery Tiny Rebel. It's brewed with Maris Otter. This much-loved variety of a specialised, domesticated grass could not have wished for a better birthday present.

10. The Mother Field

Somewhere in north Norfolk lies the most precious six acres of malting barley in the world: the Maris Otter Mother Field.

When Robin Appel and Roger Banham rescued Otter, they faced the problem that it was still full of the impurities that had seen it removed from the approved barley varieties list in 1989. The National Institute of Agricultural Botany set the standards for a true and healthy barley variety, so they were well placed to start cleaning up Maris Otter. There were people still working at the institute who remembered Otter from its sixties heyday, and they still had the original botanical descriptions of it on file. After starting with just a few pure grains, in 2006 they handed back a spruced-up Otter to Banham's, and taught the grain merchant how to keep the sample pure.

Using a more sophisticated version of the traditional idea of taking the best seeds and planting them over, they approached farmers they trusted to plant two plots on the Icknield Way, and one of them is here on Manor Farm near Grimston, just north-east of King's Lynn, a few miles inland from the Wash. The grain grown in this field doesn't make beer: it's used exclusively to plant other fields nearby. They in turn grow grain that is used to plant still more fields, and it's these that grow the Maris Otter that brewers buy. Every single Maris Otter grain now used in brewing anywhere in the world can be traced back directly to either this field or its sister plot, down near Warminster, where Robin can keep an eye on it. But this one, here in north Norfolk, is the one that has the romance built up around it.

This romance means that, inevitably, the Mother Field is described as being at a secret location, but it's no secret that Roger Coe has been nurturing Maris Otter on his farm for the last forty years. The farm started growing it in the 1970s, but stopped as demand dwindled. It returned in 1992 when Banham's and Robin Appel revived it, and has been grown here ever since.

This location is the perfect place for barley – and Maris Otter in particular. While barley was grown across the country in the seventeenth and eighteenth centuries, it thrived best in various areas along the Icknield Way. In the middle of the eighteenth century, when large-scale brewing was being born in the newly industrialised cities, Hertfordshire increasingly became famous for brown malt, while Norfolk began to specialise in pale. Crops such as wheat took too much out of Norfolk's light soil, and barley was rotated with turnips, which were grown as food for livestock and also 'cleaned' the soil ready for barley to go in. This rotation drove the development of farming in Norfolk, which became increasingly reliant on London's brewing industry as names like Whitbread grew to become the first industrial-scale breweries. As brewers realised pale malt gave much better extract than darker malts, its popularity soared. By the end of the eighteenth century, a third of arable land in Norfolk was under barley destined for London brewhouses, and the quality of Norfolk barley became highly prized.

One of Roger Coe's close neighbours, Teddy Maufe, has made barley farming his life's work. His crop of Maris Otter is malted by Crisp at Great Ryburgh, from where about a quarter of it goes to local microbrewers. Teddy boasts of being able to give brewers the precise grid reference where their barley was grown. The Iceni tribe were growing barley for brewing here 2,000 years ago, and Teddy believes this part of the world should be as famous for its barley as Bordeaux is for its grapes. 'It's the perfect *terroir*: the soil is light and sandy, and there's a lot of sunlight,' he told me when I visited his farm a few years ago. 'But the *haar* that rolls in from the North Sea keeps the climate cool and moist – it keeps the temperature at about 15 degrees Celsius when it should be closer to 30, allowing the grain to ripen for longer before it dries out.'

Teddy has a real ale shop on the farm that sells all the beers brewed with his barley, and has recently installed his own micro-maltings. Surely a microbrewery, enabling the process from grain to glass to happen without the barley leaving the farm, can't be far behind.

But I don't have time to visit Teddy again today: after a quick sandwich at Crisp Maltings, Frances Brace is driving me to Roger Coe's farm for the harvest of the Mother Field.

✿ ✿ ✿

Frances is a long-standing PR strategist in the brewing industry who I've worked with for years. Early in 2015, she included me on a press circulation list about the year of celebrations for Maris Otter's fiftieth anniversary. She's working with Crisp to promote various events, and when I responded that I'd be very keen to find out more, she roped me in. They're making a film of the whole Maris Otter story, of which today's harvest is a key part. In return for agreeing to do a bit of interviewing on camera, I've been allowed to come to the 'secret' Mother Field to watch.

As Britain's climate continues to unravel and randomise, judging the correct time for harvest is becoming a stressful enterprise. There's a saying in barley farming that it takes 'eight weeks from ear to shear'. When it's first in ear, the barley is green and the head stands upright. As the grains grow, the stalk dries out, and the ear hangs over and droops down. The perfect time to harvest – the time when the crop is properly 'fit' – is when the ear hangs so heavy that it rests flat against the straw that supports it. But while you're waiting for that to happen, the bonds between the individual grains and the plant begin to weaken. Barley has evolved so that it wants the wind to carry the seeds away when they're ripe, which is the opposite of what human harvesters want. While you're waiting for it to become fully fit, a strong wind or heavy rainstorm could separate the seeds from the straw and you've lost your entire harvest, as Beaven grimly recalled happening so often in the late nineteenth century. Also, you really want the crop to be dry when you're harvesting, so rain showers can delay things, possibly until it's too late. We've been on tenterhooks for a couple of weeks now, waiting for the final go/no-go decision on the harvest. By the time Frances phones me and says, 'Drop everything, it's tomorrow – it's definitely on', the Mother Field harvest has been scheduled and cancelled three times.

The location of the Mother Field may or may not be secret, but by the time we've followed a couple of other cars down winding lanes with high hedges to get to it, I have no idea where I am, and there's no signal on my phone.

The hedges, which help protect the crop from those dangerous winds, certainly give the bottom end of the field a curious air of seclusion. The field is on a gentle slope, and the barley is drilled in rows going up and down the hill. In the centre of the field there's a curious bald rectangle, sort of like a firebreak, kept completely free of vegetation. It marks out the boundary of a square area of six acres, a field within a field – the Maris Otter Mother Field. The firebreak is there to prevent any other grains getting in and cross-contaminating the crop. From when it starts to grow to the point it's harvested, the crop is inspected by people with magnifying glasses walking up and down the rows, making sure nothing is growing there except Maris Otter barley, and that no cross-contamination can happen.

I can't wait to get up close to it and take a good look. Roger Coe, a big, tall man in his sixties who strikes me as a cross between a farmer and a fit-for-his-age company CEO, leans in with me. 'It's *just* fit,' he says. 'It's well nicked over, but see how there's still some curve in it where it's hanging down? We want it right flat down against the straw. Ideally it could do with another week, but we can't risk leaving it any longer.'

The harvest of the whole Maris Otter crop takes about two weeks. 'In that hot summer of 1976, we were all finished by 2 August,' says Roger, 'but we had a very cold spring this year so we're quite late – here we are on 5 August and we're just getting started. There's a lot of chalk in the soil, and it holds the cold in spring. It's different where the soil has a lot more sand, so we actually filter sand into the soil here. With most crops you'd be trying to filter it out.'

There's a big, bright yellow combine harvester already at work on the left edge of the Mother Field plot – everything outside the firebreak has already gone. It's mesmerising to watch. A big roller at the front cows the barley ears into submission as clippers slice their stalks about four inches from the ground. A screw then draws the barley up into the guts of the mechanical beast, where it's rubbed and sieved to separate the grain from the chaff. The grains fall through plates and are sucked up into a big hopper at the top. The chaff is spewed out of the back in a brittle cloud.

The harvester creeps down the hill towards us having gone once up and down, and comes to a halt. In its wake are clusters of hollow, dry stems that are surprisingly widely spaced, pale gold with the odd one that's vivid yellow. From above they look like wooden drinking straws, and they give a nice swish and crunch underfoot, all brittle and dry.

The front wheel of the combine harvester is exactly the same height as I am.

'Would you like to ride in the cab for a bit, Pete?'

What do you think?

Up in the cabin I'm looking at a set of computerised controls and readings that remind me of the bridge of a giant ship. The illusion of being at sea grows even stronger when I look out of the concave windscreen that slopes down and draws the gaze with it to the field below. The barley falls before us, endlessly, and we're like a ship's prow ploughing through waves. 'It's addictive,' says the young farmer driving, after warning me not to touch anything. 'You get people saying "I'll just sit with you once up and down", and before you know it you've done the whole field together. I often look at a big field and think, "This is going to take forever", and then you've done it.'

He shakes his head and gazes at the waves. 'Totally addictive.'

I only get to go once up and down, because there's a big queue for the passenger seat. People are filming the combine, chatting in high-pitched, laughter-filled voices, and taking photographs of the big, stupid grin on my face.

Barley

And then it's done.

The combine harvester costs £150,000 new, and depreciates in value by £10,000 a year. It sits in a shed for nine or ten months of that year. 'It's nice to see it out,' says Roger Coe, master of understatement.

Frances approaches and tells me it's time to keep my end of the bargain and shoot the video. I'm perfectly happy to do so. Forget the book – I've just had a go on a combine harvester and it was awesome and right now I love everyone in this field and firmly intend to move to Norfolk and become a farmer. I might pick up a few tips from the interview.

Frances positions us against the freshly mown field with the combine placed strategically in the background. Roger Coe, the farmer, and Roger Banham, the grain merchant who persuaded him to help revive Maris Otter, are standing next to me, half facing me, half facing the camera, at forty-five-degree angles. Frances looks nervous. 'They're farmers,' she said to me on the way over here. She paused, hesitated, as if trying to choose the right words and then giving up. 'Just . . . do the best you can,' she finally said.

Roger Banham is a bit older than Roger Coe, short and stocky with a deeply lined face that's set, intentionally or not, in an expression that says, 'I'm busy, so don't waste my time.' I decide I'll come to him later, but I've been having a nice chat with Roger Coe and decide that Frances has been worrying unduly.

When we're rolling, I put on my energetic, speaking-for-the-telly voice and say, 'So! Here we are at a secret location in the Norfolk countryside! Roger Coe, tell me, what's so special about the field we're standing in just now?'

Roger shrugs his shoulders and says, 'Nothing, really,' looking between me and Roger Banham, waiting to see what's going to happen next.

I try again. 'Right! So, obviously, the field itself is just a field, but what's special about what we have *growing* in the field? IN THE MIDDLE OF THE FIELD?'

My forced grin is starting to slide. My eyes are so wide my eyeballs are drying out. But the Rogers are set in stone, if stone could look like it would rather be anywhere else than here.

Roger Coe looks at me oddly, like I've said something surprisingly stupid. 'It's the Maris Otter Mother Field.'

'And what does that *mean*, exactly?'

With incredible reluctance, and as few words as possible, he explains the concept of the Mother Field. I sense this is going to be a short piece and turn to Roger Banham. 'And, Roger, you're the grain merchant who helped revive Maris Otter. What is it about this particular barley variety that's so special?'

I'm rewarded with another incredulous, impatient stare, and a brief answer about Maris Otter's fitness and how it makes great tasting beer. And that seems to be as much as we're going to get. They're farmers. They're practical and economical, doing what has to be done and no more. I smile apologetically at Frances, and we cut.*

By the time we've finished, the Mother Field crop has been loaded into the back of a deep blue trailer affixed to a tractor. I gaze at the pile of grain. In three years' time – possibly around the time you finally get to read this – every single beer in the world made from Maris Otter barley will be brewed with grain descended from this trailer-load (or the other one like it down near Warminster, I guess) and that's entirely due to the efforts of Robin Appel, Roger Banham and farmers like Roger Coe. Contemplating this, giving an interview to camera seems pretty unimportant.

11. The Birthday Party

Despite my failure as an on-screen interviewer, Frances Brace asks me if I will continue to help her with the celebrations of Maris Otter's fiftieth birthday. There are activities all through the year, including a parliamentary event, and a competition to find the UK's best Maris Otter grower. But everything comes to a head in September, at the Maris Otter Beer Festival in Norwich.

To commemorate the anniversary, fifty brewers from around the world who love this venerable barley variety have each brewed a brand-new beer with it, and each of those beers is to be available at a one-off, unique beer festival over three days. I've been asked to say a few words, and to introduce

---

* I'm recounting this from memory, so I may have got the details slightly wrong, but that's definitely the gist of it. I have a copy of the Maris Otter fiftieth anniversary video and watched it to check, but for some reason my interview with the two Rogers didn't make the final cut.

a panel of speakers including Teddy Maufe and Mark Banham, Roger's son, who has now taken over the Banham company reins.

On the surface, it looks like any other beer festival: the building is an arts centre that looks like it used to be a church. There are long trestle tables down each side, with racks of ale casks behind them. There's a raffle and a stall of beer memorabilia, some insanely good pork pies and a bottle shop selling beers at bizarrely reasonable prices.

But the tasting notes in the programme form an extraordinary love letter. As you'd expect, the majority of beers here are from traditional English real ale brewers, but more modern craft brewers are here too. Maris Otter cuts across boundaries, and everyone who brews ale seems to revere it. Brewers have travelled here from the United States, Spain, Japan and New Zealand. All of them buy Maris Otter from Crisp Maltings. All offered to fly over, brew a real ale on someone else's kit in the UK and give their own interpretation of what Otter can do, here in its homeland.

The centre of gravity of the whole thing is pale ale at around 4 per cent ABV. Here, the balance of hop and malt character works as only a British cask ale can. There's subtlety and depth. The malt flavour is full and round, and it makes me realise how much I usually focus on hops when I'm tasting beer, giving little thought to the malt. As you might expect, Arcadia Ales, an American brewer, gives an American-style expression of Otter's versatility – their Sword of Damocles is a heavy, bruising IPA. Maris Otter provides a strong enough backbone to withstand an outrageous assault of hops.

Some of the British brewers have gone for American-style beers too. Hastings Beer Co. again nod to the 'sweet, full-bodied backbone' that Maris Otter gives their IPA. There's a botanically infused 'Black IPA' from Nottinghamshire, 7.4 per cent Ragnarok from Scotland, a honey and mustard sour beer from the West Midlands, and an 'Imperial Pilsner' from Wales.

Each of the tasting notes in the programme gives special credit to the barley. Hops are driving the interest in craft brewing right now. But for the guys at Crisp Malting, 'Hops are just the lipstick on beer. Barley is its soul.' This anniversary has prompted brewers to think about malted barley more carefully than they normally do, and the quality of the resulting beers is uniformly excellent. The beers here are thoughtful and restorative. They demonstrate that good old Maris Otter can adapt perfectly to the demands and imaginings of modern craft brewers. And show again what I saw was the reaction to Chevallier, too — good beer is still about romance, history and a sense of place. This is what gets brewers and drinkers, old and new, excited about what's in their glass.

Frances calls me over to the foot of the stage, where the dignitaries are gathering. I just need to get this duty out of the way, then I can enjoy more of these fabulous beers. As we gather, I recognise Roger Banham from our day together in the Mother Field a few weeks ago. He's talking to another man of roughly the same age, and their body language suggests they've been doing business together for decades. As I walk over to say hello, Roger doesn't return my smile. Instead he raises an eyebrow, points at me, turns to his friend and says, 'Here's that bloke I was telling you about. Asking me all these stupid questions. Calls himself a beer writer, but he doesn't know anything about Maris Otter. I had to explain it all to him. Didn't know the first thing.'

I briefly consider explaining to them why I was asking such simple questions back on our interview day. But looking at their hard, impassive faces, I realise that whatever I say, it'll be me that comes off looking stupid. I smile and shrug, and get on with the bit that's keeping everyone from more beer.

12. The Flavour of Smoke

I've never really been that bothered about Schlenkerla, the smoked beer that made the German town of Bamberg famous. Like Cantillon, the equally esoteric 'champagne of beers' created in a Brussels suburb, the reverence of its hardcore fans has always put me off a little. For me, these brands have always been beer's answer to progressive rock: complicated and aloof, celebrated more for the *idea* of them than their actual delivery. When the Jolly Butchers, the first craft beer pub close to my house, opened in 2010, the owner, Martin, proudly showed me the Schlenkerla tap on the bar. 'I'm having it on permanent,' he boasted.

'But no one really likes it,' I said. 'It tastes of bacon and smoked cheese. It's a *posturing* beer.'

'Nah, you're wrong. It's a sign that we're a serious craft beer pub. We're the only place in London that has it on permanent. Sends a message.'

It was gone a month later.

Smoked beer is a minority interest, something we're supposed to like if we're really into our beer, but secretly don't, apart from a few fanatics.

And now I'm sitting in the Schlenkerla brewpub, the place where the beer was brewed until it moved to a bigger facility recently, in Bamberg, the legendary beer city in Franconia, northern Bavaria. It's my first time here because, smoked beer aside, I've never really clicked with German beer or beer culture before now. People speak of Bamberg in reverential tones, and I've always assumed that this was part of the posturing that goes with pretending that smoky bacon is your favourite flavour in a beer. I feel like I've got a front-row seat at a King Crimson reunion gig: I appreciate that it's very special, but it's someone else's special.

The pub itself is wonderful, though, and does a great deal to challenge my prejudices even before I order my first beer. Bamberg is a beautiful medieval town straddling the Regnitz river. If there's one picture of Bamberg that's always used to evoke the place to tourists, it's of the *Altes Rathaus*, the old town hall that sits on a bridge halfway across the river, perched on a small rocky island, which gives the whole place a fairy-tale look. The walk to the pub from my hotel is enchanting, and a large chunk of the town was declared a UNESCO World Heritage site in 2003.

The Schlenkerla pub is also high on the list of tourist attractions, whether you're a fan of smoky beer or not. There aren't many traditional pubs that could match it for its welcoming, homely atmosphere, and for the first time in all my travels around the world of beer I realise that the British Isles don't have a monopoly on the cosiness that defines an autumnal local pub as opposed to a bar. Schlenkerla traces its origins back to a tavern first recorded in 1405, and the cellars survive from that time. Like all ancient buildings that are still in use, the rest of it is a patchwork added to and repaired over years. It was destroyed and rebuilt during the Thirty Years' War, but remains a traditional-looking, half-timbered building with pretty turquoise shutters and window boxes of geraniums bursting forth. Inside it's all blackened, sagging wooden beams and mullioned glass with tiny panes that look like the bottoms of beer bottles. Schlenkerla follows what I'll quickly learn is a standard layout for the Franconian brewpub: the *altes lokal* is the big main bar full of communal tables, and on the other side of the building there are three other rooms that open depending on how busy it is. But the main action is in the wide corridor that divides them. There's a small serving hatch ostensibly catering for people popping in for carry-outs, but as is often the way with haunts like this, it seems to be the spot the locals choose to hang out instead of the main rooms. The double doors to the street are never still, swinging and thudding every few seconds. I feel like I've been coming here for years.

The brewery was founded in 1678. In the middle of the eighteenth century it was taken over by a man named Johann Wolfgang Heller, and its official name is still Heller-Bräu. But in 1877 a new owner, Andreas Graser, arrived at the tavern. Graser had a peculiar gait due to some handicap or injury, and the locals dubbed him 'Schlenkerla' – *schlenkern* is a Bavarian dialect word that translates as 'to swing' or 'to dangle', and 'the dangler' soon gave his name to both the tavern and the beer it brewed.*
The beer is now brewed at a larger site half a mile away, but this is still the spiritual home of *Aecht Schlenkerla Rauchbier*, or 'the original Schlenkerla smoked beer'.

'Original' is of course a matter of interpretation. The beer gets its distinctive character from a malting process in which germinated barley is kilned over a wooden fire and develops a vivid smoky character. Today this is a specialised skill, creating a product that's an acquired taste, just like how Islay whiskies gain their distinctive character from the malt being dried with peat. And just like Islay malts, it's a throwback to a time when maltsters didn't have much of an alternative. Wood used to be a standard choice for kilning malt, and maltsters did what they could to remove the character of smoke. When you look at the innovations that were patented to keep smoke away from malt, and the joy that met the arrival of coke-fired kilning, wood smoke in beer clearly wasn't a popular flavour. But beer has something for everyone, and some people clearly liked it.

Schlenkerla brews a variety of different beer styles, all with a greater or lesser degree of smoky character derived from adding more or less smoked malt to the grist. I realise I can't remember which is the one that is sold around the world simply as Schlenkerla, so I order the Marzen to see

---

* The brewery website warns that the beer, at 5.1 per cent ABV, can make you 'schlenker' quite a bit. I'll leave you to draw your own conclusions about what the whole story of the Schlenkerla name adds to the ongoing debate about the existence or otherwise of the German sense of humour.

what that's like. It's served directly from a wooden barrel on the bar, and pours a dark, chocolate-brown with a good two or three inches of foam I smell smoked bacon and smoked cheese on the nose, and for the first time I question my senses: am I smelling wood smoke here, or smoked foodstuffs? What is the aroma of smoke itself as opposed to something that has been smoked? Whatever it is, there's more than smoke here. There's also a big malt character giving aromas of chocolate and caramel, and the richness of it reminds me of a Belgian Dubbel, one of my favourite beer styles. On the palate it's all about dark flavours: echoes of roasty Guinness, the sweetness of a brown ale, rich and round. The smoke is really more of an aftertaste, bitter and wistful. It's easy to believe that this is what a typical beer tasted like 500 years ago. This might still be scary to many drinkers, but I'm really enjoying it.

Schlenkerla Marzen demonstrates the value of perseverance, and I'm clearly not the first person to be converted on this spot. There's a legend on the beer mats here that translates as, 'Even if the brew tastes somewhat strange at the first swallow, do not stop, because soon you will realise that your thirst will not decrease and your pleasure will visibly increase.' The brewpub's website develops the theme, in tones that would alarm marketing regulators in most countries:

> *The connoisseur drinks it slowly with relish, but steadily and purposefully. He knows, that the second "Seidla" (half-litre) tastes better than the first, and the third even better than the second. He drinks during the morning pint and during the afternoon break. He drinks it in the evenings, drinks it alone and with company, especially with company, as "Aecht Schlenkerla Rauchbier" makes one talkative and exuberant. It brings together the local with the stranger . . .*

Later, when I check, I'm shocked – but not really – to discover that this, the Marzen, is the classic Schlenkerla I thought I hated. German beers don't age or travel well as a rule, so I convince myself it must be the freshness that's making the difference. It looks like I'm going to have to make the Schlenkerla brewpub my new local.

Smoked malt is not the only 'speciality malt', and Schlenkerla is not the only maltster and brewery that makes it. Bamberg is also home to

Weyermann Malting, the most high-profile speciality maltsters in the world. Weyermann sell a wider range of malts than any other company, and they're all made in-house here in Bamberg. The huge, striking red-brick building dates from the turn of the twentieth century. It's an extraordinary sight, similar in shape to a British Victorian-era factory, but garlanded with baroque towers and buttresses. From a hundred yards away, it looks like a palace from a *Flash Gordon* movie.

Beate Fersti, the press officer for Weyermann, greets me in a modern visitors' centre at the edge of the sprawling complex. I'm here with Charlie Gorham, who works for Charles Faram, British hop merchants who have come over for a big industry exhibition down the road in Nuremberg and the annual Weyermann party this weekend. There's a notice in the window on bright yellow paper, written, like the emails Beate has been sending me, to confirm the details of the trip, in bright red Comic Sans:

WELCOME!
PETE BROWN
BEER WRITER
AND OUR GUESTS FROM
CHARLES FARAM
UK

Weyermann is a family company, established in 1879 by Johann Baptist Weyermann and run today by his great-granddaughter, Sabine. And while many companies tell you they're family run and family owned, this one doesn't need to. Beate greets me warmly and ushers me through to a bar area where my name has already been written in a guestbook, ready for me to add a comment later. Then she takes me through the history of the company. Almost every presentation I've seen on this kind of subject over the last twenty years has been done on PowerPoint slides, but not here: this is Weyermann, and instead of slides we have a series of family style photo albums.

The bright-red-on-yellow theme is carried through everywhere you look, from the distinctive logo that looks very similar to the VW badge ('Everyone says that, but it was designed for our fiftieth anniversary and so is older than Volkswagen!') to the lemon-yellow tiles and bright red grouting on the walls in the main plant, to every piece of paper. When Beate speaks, it's impossible not to hear her spoken words in the same font. 'The yellow symbolises the barley, while the red represents the building,' she explains. It's incredibly tight and consistent branding, executed in a style no brand management professional would ever contemplate. It's utterly insane and entirely effective, just like the best families.

Weyermann produces 100,000 tonnes of malt a year, and exports 80 per cent of it. In total they sell to 4,000 brewers, who between them make 50,000 different beers using Weyermann malt. Their business transformed after Sabine visited the United States in 1993, encountered the burgeoning American craft beer scene and thought, 'We have to be here!' American craft brewers remain their biggest customers.

The initial stages of the malting process here are similar to, but on a much bigger scale than, anywhere else I've been. After a certain point, it differs quite dramatically. Rather than just kilning the malt for longer or at a higher temperature, Weyermann uses a combination of kilning and roasting. The kiln takes malt as far as caramelisation, while roasting drums, which can also make caramel or crystal malts, also – you guessed it – create roast flavours. It's a curious distinction. Some malts are just kilned after germination. Others are kilned then roasted, and some go directly from the germination floor to the roasting drum. Still others aren't malted at all, but roasted, unmalted grains, treated no different from coffee beans.

As well as barley, Weyermann also works with rye, wheat and spelt. Many of the kilned malts, and all of the roasted varieties, provide colour, flavour and aroma to beer, but no fermentable extract. They'll be used as only small percentages of the total malt bill, but will still define the character of the beers they help create.

I'm now familiar with testing, wetting, germination and kilning, but the roasting aspect is new to me. Johann Baptist Weyermann started his business with one roasting drum under a tarpaulin, and one employee. The original drum is still on display in the heart of the complex, a metal cylinder with a flue on top and a winch handle that turns the drum inside.

It couldn't be more different now. The roasting drums are about twenty feet long, made of thick stainless steel and suspended about six feet off the ground. They spin constantly, and an intricate network of paddles inside continually stir the malt. They're on twenty-four hours a day, 365 days a year. Depending on the variety, the malt spends two to three hours being agitated and heated to temperatures of 240 to 260 degrees Celsius (161 to 500 degrees Fahrenheit). The temperature and length of time is crucial to get precisely the right malt, and even though the machinery is advanced, the skill of the maltster still has a huge role to play. Some of the maltsters have been with Weyermann for forty years.

Weyermann have developed the **Weyermann® Malt Aroma Wheel®** on which they map each of the malts they produce. The centre of the wheel divides into six sections: roasted aromas, smoky aromas, fruity/nutty aromas, malty aromas, caramel aromas and taste. Each of these then subdivides, so fruity/nutty splits into vanilla, raisin, hazelnut and almond; smoky into wood smoke and clove, and so on. They've actually created several of their own new malts here, each protected by that cheerful red ® wherever it's written. Weyermann® CARABOHEMIAN® provides an intensified caramel aroma and notes of caramel, bread and toffee on the palate, and is specifically designed for darker, fuller Bavarian dark lagers such as Bock and October beers. Weyermann® CARAFA® SPECIAL uses de-husked roasted barley to give a milder, smoother body to porters and stouts. Weyermann® CARABELGE®, designed for Belgian styles such as Tripel and Dubbel, has a restrained caramel character as well as notes of dried fruit and nuts. None of these is recommended as the main malt in a beer. Weyermann advises using CARABELGE® to make up no more than 30 per cent of a beer, while CARAFA® should be no more than 1–5 per cent.

As well as having a dramatic influence on flavour, aroma and colour, some of these malts can have hidden effects on the quality of a beer. Melanoidin malt has particularly highly modified proteins and starches that help promote flavour stability and give a smoother mouthfeel. Stick 1–5 per cent of acidulated malt, which has had lactic acid growing on it, into your pilsner mash and it will lower the pH and improve both the mash working and the fermentation, stabilise the flavour and round out what's already there.

I'm scribbling all this down while looking at a sample box of different speciality malts, lingering over the palette of rich reds and browns. 'And this one is our smoked malt,' says Beate. I'm surprised to see that it's very pale. Every smoked beer I've had has been dark brown, and there's something about the very idea of smoky flavour that suggests the malt should be charred. But this is a slightly dirty pale malt, not even caramelised. Of course, now I've seen it, this makes perfect sense. It's about smoke rather than heat. And unlike the darker speciality malts, it's designed to be a source of fermentable extract as well as flavour. If this is roughly how malt used to be dried before we had coke-fired kilns, it proves once and for all that pale malt is nothing new, that we've long had methods to control the heat that reaches the malt to preserve its extract, even if we suffered compromises to the flavour.*

'So how do you make it then?' I ask Beate. 'Are you making it today? Can we see it?'

She shakes her head. 'The Weyermann smoked malt process is top secret,' she says. I can almost see the red ®s floating in the air.

'OK, let me guess. Would I be right in thinking that you do it like an off-set barbecue, with wood burning at one end of a chamber and air drawing the smoke across the malt without burning it?'

'No. I told you, the process is secret. I'm not going to tell you how it is done.'

'Isn't there anything you can tell me about it? Anything at all?'

She thinks, and then points across the yard. 'That's the wood we use.'

There's a pile of cut beech logs under a low outdoor shelter. I go over and look at it, nodding sagely. 'Beech, eh? Right. Right.'

Schlenkerla make no secret of their smoked malt process. There are photos of it on their website, showing a wooden fire underneath something that looks like a professional bread oven. They also mainly use beech, with the occasional bit of oak. But this is the closest I'm going to get to discovering Weyermann's secrets.

I do get to taste their beers, though. In 2003, Weyermann built their own on-site pilot brewery, the better to test and then promote their malts. Today there's a range of beer styles on tap and in bottle, including a Dunkel, an alcohol-free wheat beer, an oatmeal stout and a barrel-aged barley wine. Weyermann's own smoked beer is called *Schlotfergerla*, or 'chimney sweep'. Two different smoked malts form the main body of it, providing both extract and flavour, with 10 per cent CARAMUNICH® and 3 per cent CARAFA® SPECIAL. It's dark brown, with some nice sweetness up front. The smoke is subtle and gentle, working with everything else rather than

---

* 'Compromise' being very much in the eye of the beer-holder.

cancelling it out. The smoked malt may be pale, but I imagine it could be quite astringent if it were used on its own. It makes sense now that these darker malts are added to smoked beers, providing big enough flavours to work both against and with the smoke. Weyermann don't put smoke in everything, because they have a much broader range of malts to promote. But across a wide range of uniformly excellent beers, I find myself loving the smoky beers most of all.

I can't believe I just wrote that.

13. 'Lager' Isn't Just Lager

Bamberg is chock full of breweries, pubs and brewpubs. It's a small town and yet it once boasted sixty-five breweries. Franconia is big barley-growing country, and if the broader region of Bavaria were counted separately from Germany it would have the highest per capita beer consumption of any country in the world. The traditional brewpubs that remain all follow a similar design, almost like a traditional British coaching inn, with the entrance from the front to the courtyard behind now closed in to form a corridor like the one in Schlenkerla.

Speziale has wood-panelled walls, with ancient beams holding up a wooden ceiling. There are coat hooks along the wall, which you're expected to use rather than putting your crap on the chair next to you at the communal tables. All pubs should be like this. I wish we could trust each other enough at home in Britain to do the same. The lager here is very lightly smoked, amber in colour with a light savoury character that fleshes out the biscuity pale malt.

In Mahr's Brau, the *Stammtisch* – the best table, formalised as such by a small plaque – is by the window, and seating there is by invitation only from the pub's self-appointed group of regulars. Old men enter and rap twice on the table, announcing their presence, before they sit down and put the world to rights. The Kellerbier here is fresh, unfiltered and unpasteurised, amber in colour and with a thicker, juicier mouthfeel than the usual Helles I've been drinking so far in Germany. Delicate cereal flavours balance a lightly citrus hop. It's a wonderful beer, simultaneously comforting and enlivening.

Finally, before I have to leave I cross the road to Keesman, the lightest and airiest of all the Bamberg brewpubs, and opt for a Bock, as it's the season for Bocks here in mid-November. It's as pale as a pilsner and tastes rich but not strong. There's no alcohol burn, but there is an assertiveness, a warning that you can't drink it the way you would most beers of this colour.

I arrived here believing that Bamberg was all about smoked beer, and that smoked beer was strong and heavy and alienating and poseurish. As I catch the train down to Nuremberg to talk to hop merchants and their customers at one of the world's biggest brewing conventions, I leave having fallen in love with both Bamberg and smoked beer, and with a new appreciation of the diversity of speciality malt and the ingenuity of German brewing.

All the beers I've tasted have been lagers, and most beer drinkers – both friends and foes of lager – believe that lager has a uniform style full of interchangeable brands. Many of the lagers with which we're most familiar are brewed using only pale malt. Some of the bigger commercial brands cut this with other cereals like corn or rice that are not only cheaper, but also contribute less flavour. Bamberg's lagers offer an astonishing array of flavours, and the main difference between them is the mix of malts used.

German brewing is still bound by the *Reinheitsgebot*, a purity law that states hops, barley, yeast and water are the only ingredients permitted in beer. Some brewers believe this is a restriction that enforces a monotone beer culture across the country. In Bamberg, the beers play tunes with malted barley like nothing I've experienced before.

If hops are merely the lipstick on beer, as Dave Griggs at Crisp Malting argues, then I don't accept that barley is beer's soul. It's too big, too present, for such an esoteric concept. Barley is beer's body, its bricks and mortar, its Hodor or Hagrid. It contributes the sugar that gets fermented into alcohol, surrendered so reluctantly by the barley grain, and it defines beer via its body and basic building blocks of flavour. Behind the scenes, its proteins and starches help create stability of flavour, good head retention and workmanlike details like that. And because of this, malt gets overlooked. Curious brewers and drinkers tend to start off with hops, and then move on to exploring yeast and bacteria, because the flavours are more dramatic, and because it seems more interesting than stocky old barley at the back, propping up everything else, providing the 'solid backbone' against which the hops can show off. We take barley, and malting, for granted. In barley was the birth of brewing – we were making beers from barley thousands of years before anyone threw a hop in to see what happened – and possibly also the birth of civilisation itself.

But malted barley has a subtlety and dexterity that belies its size. It's capable of being artistic and graceful, creative and surprising. Outside beer, we see barley as a lesser grain than wheat, suitable for animal feed but not good bread. Cynics argue that its promotion in beer is simply because the nobler grain of wheat had a higher purpose. But barley can do things in beer that wheat never could. And in the hands of a skilled maltster, it becomes an art that even the winemaker's grapes could never hope to emulate.

THREE

Water

'In most cases, the very purest and finest water is, for brewing, the worst of all.'

GEORGE WATKINS,
*THE COMPLEAT BREWER; OR, THE ART AND
MYSTERY OF BREWING EXPLAINED*, 1760

1. The Forgotten Ingredient

Most brewers and even many beer drinkers have their favourite ingredient, the one they really get obsessed with. For most drinkers today it's hops. Young craft brewers impatient for a new challenge are turning increasingly to yeast, particularly the challenges of using wild yeasts and other micro-organisms in brewing. For a few, it's malt. But you rarely hear anyone talking passionately about brewing water.

Among drinkers, when I do my pop quiz about what beer is made of, water is without fail the last one people get, even though it accounts for at least 90 per cent of what's in the drinker's glass. If water were sentient and aware of this, it might ripple its surface in a manner vaguely reminiscent of a Gallic shrug and say, 'It's all right, this always happens. I'm used to it by now. I mean, you'd all be dead by the end of the week if I wasn't here but fine, no, you go on talking about how much you love hops, don't worry about me.' Water, like air, is so essential we take it completely for granted, to the point of forgetting all about it.

It's also worth noting that in most beer water is the only one of the four central raw ingredients that ends up in your glass. This is another problem with trying to understand beer: what it's *made from*, and what it's *composed of*, aren't quite the same thing. This can be a little confusing, and it has all of us making mistakes on a regular basis.

As we now know, beer is made from hops, barley, yeast and water. But when you raise a glass to your lips, it doesn't contain any hops or any barley, and it's unlikely that it will contain any yeast. It is mostly water, and probably between 4 and 6 per cent alcohol. The water contains flavour and aroma compounds extracted from the barley and the hops. It contains alpha acids and essential oils drawn from the hops, but not the hops themselves. It contains gluten, also extracted from the barley, an amount of unfermented sugar, and most likely some dissolved carbon dioxide, created by yeast or added by machine. It's a cocktail of compounds derived from the raw ingredients, altered by alchemy, rather than the original ingredients themselves. Water is the only constant from raw ingredient to glass, as well as the medium within which the transformation happens, and the medium that delivers everything created by the other ingredients and the brewing process to your mouth.

I've already described malt as the building blocks, the body of beer, whereas I've heard others talk about malt as the canvas on which you paint your flavours. That doesn't work for me, given that malt is already rich in flavour and colour. For me, water is the blank canvas upon which all the other ingredients express themselves. Without water, you've got some seeds, leaves and fungus in a glass.

But, of course, it's not as simple as that.

If you're interested in becoming a brewer and you're looking for a little more weight in the science bits than this book provides, you should immediately check out the 'Brewing Elements' series. This comprises four excellent books published by the Brewers' Association in the United States: *Malt*, *Water*, *Yeast* and *For the Love of Hops*, each written by an expert in the field. They're aimed at brewers of all levels, and contain sections such as the history of malting or the flavour characteristics of hops that are also of interest to the non-brewer. All four are written as clearly and accessibly as they can be. But the first page of the first chapter of *Water: A Comprehensive Guide for Brewers* contains a warning:

> *It should be understood that this is a technical book that is not intended for the novice. Brewers should have a working knowledge of grain brewing techniques, including mashing, lautering, and expected yields to fully appreciate the discussions in this book. Brewers should also have a basic knowledge of high school level chemistry in order to understand the concepts discussed here.*

No other book in the 'Brewing Elements' series carries such a health warning. Water, so simple on the surface, is arguably the most technical and difficult-to-understand element in beer. The list of key figures and tables in *Water* quickly tells you why: 'A Quick Note About pH and Buffers'; 'General Solubility Rules for Ionic Compounds in Water' and 'Carbonate Species Mole Fraction vs. Water pH @ 20°C' suggest even to the most clueless of non-chemists that H_2O is only a tiny fragment of what water means to the brewer. That's why brewers refer to their canvas as 'liquor', to distinguish it from mere water.

2. Made of More

A page or two after giving their health warning above, authors John Palmer and Colin Kaminski comment, 'Beer is the most complex beverage known to man, and the role of water in brewing is equally intricate'.

It's an interesting, challenging sentence that turns convention on its head. If you don't think much about it, beer seems like a very simple and straightforward beverage, and surely water – plain, simple water – is its most basic component. But as we're learning, beer is indeed complex. There are mysteries and miracles in each of its four main ingredients. When you look at a glass of crystal-clear water, it's hard to imagine the chemical complexities that are going on in there, and difficult to comprehend them even when they're explained.

Let's start with an aspect you almost certainly already know about, but probably don't give much thought to: the softness or hardness of water, because this has a significant influence on the beer it becomes.

The sugars and flavour compounds from barley, hops and yeast are not the first elements to get into the brew. When rain falls, it's usually 'soft', which means it has nothing dissolved in it save for some carbonic acid which it picks up from being in contact with carbon dioxide in the atmosphere. When it hits the ground, it comes into contact with rocks and minerals, some of which – usually calcium or magnesium – dissolve into it. The ions from these minerals determine whether the water stays soft or becomes hard. Hardness can be temporary or permanent. Temporarily hard water contains hydrogen carbonate ions. If the water is boiled, these break down into carbonate ions that react with the dissolved calcium and magnesium to form solid precipitates such as the limescale (calcium carbonate) you get in kettles in hard-water areas. Permanently hard water contains dissolved sulphate rather than carbonate ions, and these don't behave the same way, so the water remains hard even when boiled. This difference in temporary and permanent hardness has big implications for different styles of beer.

There are pros and cons to both hard and soft water. We find hard water more pleasant to drink – it has a different mouthfeel, and those calcium and magnesium compounds are also a useful part of our diet. But the dissolved calcium and magnesium ions react with soap to form a scum, so soft water is much better for bathing, showering or household cleaning and laundry. Hard water also leads to a build up of residue in pipes. So in a perfect world, at home you'd have soft water coming out of your taps and hard water – mineral water in other words – to drink.

Hard water is usually also the best for brewing beer. A base level of hardness improves the processes of mashing and fermentation, and helps give some clarity to the finished beer.

But hardness is relative, and different styles of beer work best with differing degrees of hardness. The relative hardness or softness of water drawn from the ground has played a major role in the development of some of our favourite beer styles, anchoring them to the places in which they evolved. Hardness is entirely dependent on what happens to the water between it falling as rain and it being drawn from a well, spring or reservoir. And that changes depending on the geology of your location. If we're talking *terroir*, never has the word been more apt than for water itself.

A perfect example is one of the most iconic beer brands in the world, a brand that, for everyone who drinks it, is romantically linked to its *terroir*. So I decide to get a crash course in water chemistry – and its implications for brewing – by visiting the laboratory at the Guinness Brewery at St James's Gate in Dublin.

I chose to come to Dublin partly because the facility here is the centre of excellence for a brand that's brewed and sold all around the world, and partly because people often attribute the romance of Guinness, and the endless debate about whether it really does taste better in Ireland, to the notion that it is brewed using the water from the River Liffey.

This last point is dealt with swiftly as soon as I arrive. Eibhlin Colgan, the brand's full-time archivist, tells me that Liffey water is not and never has been used for brewing. 'It's tidal, completely unsuitable for human consumption. It was useful as a form of transport, though, and that shouldn't be underestimated.'

Eibhlin heads to the archives to prepare some stuff for me, while I grab a coffee with Feodora Heavey, a brewing scientist whose colleagues speak about her in tones of awe. As soon as I contacted Guinness and told them what I was looking for, Feodora was deployed to try to teach me the basics. Over the course of an hour, Feodora does a remarkably good job of making me understand this most technical element in beer – or making me *think* I do at any rate.

Just as I'm getting comfortable with the chemistry behind hard and soft water, Feodora ups the ante by introducing the concept of pH. The pH scale was devised by Søren Sørensen at the Carlsberg Laboratory in 1909, and an understanding of the acidity or alkalinity of water is also crucial to successful brewing. Getting the right pH in the water is vital for the enzymes in the malt to work.

Once barley has been malted and kilned, the enzymes have been activated and the starches have been broken down into smaller units, but the conversion of starch into simple, fermentable sugar hasn't yet happened. This only starts in the mashing process, when the malt is added to water in the mash tun, the first stage of brewing beer. The water has to be kept at just the right temperature for enzymes to work – usually between 65 and 72 degrees Celsius (149 and 162 degrees Fahrenheit): any hotter would risk killing the enzymes. The mash lasts for about an hour, during which the porridgelike wort is constantly agitated. The enzymes are busy converting the starch to sugar, and the water is dissolving that sugar. But as well as the mash being the right temperature, it also has to be the right pH. This would be relatively straightforward if you could work out the optimal pH level and just make sure the water you were pouring into the mash tun had it. But the problem is, when they mix, the malt changes the pH of the water it's soaking in. So brewing scientists like Feodora have to work out what the ideal pH of the mash will be, calculate what effect the malt will have on the pH and get the water to a pH where, once it's been changed by the mash, it's perfect for the mash. Easy.

The degree to which the malt changes the pH of the mash depends on the mix of different malts being used, or 'malt bill'. And this makes mash pH trickier for Guinness than most, because as well as using malted barley, Guinness gets a lot of its character from unmalted, roasted barley.

Early brewing records confirm that Arthur Guinness began by brewing ale and porter,* and his logbooks refer only to brown and pale malt. The

---

* There are various points of view on the difference between porter and stout, and most people I know who say they are clear on what that difference is disagree with other people who say they know what the difference is too. Both are dark, malty beers. From Guinness's point of view, they used to brew something called porter, and then went on to brew something darker and richer, which they referred to as 'extra stout porter', which eventually became known as just 'stout'.

last ale brewed was recorded in 1799, and in 1806 a 'superior porter' is mentioned. Guinness began using a patented black malt in 1819, and released their 'extra stout porter' in 1821, soon after which it became known simply as stout. Unmalted roasted barley (there was no point malting it to activate the enzymes if you just wanted to cook it for a specific flavour) would have provided the extra, deeper level of flavour stout drinkers wanted, but this was illegal until the Free Mash Tun Act of 1880, because brewers only paid tax on malted barley and Customs and Excise didn't think it was fair to dodge this by not actually malting your barley. Over the ensuing decades, brewers of stout, including Guinness, gradually began to switch from black malts to roasted barley, and Guinness is now the biggest roaster of barley in the world. Unmalted barley grains are cooked in big roasting drums like the one I saw at Weyermann, following the same principle as coffee roasting. And, like coffee, roasted barley is quite acidic.

Completely pure water is pH7, which is neutral. Roasted barley drives that up into being acidic. But as Feodora explains, the water at Guinness is quite alkaline, so in the mash tun, with a bit of luck and a lot of judgement, it balances out.

The science of predicting and controlling the pH of the mash by understanding the interaction of water and malt is still very much in development. 'If you don't have the right conditions the enzymes won't be happy,' Feodora says. 'We have to create the right environment for them, just like we do for yeast. We understand what they like, but we still don't know why.' Which means that even here at one of the most advanced brewing labs in the world, water treatment is still very much a process of trial and error.

'We blend water to the right specification, and it's hard to get right,' says Feodora. 'The high alkalinity of our water makes the job easier. But we also work with chocolate malt, and that likes a bit more acidity. On top of that, we now have a new brewhouse here – Brewhouse Four – and with that new equipment we had to rework everything to get the same results as before. We also brew ale and lager in there now, and those beers require water with a slightly different profile.'

In addition to all this, Diageo, the company that owns Guinness, doesn't just brew Guinness here in Dublin. All the different breweries around the world need the same conditions to the greatest extent possible. That doesn't necessarily mean getting the same pH profile in the water everywhere, but it does mean getting the same conditions in the water by the time it's in the mash tun, so the enzymes can do their job.

Could it get any more complicated? Well, as a matter of fact, yes it can. Water's pH is influenced by its hardness. It's not quite the same thing, but hard water creates the right conditions for alkalinity, and soft water creates the right conditions for acidity. That means the whole character of the water depends on its provenance, what kind of soil, rock and shale it seeps through on its journey to the brewery. And just as hops and barley change over time as well as from place to place depending on the weather, so the composition of water can change depending on the level of rainfall in a given period. Guinness check their brewing water twice a day, every day.

When I began my research I was expecting to learn more about the contribution of water to flavour in beer. I thought I was clever for even being aware that water *could* affect the flavour of beer, and that was what I was thinking of when I arranged this visit. But the whole subject of water and mash chemistry has ambushed me so dramatically that I'm still trying to process it and have forgotten all about flavour until Feodora raises it.

'The flavour impact is also more complex than you might think.'

Of course it is.

'Let's say, for example, that you have a high concentration of sodium, say, twenty parts per million. It can impact sweetness before it turns salty. The ratio of sulphate to chloride can affect whether you perceive a beer as bitter or malty, full or dry. Zinc, potassium, sodium and calcium all have flavour properties that can be good in small concentrations, but produce off-flavours if there's too much. Chloride mellows out the beer and gives it a rounder flavour. To work out whether the water is right or not, we do sensory testing of the water in a controlled environment. You turn off the lights to double-blind people, making sure they're responding only to the flavour and no other influences. We want to get the perfect Guinness profile, making sure the right attributes are there, and technical taints are not. We want roasted, nutty, caramel and toffee flavours, a creamy, lactic mouthfeel with a touch of acidity. The minerality can contribute to a creamy mouthfeel. If we didn't have water with that profile, it wouldn't taste the same.'

'How do you isolate any differences in the flavour of the beer back to a specific ingredient, such as water?'

'It's difficult to tell in the finished beer, so you have to use . . .'

No, let me guess.

'. . . trial and error.'

I thought so.

This all means that when big lager brands tell you they're brewed using only pure fresh mountain spring water, they're probably either lying or producing inferior beer because of it. But having said that, and having painted a picture of water as a dense soup full of ions, acids, alkalides and dissolved mineral deposits, it's worth reminding ourselves that brewing water has to be clean – and cleanliness for brewing means something different from cleanliness for drinking water. Brewing liquor should be free from chlorine as well as other, more obvious contaminants, so even mains water has to be treated before it's used in brewing. Good brewers who don't have access to perfect brewing water use a process of 'reverse osmosis' to strip the water back to purity, before adding back in the salts they need.

Of course, a brewery uses far more water than just that which ends up in the beer. It's also used for cooling and, especially, cleaning. Going back to the pros and cons of hard and soft water, a brewery wants softer water for cleaning than it does for brewing, so if you're taking all your water from one source, it probably needs to be treated in different ways depending on what it's being used for. Those who know better than to suggest Guinness is brewed with water from the Liffey speak knowledgeably about the remarkable properties of the water from the well on-site at St James's Gate, but they're just as wrong as the Liffey fans. The well water, like the Liffey, is brackish, and where it has been used in the past it's only been for cooling.

Every commercial brewery is keenly aware of their ratio of water used to the volume of beer brewed, and that ratio is dramatic: traditionally, between five and ten pints of water are used for every pint of beer brewed. That means for every pint of beer, between four and nine pints are either being boiled off into the atmosphere or going down the drain and into the water supply, and that creates another headache for the brewer. Waste water will be dirty or full of yeast, and brewers can be penalised for putting too much crap back into the system, meaning more modern breweries are exploring different methods for pre-treating their waste water before releasing it. And as such large consumers of water, they can't take their supply for granted. In 2011, a drought began in California that was still going strong when this book was being written in summer 2016. Brewers like Bear Republic, who wanted to expand to meet demand by doubling their capacity, were told by city authorities that this was impossible. American brewers began investing in water conservation – between 2009 and 2014 the Anheuser-Busch Brewery in Los Angeles reduced its water consumption by 31 per cent, and many brewers are now bringing the ratio down closer to three pints of water used for every pint of beer brewed. But conservation is only half the story. In early 2016, the Half Moon Bay Brewing Company just south of San Francisco launched a beer that had been made using NASA technology to recycle 'grey water' – the stuff that comes out of sinks, showers and washing machines.

Water is fundamental to beer, by volume easily the most important ingredient, and that volume only accounts for between 10 and 20 per cent of all the water a brewery needs. Water supply is the most important factor in the location of a brewery, and a key part in the whole history and development of Guinness in Dublin.

St James's Gate was one of the main entrances to medieval Dublin. Just outside it was an area known as The Liberties, home to merchants and artisans who didn't want to be governed by city regulations. It was also next to the watercourse that flows to the city from the Wicklow and Dublin mountains to the south. The River Dodder and the River Poddle make their way through Dublin and down to join the Liffey, and over time they've been added to with channels and eventually the Grand Canal leading to the city basin, a man-made reservoir that fed Dublin's needs for most of its history.*

Guinness has detailed records stretching all the way back to the lease Arthur Guinness signed when he took over what was then a modest brewery from its previous owner, Alderman Sir Mark Rainsford, in 1759. The property was on 'the ground known as the Pipes', thanks to its proximity to the pipe wall or city watercourse. Records from the previous century show seventy different breweries and distilleries in Dublin, and most of them were located here. Water rights were an important aspect of the lease.

---

* The main source of Grand Canal water was St James's Well up in the mountains, the same St James who gave his name to the gate there, and the same St James who is also revered in Santiago de Compostela in northern Spain. St James's Gate was the starting point for a pilgrimage to Santiago de Compostela, and the location of epic medieval feasts. The saint's feast was celebrated at the well on 25 July. In the early seventeenth century, one traveller, Barnaby Rich, was shocked to find only ale on sale at the fair, and a 'multitude of rascal people' enjoying it.

The dispute between the brewery and the City of Dublin over water rights is a defining moment in the history and culture of Guinness. Arthur Guinness the man is a cornerstone of Guinness the brand. The company reveres him as an entrepreneur and visionary, a man of character who stood up for what was right.* In 1773, a committee 'appointed for better supplying the city with pipe water' began to take a closer look at the behaviour of several brewers around St James's Gate, including Arthur Guinness. Guinness insisted on his right to take water from the city basin, but the committee found that many of the pipes leading from the watercourse were larger than regulations permitted. In court, the Corporation of Dublin found that the land on which the watercourse ran belonged to the city, not to the tenant of the brewery, and instructed that the watercourse leading into the brewery should be filled in.

The committee informed Guinness of their intention to do so on 10 May. According to their report, Mr Guinness 'gave for answer that the water was his, and he would defend it by force of arms'. The committee replied that they 'were not to be intimidated from the execution of their duty by threats, but would certainly proceed to accomplish it', to which Mr Guinness responded 'come and have a go if you think you're hard enough' – or, rather, he 'invited them to try how far their strength would prevail'.

So the committee men prevailed upon the local Sheriff, who sent two of his men with them. They began to destroy the water channel, and were quickly confronted by an employee of Mr Guinness who 'offered some obstruction' before 'being removed by Mr Sheriff threatening to send him to Newgate'.

---

* This is very handy for a beer that many drinkers perceive as being strong, thick and challenging. In fact Draught Guinness – the main beer the company makes, for there are many different Guinnesses – is surprisingly light and easy to drink (and has fewer calories than the equivalent volume of lager). But we're led by the eye, and at first sight Guinness looks forbidding. In mainstream beer culture it's a 'proper drinker's drink', not for the faint-hearted. This creates a curious problem for the brand: people want to be seen as Guinness drinkers because they think it makes them seem more substantial, but if everyone who claimed to drink Guinness really did so, as often as they claim, Guinness would be by far the biggest beer brand in the UK. In Nigeria, where Guinness is also brewed and drunk widely, it's viewed as a real man's drink that puts lead in your pencil, and the folklore is that if a woman is in the mood for sex, she leaves a bottle of Guinness out for her husband for when he comes home, and heads to bed. The fact that Arthur Guinness was a powerful, successful man is a dream to marketers celebrating the virtues of the drink.

But the delay had given time for Arthur Guinness to arrive on the scene himself, 'who violently rushed upon them wrenching a pickaxe from one and declaring with very much improper language, that they should not proceed'. The committee 'expostulated on this impropriety' and the labourers were ordered to proceed, but Arthur Guinness 'stood with the pickaxe in the way and prevented them, and declared that if they filled it up from end to end he would immediately open it'.

Guinness stood his ground, and the legend of Arthur was born. There followed a long-running legal stand-off, which Guinness resolved 'in order to avoid expense' by securing the water supply he needed, on his terms, for the payment of an annual rent of £10.

As both Guinness and Dublin grew, the water supply changed. The city takes its water today from a large reservoir in County Wicklow, and Guinness now draws all its water from the municipal supply. In the days of the old Grand Canal, brewers couldn't yet measure accurately the hardness and pH of the water, so there's no way of knowing if today's water is the same as that used by Arthur to perfect his stout. But the Dublin Mountains are part of the same range as the Wicklow Mountains, divided by a county line, so Arthur's liquor was probably at least similar to the hard, alkaline water Guinness enjoys today.

Knowing what we do now, we can see that water was an invisible hand guiding Guinness's fortunes. Would Guinness be the global success it became if Arthur had set up in a different city, trying to brew the same beers using a different water supply, where the alkalinity and hardness weren't quite right so the enzymes didn't perform quite as well and the mouthfeel and bitterness of the beer were just slightly different? We'll never know. But the best brewers of the past were able to take credit for the excellence of their beers when much of it was due to the unseen, unknown chemistry of the water most drinkers never thought about, and still don't. The brewers of today understand and shape that water chemistry as part of their job. But many of them do so in locations that, just like St James's Gate, were originally chosen because brewing just seemed to work there.

If you're ever wondering why some cities have reputations for brewing excellent beers, a dismissive shrug of 'maybe it was something in the water' actually hits the mark.

3. Three Hundred Metres Down

The first brewery trip I ever went on was a visit to the Budweiser Budvar Brewery in České Budějovice, southern Bohemia, in the Czech Republic. One aspect of the brewery tour stood out in my memory more than anything else.

Our tour was conducted by Josef Tolar, who at that time had been Budvar's head brewer for twenty years. Before we even entered the brewery, Mr Tolar stopped us in the yard by a shiny metal cylinder and told us this was the water supply, pumped from 300 metres below ground. 'The water here is extremely mild, very soft,' he told us in slow, precise English. 'What is important, perhaps, is that this water is free from any adjuncts, or sterilisers, or chemistry. When the water is collected from the earth, really it is nine thousand years old. We are pumping water that has had no contact with civilisation, no contact with chemistry, with agriculture, or with any other part of human activity.'

It was a hell of a sales story. Thirteen years later, when I decided I wanted to learn more about brewing water, I asked Budvar if Mr Tolar would be available to expand on the subject a little more.

České Budějovice is about ninety miles south of Prague. It's very near the borders of both Austria and Germany (more specifically Bavaria) and has been exporting beer to those countries since the twelfth century. After the Battle of the White Mountain in 1620 – one of the opening salvos in the Thirty Years' War – it was part of the Austro-Hungarian Empire, within which the official language was German. Czechoslovakia gained its independence in 1918, and Czech names slowly began to swap places with German names on maps. Hence the town of Pilsen became Plzeň and, more dramatically, the town formerly known as Budweis became better known as České Budějovice.*

---

* In German, Budweiser literally means 'from Budweis'. If you want to read more about how American brewers Anheuser-Busch stole the name, said on record in a court of law that they'd named their beer after the town of Budweis and then flatly denied they had ever done so, broke numerous promises about how they proposed to use it and then fought aggressive legal battles around the world with a small Czech brewer to try to prevent them naming a beer after the town in which it was brewed, it's all in my book *Three Sheets to the Wind*.

Being part of the Austro-Hungarian Empire did have some advantages for Czech brewers. When a new blonde lager called pilsner was first brewed in 1842, it spread rapidly across Europe to become the most popular and celebrated beer style of its day, and any day since, leaping from there to account for 90 per cent of the world's beer by the late twentieth century.

But in Czech towns such as Budweis / České Budějovice, the coexistence of Czechs and Germans was politically tense. The 1890 Census in České Budějovice showed that there were 11,117 Germans living there compared to 16,271 Czechs, but the Czechs had no political representation. In order to gain political influence, the Czechs realised they needed economic influence first. Most of the big businesses in town were German-owned and run, so the Czechs set about creating rivals to them.

In the 1890 Census, the German-owned Civic Brewery put enormous pressure on its (mostly Czech) employees to claim German as their primary language.* When they protested, the management told the Czech workers that if they didn't like their jobs they were quite welcome to set up a brewery of their own. So they did, forming a committee to create Czech Joint Stock Brewery in České Budějovice.

A decisive factor in the siting of the new Joint Stock Brewery was water analysis. Boreholes revealed that the water in a northern suburb of town (confusingly named Prague) was perfect for brewing the pilsner-style beers sweeping Europe. Two wells were dug on the site: one to a depth of twelve and a half metres to supply water for cooling, and another to twenty metres to supply brewing liquor.

As the date of the first brew's release approached, the German-owned press mounted increasingly fierce attacks on the 'undrinkable' beer no one had even tasted yet, and water was their focus. The *Budweiser Zeitung* wrote, 'Germans will not drink Czech beer brewed from filtered river water as they don't want to get upset stomachs!' The Czech press fought back, time and again, with the *Budivoj* responding, 'With this article the *Budweiser Zeitung* has once again put its foot in its mouth as the Czechs

---

* The Civic Brewery was founded by the Germans in 1795 and was brewing 'Budweiser Bier' from 1802. It was exporting 'Budweiser Bier' to countries including the United States from 1875. So while they might be the villains in this particular story from Budvar's perspective, it complicates the ongoing legal situation somewhat that Budvar's local competitor was actually the 'original' Budweiser.

will not do it this way and have for a long time been avoiding beer from the Civic Brewery that is brewed only from filtered river water. The Czech beer will be brewed from well water.'

The first beer was brewed in October 1795, but because of the long lagering time that was typical of the day* it didn't go on sale until Christmas. Thanks to its perfect brewing water, Saaz hops and soft, Moravian barley, the beer's impact was immediate. By 1897 the Joint Stock Brewery's beer was being exported to Prague, Vienna and Trieste. The Civic Brewery renamed its beer Samson, struggled to compete and went into decline.[†]

When the Joint Stock Brewery was first built, the shareholders assumed the water supply from the shallow wells would be sufficient. But they were soon expanding, and the amount that could be drawn from 20 metres down wasn't enough. Samson was indeed using filtered river water by this time, in the age-old tradition of accusing your opponents of doing something bad and then doing it yourself while everyone is looking their way. The ground around the river was sandy, and that limited the scope of any wells

---

* Lagering – the conditioning of bottom-fermented beers – doesn't really fall within the remit of this book, but it's a vital part of the Budvar story. Traditionally, lager beers (from the German verb meaning 'to store') were aged for around three months before being released.[‡] Modern cost pressures and modern technology have caused this period to be dramatically reduced. I've been told by a former brewer of one famous 'premium' lager brand that as late as the 1990s was boasting of its twenty-eight-day lagering period, is now brewed, 'lagered' and packaged within seventy-two hours, and that in his opinion, this dramatic cutting of corners results in the presence of unwanted alcohols that are responsible for worse hangovers than other beers. This may also explain this particular brand's unfortunate association with domestic abuse. Budvar still matures its lagers for three months, just like that first brew in 1895. It suffers no such associations.

‡ Less well known, and certainly less celebrated, is the fact that British ale styles were also stored for long periods. Porter was stored in large vats for up to a year. India Pale Ale famously enjoyed a particularly special maturation process on its six-month journey through the Atlantic, round the Cape of Good Hope and up through the Indian Ocean. But IPA that was intended for domestic consumption in the UK was aged for up to a year. The temperature and subsequent effects of maturation were different for each style, so while it's tempting to say 'all beers were lagered' in the original meaning of the German word, lagering now means something more specific. But traditionally most premium beers were stored before consumption. What we now refer to as real ale – live beer served fresh from the cask a few days or weeks after brewing – is often referred to as beer as it's always been made, but it's a relatively recent innovation dating back to the 1870s.

† Samson is still brewed in the town today, but is often simply referred to as 'the other brewery' by certain residents.

that could be dug there. The issue for an expanding, successful brewery was that, away from the riverbank, České Budějovice sat on solid rock.

When Czechoslovakia gained independence at the end of the First World War, the whole brewing climate changed. Independence was great; the loss of the big single market of the Austro-Hungarian Empire wasn't so good, and the Joint Stock Brewery looked to modernise and find new markets. They consulted Professor Karel Absolon, the foremost geologist of his day, who had previously mapped the terrain of large parts of Moravia. Absolon observed that České Budějovice sat in a natural basin. The layer of rock ran 300 metres deep, and in the basin every geological layer was lowered compared to the ground around it. Absolon advised the brewery that in other, similar sites he'd mapped, such basins collected water beneath the rock. Because of its consistency, water took thousands of years to trickle down through the rock to the underground reservoir below, and when it got there it was remarkably pure and soft, having picked up very few mineral deposits along the way. This would, in theory, make it perfect for brewing pilsner-style lager beers.

That was all well and good, but drilling through 300 metres of solid rock was no easy feat. It wasn't cheap either, and the shareholders were hesitant. But tests suggested the water was there, and that it was perfect. In 1923, the brewery dug its first artesian well, drilling down manually with a rotating drill. The first well didn't go all the way through the rock, but still far enough to access a water source. But the walls of the well began to cave in, and in 1928 a second well was dug to a depth of 212 metres. Feeling increasingly confident, in 1930 they dug a third well to 300 metres, and into a massive aquifer, just as Absolon had predicted. At the same time, the brewery built a state-of-the-art laboratory that, among other functions, could analyse the underground water. It was absolutely perfect for pilsner-type brewing.

'It was a stroke of good luck to find such water beneath the brewery,' Josef Tolar tells me. 'We are saving money now, but we spent it on drilling the wells.'

Mr Tolar* started work for what is now the Budweiser Budvar Brewery in 1965, thirty-five years after the 300-metre well was completed. He worked

---

* Even now, thirteen years after I first met him, I still feel like I must refer to him as *Mister* Tolar.

in various functions, mainly in laboratory analysis, under what he now refers to euphemistically as 'the previous regime', before becoming brew-master in 1985. Under Soviet rule everything was organised regionally, and all the breweries in southern Bohemia were united in one group owned by the state. The lab at Budvar worked for ten breweries across the region. If there's anyone who can tell me about Czech brewing water, it's this man.

Mr Tolar retired in 2008, but is retained with an official title of 'Advisor to the Directors'. Well into his seventies now, his thick, dark hair is finally greying. 'I still have my room, my desk in the brewery,' he says. 'It is pleasant for me that the directors ask for my opinion. It's pleasant to have a chance to speak. But it is also a responsibility. If you are part of a big international unit you know you are only going to be in your role for three to four years. I am not friends with such practices. If you destroy the company but you have a very big profit in that time, you are a hero. It's not healthy, because continuity is important.'

Mr Tolar's predecessor was brewmaster for twenty-five years, Tolar for twenty-four. 'At one hundred years from the foundation of the brewery I was proud to say that for half of its existence, the quality and technology was influenced by two people only. Czech drinkers are conservative and traditional. Producing a product that has been sold for decades, you are giving people the same product as their father, their grandfather. You make decisions that will have influence for forty or fifty years.'

Sinking wells through 300 metres of rock rather than simply taking water from the river – especially in an age where water chemistry was better understood and treatment of water for brewing was becoming com-monplace – seems like one such decision. Mr Tolar has made many similar long-term decisions of his own, but perhaps none as fundamental as this.

He takes me outside the main brewery building to see what he refers to as 'the reservoir'. I'm looking around for a body of water, perhaps some anglers or canoeists, and then realise he's pointing out two large stainless steel cylinders, each about forty feet high and similar in width. They sit amid neatly cropped grass as carefully manicured as a bowling green. Next to them sits a smaller structure whose base is a circular stone wall, like a fairy-tale well. Metal plates cover the top of the well, and a thick steel col-umn rises from the centre, a glass cylinder in the middle of it, before it runs into a network of pipes leading into the big cylinders of the reservoir. The whole apparatus is encased in Perspex. Like much in this brewery, there's a sense that it doesn't need to be as pretty as this, but that standards are standards, and everything has to look the part as well as working properly.

There are now eight or nine different boreholes across the town, but this is the main one, running to a depth of 307 metres. It was renovated twenty years ago, and the size of the tanks increased. We can hear the hissing of the pump, and, though you can't really tell, what we're seeing in the clear central column is water being pumped from 307 metres below us at a speed of fifty-five litres per second. It rarely stops: if it were to stop and start, this would disturb the sands around the water source. The reason we can't actually see the water moving is that there's nothing in it, no visible particles or haze rising through the central column of the well, and that's how we want it to stay.

'Perhaps it could be mentioned that for decades of years, water from underground was free,' says Mr Tolar. 'But permission had to be gained because now, everything underground is owned by the state. We have permission to extract the water, but no one else is allowed to use it.'

The water is so pure that absolutely no treatment is needed – nothing is added, and there's no sterilisation. Between the steel reservoirs and the brewhouse it's filtered through sand in case any particles have managed to get into it while it was being stored, but that's it. In this most fundamental of brewing disciplines, Budvar gets a free pass.

'When our grandfathers went to Professor Absolon, he gave them the analysis of the water from similar locations. This water is very mild, the best for brewing lager beer. Hard water influences the character of hop bitterness. It makes it more aggressive, less smooth. When we were experimenting with the Žatec [or, in German, Saaz] hop we wanted soft water to work with its delicacy. It is a stroke of luck to find such water beneath the brewery.'

Joe Tolar's delivery in his second (or maybe it's his third or fourth) language understates that point quite beautifully.

There are various scales around the world that measure the hardness of water. At Budvar they use a German scale that measures degrees of hardness, with one degree being ten milligrams of calcium oxide per litre, or 17.848 parts per million. On average, water scores around 8 to 10 on this scale. The excessively hard water of Burton upon Trent scores 25 degrees or higher. The water from Budvar's wells scores just 3.5.

Outside the UK, other countries have a much more sophisticated understanding of the minerality of water and the difference it makes. It's recommended that mineral water is not fed to babies or toddlers, because high levels of some minerals, such as sodium, aren't suitable for them. Some specific brands that are low in sodium are sold specifically as baby water, and up the road in the capital city of Prague it's a matter of civic pride that the tap water is so pure and soft it's often referred to as baby water. It's no different here. 'In Germany and Switzerland, bottled water undergoes a battery of tests before it goes to supermarkets to make sure such elements aren't present,' says Mr Tolar. 'In our water, these elements are so low they do not even register on such tests. It means we could use such water for the production of water for babies. This is an excellent positive for us.'

Pilsner-style lager is definitely not for babies, but it's one of the lightest and most delicate beer styles – and that also makes it the most unforgiving. Everything has to be just right in a pilsner – there's nowhere for mistakes to hide. It's finely balanced, and when it's perfect, rather than being tasteless like many commercial lagers, it's definitely flavourful; some might even say it's assertive. But it's like filigree lace compared to the solid, heavy blocks of an IPA or stout. Pilsner gives the lie to the notion that delicate flavours are the same as dumbed-down or absent flavours. It's satisfying and quenching and invigorating and calls you back again and again.

Like any beer, pilsner benefits from a bit of calcium, which helps improve clarity, but if there's not enough the long lagering times that are traditional around here will take care of that. Žatec hops, which just happen to grow nearby and are widely revered as the world's greatest lager hops, also need this kind of soft water to shine properly. Everything fits.

Mr Tolar doesn't refer to the water as being perfect for pilsner brewing, and he doesn't refer to the beer as pilsner-style beer, 'for obvious reasons' – the main one being that *Pilsner Urquell* is Budvar's biggest competitor in the Czech Republic. But beer from České Budějovice is still what we would refer to internationally as Czech-style pilsner, the style having grown and diversified, the interpretation of it having been stretched and too often abused and bastardised. It's a happy accident that all the right ingredients just happened to be close together, that production techniques such as lagering helped enhance the beer created by them, and that the local preference just happens to chime with the character of that beer.

Or maybe it's not an accident at all. Maybe it's evolution, natural selection. Golden lager emerged as the dominant beer style here because it suits the land and the water, the brewing liquor that is the union between the other local ingredients. People here like that style of beer because it's the style that worked best here. Just as with stout or IPA, as different beer styles developed some came and others went, and before we understood what water chemistry was those beers that have endured did so because they found their natural habitat.

And different habitats resulted in the prosperity of very different beers.

4. The 'Beer City'

When Alfred Barnard travelled around the UK in the 1880s while researching his epic three-volume *Noted Breweries of Great Britain and Ireland*, the town of Burton upon Trent took his breath away:

> *Nothing can be more interesting than the view of the "Beer City" from the hill, with its tall chimneys, mammoth buildings, and numerous spires . . .*
>
> *We passed no less than four large breweries, all within a quarter-of-a-mile of our hotel, whose lofty buildings, water towers and tall chimneys seemed to hem us in on every side. As we proceeded, a smell of beer, and the odour of hops pervaded the air, whilst burly brewers met us at every turn. Here and there, engines glided noiselessly about, dragging trucks heavily laden with casks, and the clean streets were full of animation and life.*

In this description, Barnard was echoing the impressions of the *Burton Daily News*, which in 1872 described the town as 'a congeries of breweries, in the interstices between which and around their edges a town has diffidently grown up, and exists on sufferance, while the ground on which it stands is not required for brewery purposes.'

Burton was the most famous brewing town on the planet and home to the world's largest brewery. The red triangle of Bass was Britain's first ever registered trademark, and was as recognisable around the world then as the McDonald's golden arches or Nike swoosh today. But Bass was just one of around thirty breweries in this tiny Midlands town. Many of the biggest names in London brewing – the world's first industrialised breweries – had set up satellite operations here, brewing beer in Burton and sending it back home to the capital on newly laid rail links.

No town in the world before or since has ever been as dominated by brewing as Burton was at its peak, nor has any other town or city ever had greater importance on the global brewing stage than Burton had at the time of Barnard's visit. India Pale Ale (IPA) was the most celebrated, fashionable beer in the world, and no other town or city could brew better IPA than Burton.

IPA was brewed for export, and Burton had long enjoyed a reputation for brewing beers that kept well. Export beers tended to be stronger than their domestic counterparts, and Burton made good strong beers. No one really knew why, but many speculated. In 1789, James Pilkington's *A View on the Present State of Derbyshire* contained a letter from Erasmus Darwin – Charles Darwin's grandfather, who lived in nearby Lichfield – on the relationship between water hardness and beer:

> *I cannot leave this account of calcerous or hard waters without adding; that . . . hard waters make stronger beer than soft ones. I appeal to the brewers of Burton for the fact, who have the soft water of the Trent running on one side of their brewhouses; and yet prefer universally the hard or calcerous water supplied by their pumps.*

In linking water to beer quality in this way, Darwin was ahead of other thinkers of his time, even those in the brewing industry itself. George Watkins, author of *The Compleat Brewer; or, The Art and Mystery of Brewing Explained*, published in 1760, wrote:

> *Water may be distinguished into four kinds: Spring, River, Rain and Pond; and what is the worst in appearance often makes the best drink . . .*
> *The brewer . . . will find it true that very soft water, such as rainwater, and that of ponds, and very hard, such as that of springs and wells, are proper in but a few cases; and that for high-coloured drink, river-water is the best, and for the pale kinds, that of brooks or rivulets, with a swift current.*

The Trent Valley is a broad trough, hollowed out of Triassic rock and covered by layers of sand, shale, silt, gravel, chalk and mudstone. These deposits, known as marls, have a dramatic effect on the water that seeps through them, giving it a mineral composition that turns out to be perfect for pale ale.

Throughout the eighteenth century, as both pale ale and exports of beer from Britain grew, Burton acquired its reputation for brewing beers that were bright, clear and strong, and stood up well to the rigours of travel. Scholars like Darwin came close to the reason why with their speculations on the merits of hard water, and in 1830 the secrets of Burton's brewing water were finally revealed thanks to a scandal that rocked Britain. In 1830 the Society for the Diffusion of Useful Knowledge* published a treatise, 'The Art of Brewing', which claimed that Burton brewers created the special character of their ales by adulterating them with salt, steel, honey, prunella, jalap, sulphate of lime and black rosin.† The Burton brewers sued for libel and won, after producing affidavits from chemists who had analysed their brewing water and found that it contained high levels of calcium sulphate derived from the gypsum deposits in the gravel and the wells. The author of the article, David Booth, said he hadn't known this, and that in his attempts to recreate the character of the beer he'd only been able to get close to it by adding various 'noxious' ingredients.

Thanks to Booth's libel, the world now knew that what made Burton's beers so special were mineral deposits in the brewing water. But this didn't stop another expert, far more qualified than David Booth, from making the same mistake years later. Anselme Payen – the French chemist who achieved brewing immortality by being the first person in the world to

---

* Set up in 1826 with the aim of disseminating scientific knowledge in an inexpensive and democratic way to people who hadn't had the benefit of formal education. By 1840 it had failed, perhaps because, as demonstrated here, its knowledge turned out to be not all that useful, or possibly because it didn't contain enough pictures of cats.

† I have no idea what half of these are. But the accusations weren't as outrageous at the time as they sound to us now. Adulteration of beer was commonplace. In my research on this topic for *Hops and Glory*, I came across a book with one of my favourite ever titles: *A Treatise on Adulterations of Food, and Culinary Poisons, Exhibiting the Fraudulent Sophistications of Bread, Beer, Wine, Spirituous Liquors, Tea, Coffee, Cream, Confectionery, Vinegar, Mustard, Pepper, Cheese, Olive Oil, Pickles, and Other Articles Employed in Domestic Economy. And Methods of Detecting Them*, written by Friedrich Christian Accum and published in 1820. It reads like a food standards report written for the *Daily Mail* by Stephen King in a bad mood.

identify enzymes – blotted his record as a brewing chemistry expert when he accused Burton's brewers of achieving the special bitterness of their beers by adding strychnine to them, an accusation he made during a lecture on hygiene in Paris in 1852. Burton's brewers threw open their doors and offered up samples of their beers to chemists around the world, at the same time as demonstrating that there wasn't enough strychnine in the world for them to bitter their beers in the way suggested by Payen. Once again, the beers were found to be absolutely pure.

The scandal proved to be the perfect advertisement for Burton beer, at a time when glass was becoming increasingly affordable and the colour and clarity of beer was becoming more important than ever before. Pale ale was the fashionable drink of Victorian Britain, right around the time the British Empire reached its peak. Burton had been scientifically verified as the incomparable champion of the world's new favourite beer, and became the world's beer capital.

As I learned on my visit to Guinness, the minerals dissolved in water have two main effects on beer, closely related to each other. They influence the brewing process itself, and they influence the flavour of the finished beer, interacting with the other ingredients. The perfect water specification, the amounts of different minerals dissolved in it, changes depending on what kind of beer you're brewing.

If you're making a strong pale ale, ideally you want a high concentration of calcium ions. This reduces haze and helps the beer to clarify better, and minimises the extract of coloured material, all of which emphasises and accentuates a bright, pale, hoppy beer. Magnesium can also add bitterness, but it can be the wrong kind of bitterness unless it's countered by calcium, which should always be higher. A good level of bicarbonate is also desirable, as this helps control pH and gets more out of the hops. You want low levels of sodium, potassium and chloride: sodium and potassium both contribute saltiness, whereas sodium and chloride both give a fuller, more mellow palate, which is fine for other styles, but not necessarily for a dry, zippy ale. What you want instead is a high level of sulphate, which gives a drier flavour and works well with the hops to enhance their bitterness. Sulphate would be Josef Tolar's worst nightmare at Budvar, making his treasured Saaz hops come across as harsh and astringent. But it's great for hop-forward pale ales. Bearing all that in mind, a comparison of some of the key minerals in the

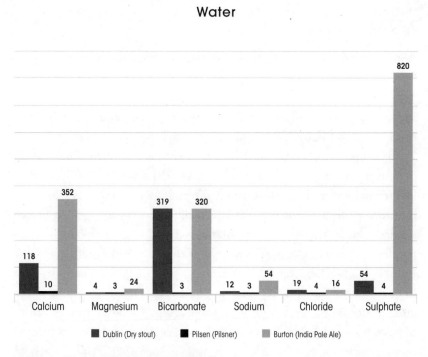

Water profiles from famous brewing cities
Dissolved mineral content (parts per million)
Simplified from Palmer and Kaminski, *Water: A Comprehensive Guide for Brewers*

three centres of brewing excellence I've visited while learning about water paints a dramatic picture.

All that sulphate in the water from the marls creates a pale ale with a drier flavour and a more enhanced hop bitterness. According to a contemporary account in the history of the Mann, Crossman & Paulin brewery, in its heyday Burton pale ale was 'a bright sparkling bitter, the colour of sherry and the condition of champagne'.

Burton water was perfect for a strong, hoppy pale ale designed for long-keeping and export. Another curious aspect of beer exports was the 'ripening' or conditioning of beer once it had left the brewery. When the *Pall Mall Gazette* visited Bass, Ratcliff & Gretton's ale stores in St Pancras station, the manager, Mr Bailey, told them 'the best ales need a little age on them'. Contemporary accounts of the arrival of Burton ale in India talk about it being 'perfectly ripe', which, when described, echoes the champagne comparison above. IPA was also exported in great quantities from Edinburgh's breweries, which had similar, but not identical, water to Burton's. In 1858, an agent in Calcutta wrote to William Younger of Edinburgh, complaining,

'Your beer is well known for its body. This is an obstacle to it becoming a favourite brand, it takes too long to ripen. The few casks of your last lot were fully eighteen months before sufficiently ripe to drink.' It's hard for us to identify precisely what ripeness was from contemporary accounts, but the lighter, drier body of Burton IPA seems to have enhanced it.

For centuries, brewing had been considered an art form. The analysis of Burton's water, and the explanation of what had previously seemed like magic, was an important aspect of the movement that saw brewing transformed into a science. The 1870s and 1880s were a golden age of scientific innovation in brewing that reinvented beer as the drink we're familiar with today, and Burton was one of the early drivers of that process. In 1866, Horace Tabberer Brown started work at the Worthington Brewery in Burton, aged just seventeen. He would become recognised as one of the greatest brewing scientists (indeed, some argue the recognition given to him is not enough). But it wasn't easy. Brown's earliest experiments focused on water analysis, and he met with strong resistance when trying to get hold of the kit he needed, thanks to the age-old belief in brewing as craft rather than science. Reflecting on his career decades later, he wrote:

> My chief was one of the old school of practical brewers and distinctly discouraged any suggestions I threw out as to the desirability of fitting up a small room for the purpose [of being a laboratory] . . . I soon found out that the real objection on the part of my chief was due to a fear that the display of any chemical apparatus might suggest to customers who went round the brewery the horrible suspicion that the beer was being 'doctored'. A small room was later fitted with a balance and apparatus for water analysis, but the little office in which these were placed for my use had its windows carefully obscured so that no one could see what was going on inside.

Aided by the ever more precise analysis of people like Horace Tabberer Brown, brewers of IPA who weren't lucky enough to have access to Burton wells began adding gypsum (calcium sulphate, the main ingredient in blackboard chalk and plaster of Paris) to their brewing water to increase its hardness. In *Chemistry, Theoretical, Practical and Analytical*, a part-work published in 1853 and edited by James Sheridan Muspratt, the editor suggests that any water containing a large amount of gypsum, or sulphate of lime, is the best for brewing, and goes on:

> *The Editor would suggest that when brewers in certain districts are compelled to use soft water, or that which runs off moors or fens, for want of better, they should impregnate them at second hand with gypsum, or with such limestones as are easily procurable. This plan has been found most serviceable, and the ale obtained from such artificial water has nearly equalled the renowned product of Burton.*

The word 'Burtonisation' was first used to describe this process by Egbert Hooper in his 1882 book *The Manual of Brewing*, and it's still common practice for brewers of pale ale around the world to Burtonise their water today. Burtonisation was the start of modern brewing water treatment. Wherever you are in the world, you can analyse the water you start with, find the ideal water profile for the beer you want to make and add or take away the minerals to create your perfect beer.* But those style specifications are still based on the water that occurs naturally in places like Burton, Dublin, Plzeň or České Budějovice. And there's still a sense that the real thing is better. London brewers were still coming to Burton to brew long after they could have Burtonised London water, and all these towns and cities, as well as others such as Vienna, Munich and Dortmund, are still revered as brewing centres despite the fact that the beers they gave birth to have long been brewed much more widely thanks to water treatment technology.

Some of this hankering for a specific place is the same romance in brewing that still resists giving in completely to science; that yearns for floor malting and old landrace barley varieties. But there's also the possibility that the real thing, occurring naturally, may have advantages we haven't yet discovered, that we can't yet measure. Maybe our instincts continue to guide us in ways the scientific method cannot, just as they have through most of the history of brewing. In *In Defence of Food*, Michael Pollan

---

* Although, of course, it's rarely as simple in practice. You can buy a kit that will Burtonise your water. But many home brewers and some commercial brewers neglect to test the water profile they're starting with. To give a simple mathematical analogy, it's easy to work out what you'll get if you add fifty to zero. But you'll get a very different result if you're adding fifty to minus ten or plus fifteen.

explains how, when food is processed, it loses a lot of its natural vitamins and minerals, and therefore much of its goodness. No problem, says the food industry, because now we can measure the exact composition of food and if anything is missing we can just add it back in (and boast 'Now with added vitamins!' on the packaging while we're at it). But there's a problem. Take beta-carotene, the red-orange pigment that gives carrots their colour but also occurs in fruits and vegetables such as broccoli, melon, spinach, pumpkin and mango. When we eat it in plants, it has been proven to reduce the free radicals that cause cancer. But if you take a beta-carotene supplement instead of having it in food, it doesn't work. As Pollan says, 'We don't eat nutrients; we eat food', and our attempts to build artificially something as effective as a carrot have so far come to naught. We have no idea why it works in its natural habitat, but doesn't when added artificially. Similarly, maybe there are aspects of water chemistry we haven't yet discovered.

5. The Sacred Wells

It's time for me to taste some of Burton's legendary pale ale brewing water for myself. I've tasted it many times in beer, but never from the source. Is it possible to taste the qualities in water that make it so special for brewing?

Marston's has been brewing ale with Burton well water since 1834. Its flagship brand, Pedigree, is famous among connoisseurs because the sulphates in the water are so pronounced they create the 'Burton snatch', a faint, eggy whiff that to some is the sign of true *terroir*, to others a fault, and to others still something that used to be there, but has been dumbed down recently because nothing is as good as it used to be anywhere, so it must have been, probably.

Since 1898, Marston's has occupied the Albion Brewery in the district of Shobnall. The brewery was state-of-the-art when it was built by London brewer Mann, Crossman & Paulin in 1875, when they felt they had no choice but to come to Burton and brew here if they wanted to make the pale ales everyone wanted. Twenty years later, they figured they knew how to recreate Burton's famous water well enough, and retreated to the capital. Marston's, which was too big for its previous home after merging with another brewery, moved in.

Today, the red-brick bulk of the Albion Brewery is one of the rare sights that still manages to evoke Burton and brewing's golden age. The main building follows the Victorian tower design, where you haul the raw ingredients up several floors and then let gravity help the beer flow back down various stages as it is brewed. The insides of the building have changed dramatically, but from the outside its windows, tall chimney and 1930s-style lettering on the Marston's sign give it an air of stolid permanence.

The water comes into the brewery at the boiler house, which is underneath the main brewery building. The brewery takes water from different sources depending on what it's used for. In the boiler room, four thick steel pipes stretch from floor to ceiling, each with a tap at shoulder height. One is South Staffordshire mains water, the next field well water, then deep-bore tube water, and finally water from a well in nearby Crossman Street, which isn't being used at the moment because it may be contaminated.

This highlights a further level of complication, which is good because I was starting to worry that water chemistry was starting to get a bit too simple. As I

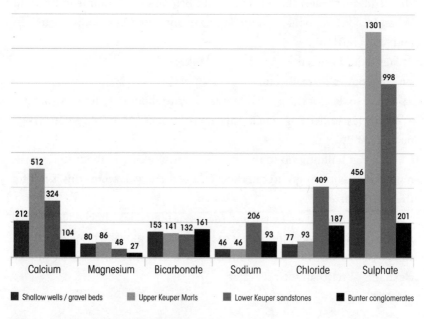

Different water compositions within Burton on Trent
Dissolved mineral content (parts per million)
Adapted from Hind, *Brewing Science and Practice*, 1938

dug deeper – in a metaphorical sense – I learned that Burton's brewers literally dug deeper as they grew. They started off digging shallow wells closer to the river, to depths of around thirty feet. Then, as both the population of Burton and the brewing industry grew, both the river and the wells close to it became polluted, and they moved further away and bored deeper to find clean water. Depending on where they dug, the mineral content varied dramatically.

This was another spur to understanding water chemistry and the development of brewing science in Burton. It wasn't enough to simply say, 'Hurrah! Our water is great because it's really high in sulphates!' and watch the money roll in. Samples from different sources had to be constantly analysed and tweaked, a reminder that even today it's not enough simply to follow a water profile by the numbers on a sheet.

Of the four taps in front of me now, the shallow field water well is the one that's mainly used for brewing, and Genevieve Upton, the Marston's brewer who is showing a few of us around, has brought glasses down for us to taste.

I'm quite nervous. My friend Paul Rudge has spent most of his career working for Molson Coors, the global brewing giant that bought Bass in 2000 and now brews about a sixth of all Britain's beer volume in Burton.* When I told Rudgie that I wanted to taste unfiltered Burton well water, he said, 'No you don't.'

'Yes, I do,' I replied.

'No, you really, really don't.'

'I have to. It's for the book. How can I write about it without tasting it?'

'Well, it's something you'll only ever do once. Make sure you have a bucket handy.'

I've been building up to this moment for weeks. I'm about to taste the most famous brewing water in the world. And now, it seems this is not for the faint-hearted.

As Genevieve turns the tap and the water pours, I'm shocked to see that it's crystal-clear. I was expecting it to be murky, or glowing orange or something. But this is the whole point of well water, isn't it? It's been filtered clean. It's purer than surface water.

---

* If you've read *Hops and Glory*, you'll remember Rudgie as the architect and saviour of my attempt to take a barrel of Burton IPA to India along its traditional sea route.

I give the glass of clear water a swirl and a sniff. It definitely has character to it. It smells earthy, and reminds me of a musty old canvas tent. It tastes a bit salty, not in a seawater sense, but more seltzerish. There's a light prickle on the edges of my tongue. It's not bad at all.

I once worked on an advertising pitch for Evian. The main things I remember about it are that we had to go to Paris a lot, and that we won the pitch. But the third thing I remember was realising how far behind France the UK is in its appreciation of mineral water. Although we're buying a lot more bottled water than we did, we still only drink about a quarter as much as the French. And while we talk about tap water being just as good, and make excuses about convenience and try not to appear too pretentious about the whole thing, the French can taste and appreciate the difference between brands – because it's not just a different brand; it's water from a different well, with a different mineral profile, and therefore a different taste if you pay close enough attention. Possibly the most striking example, and the one I use to silence any sceptics, is Badoit. It's so dry it's almost tannic, like drinking an Alka-Seltzer with extra chalk dissolved into it. King Louis XVI's physician claimed it could 'enhance the appetite, soothe digestion and lift the spirit'. I know people who buy it in by the case as if preparing for a siege, and drink nothing else. But they're far outnumbered by people who think it's disgusting.

Badoit is naturally sparkling and rich in magnesium, calcium, fluoride, and off the scale in bicarbonates. It's not the same as Burton water, which is much higher in sulphates and modest in bicarbonates, but it's in the same league of powerful, super-minerally waters. If you don't get the opportunity to taste Burton water from the well, you could still do a little experiment by drinking Badoit, and imagining making a beer with that compared to one made from pure, filtered water. Imagine not just the flavour the water adds to the whole, but also how those minerals interact with the other ingredients and play with their flavours.

'OK, so now can we taste the deep-bore water?' I ask.

'No, I'm afraid not,' says Genevieve. 'It's quite different and it's not approved for human consumption, so I'm afraid I can't let you drink it.' She looks at me with an unreadable expression, and suddenly remembers she has to go and talk to someone across the room.

As soon as she turns her back, I turn the tap on the deep-bore-tube water and half fill my glass. I raise it to my nose, and straight away it's far more pungent and sulphurous, with a distinct eggy note. In the mouth it's quite metallic, with a big, lingering, minerally aftertaste. The most ardent Badoit fans might enjoy doing shots of this at the end of a big night after several pints of their usual tipple, if they were really going for it and didn't have to get up the next morning.

It's certainly challenging, and not water I would care to drink neat, but it's not going to cause a gag reflex or anything like that. Either Rudgie's a complete wuss regarding his palate, or he was winding me up. I strongly suspect the latter.

Genevieve returns and tries to look disappointed that I've put my life at risk against her specific instructions, and then asks if we'd like to see the shallow field wells.

We exit a small door at the back of the brewery and walk across a wide playing field with changing rooms down one side. This is where the Burton Albion Under-18s team trains, but they're not here today. Instead, a bunch of overweight people in tight, fluorescent Lycra are being put through some kind of boot camp. A fitness instructor yells at them over the noise of a ghetto blaster playing the kind of tunes people put on headphones in the gym, and they fling their limbs into the air in panic.

'OK, here we are,' says Genevieve.

I look around, confused. 'What do you mean?' I ask.

She nods down. We're standing by a hedge at the bottom of the field, and running along its base is a series of rectangular steel manhole covers like you'd see in any street. An engineer from the brewery takes a long wrench to one of the covers and lifts it.

Underneath is a simple network of curved stainless-steel pipes in a hole. That's all there is, and I'm afraid that's the fullest description of it that I can give. I don't even think to take a photograph of it – it would be like photographing paint drying. It's really not what I expected after talking to Josef Tolar while gazing at his modernised fairy-tale well.

✿ ✿ ✿

Later that day, Rudgie picks me up and takes me to see one of the Molson Coors wells. The giant brewery has seven active wells in Burton, and pumps so much water from them that, if they were to suddenly stop, the new-build houses on the floodplain would soon start to submerge.

We turn into an alleyway near the train station. The concrete is cracked, with weeds and tufts of grass growing through. Inside a dun-coloured, corrugated-iron shed sits the shallow well. This one does at least look like a well. It's about ten metres wide, circular and lined with red bricks. But it's criss-crossed by wooden planks and a couple of steel girders, and clearly not accustomed to visitors.

Outside, in the middle of the shattered tarmac, sits the deep-bore well. It's a small metal box, about five feet high and ten feet long, like a telephone junction box or something you keep garden tools in, with bunches of different grasses growing around it. A network of pipes rises from it to a gantry that goes over the train station, over the main road beyond and into Molson Coors' massive main brewery complex.

I've spoken to brewers from places like San Diego who spend their lives making big, hoppy IPAs for which they Burtonise their water, and they say things like, 'Oh, man, my big ambition is that one day I might get to go to Burton upon Trent and see where it all happened, and see those famous wells.'

I feel like telling them not to bother, but I always just smile and hold it back. Burton's great breweries have all but disappeared now. Molson Coors makes a lot of beer, and keeps the Worthington brand name alive, but the town is as different from the spectacle that greeted Alfred Barnard as it's possible to imagine.

The complete lack of reverence around both the Marston's and Molson Coors wells feels at first like an insult – a slap in the face of Burton's brewing heritage, a perfect example of the town ignoring its legacy and not giving a shit what anyone else thinks, which is typical of a broader pattern here that goes beyond the remaining breweries.

But maybe this is how it should be. The history of Burton is defined by the no-nonsense, understated approach of its people. They make good beer here, using the most modern and scientific methods possible, just as they have done for centuries. When Samuel Allsopp brewed the first Burton IPA, when Horace Brown defied convention and got his laboratory equipment installed behind whitewashed windows, when Erasmus Darwin postulated on water hardness, they weren't romanticising the place in any way. They were happy to leave that to others. The water here is the best in the world for the style of beer they make. Now do you want a pint of it or not?

6. The Boiling Point

Water continues to raise questions, revealing some mysteries, while keeping others concealed in its unmurky depths.

A supply of fresh drinking water is the fundamental condition of our survival. Most of the planet is covered in water we can't drink, so supplies of fresh water have always been our primary concern as a species, and permanent settlements have always been centred around clean water supplies.

Present-day understanding of ancient knowledge about water purity depends on surviving written or pictorial accounts, so it only goes back as far as examples of these. Early civilisations knew nothing about bacteria or invisible impurities and relied on their senses to tell them if water was fit to drink or not, rejecting water that smelled bad or looked unclear. But water purification methods were in widespread use as early as 4000 BCE, and are detailed in ancient Sanskrit, Greek and Egyptian writings. The Sanskrit *Suśruta Samhita*, written around 2000 BCE, details purification methods including boiling, dipping heated iron into water, filtration through gravel and sand, as well using the seed of the *Strychnos potatorum*, or Clearing-Nut Tree, and a sacred gemstone called *Gomedaka*. The walls of the tombs of Egyptian rulers Amenophis II and Rameses II, which date back to the fifteenth and thirteenth centuries BCE respectively, feature pictures of a water-clarifying apparatus that used coagulation to purify the water, adding alum to remove suspended solids. The ancient Greeks also made widespread use of boiling, as well as the immersion of precious metals.

So we figured out that boiling water would sterilise it thousands of years ago. But we also knew there were alternatives. Boiling water takes a lot of energy, and when it became better understood, filtration was a more popular method. Which raises a couple of questions for beer: why do most beer historians assume that beer has always been boiled during the brewing process? And why do we assume that beer was vital as a safe source of drinking water because it had been boiled?

I'd always thought these principles were given. One of the central pillars of beer history, repeated by even the most rigorous researchers (and me) is that people drank beer instead of water during the Middle Ages because, having been boiled, it was safer to drink than water. Thinking about it now, one could ask, 'Well, if that's the case, why didn't they just boil the water?' which is a question I'll come back to shortly. But this presupposes that beer *was* boiled in its production.

Dr Martin Zarnkow of Technical University of Munich at Freising-Weihenstephan thinks boiling is a relatively recent innovation. 'Think about the amount of energy it takes,' he says. 'In ancient times, they didn't have oil or coal, only the sun.' (Well, and wood, but I take his point. Boiling every batch of beer would have taken huge reserves of wood.) A few years ago, Martin made an ancient beer from a Sumerian recipe. Originally confused by the recipe, he eventually challenged more than one sacred cow of brewing history and brewing science.

Sumer and Mesopotamia – now part of modern-day Iraq – were at the centre of the very first agricultural practices and the source of many of the earliest records of brewing. From his research, Martin estimates that as much as 84 per cent of cereals grown in Sumer in the twenty-first century BCE was barley, with most of the rest being emmer, a predecessor of modern-day wheat.

The recipe used volumes rather than weight, because they were easier to calculate. It called for one volume of malted barley, one volume of ground, unmalted emmer wheat and one volume of sourdough bread. This was all mixed together in water and left in warm temperatures.

'I'm a German brewer,' says Martin. 'For me it's always a hundred per cent malted barley. I couldn't understand why they used this adjunct of emmer wheat when they had so much barley. So I made my version with two-thirds malted barley and one-third sourdough, and their version with a third each of malt, adjunct and sourdough. And the three-thirds version had a much better shelf life.'

In this porridge-like mix, mashing – the process where the enzymes in the grain convert starch to sugar – and fermentation were happening at the same time. The malted barley began fermenting quickly, but the starches in the emmer hadn't yet been broken down. The enzymes from the malt went to work first on their own sugar, and after a few days they gradually began to break down the starches in the unmalted emmer wheat so those could be fermented, too. 'You had to have malting for the start of the fermentation,' says Martin, 'but not everything had to be malted. Malting is not necessary –

enzymes are necessary.' And enzymes can continue to work on unmalted grains, albeit much more slowly and later than they do on malted barley.

What this meant is that, for beers brewed in this way, the fermentation period lasted up to three weeks, compared to four or five days for a modern fermentation of 100 per cent malted barley at warm temperatures. 'All of these innovations were about extending the shelf life of food and drink. They still make beer in Africa today at ambient temperatures, and as long as the beer is still foaming it's safe to drink. While the beer is still working, the yeast protects it against other microbes. If the yeast is still alive, it won't let anything else in,' says Martin. So if beer was being drunk fresh, or over a period of a few weeks even, it needn't have been boiled in production to keep it sterile.

In northern Europe, evidence suggests beer was heated during brewing – not for sterilisation, but to get the enzymes in the barley working on the mash. But still, there's no evidence to suggest it was heated to boiling point. One method of heating the beer was to drop hot rocks in it, heated from a fire. This method is particularly appealing to the imaginations of brewers because of the likelihood that the rocks would also caramelise some of the sugars in the wort when they came into contact with it, creating some interesting flavours, not to mention the unspoken idea that dropping rocks into a big brewing vessel would have looked awesome and been a pretty cool thing to do.

In 2007, my friends Billy Quinn and Declan Moore, a pair of Irish archaeologists based in Galway, who led me from the path of righteousness when we met at a conference on prehistoric beer in Barcelona,* recreated another ancient brew based on equipment they'd found in their digs locally and conversations with ancient beer historians. Their experiment was successful, and they now make the beer on a fairly regular basis. I asked Declan if, when they make their *fulacht* beer, they use the rocks to heat the wort to boiling or not?

'No, we never heat to boil,' he replied. 'Just enough for enzyme activity. Getting to a boil and maintaining it is way more onerous and labour and

---

* It's a long and unlikely story, but every word of it is true. Check out the chapters on Spain and Ireland in *Three Sheets to the Wind*.

hot-rock intensive. We had our beer tested once and it was free from bacteria, presumably because of it being a good enough water source to begin with, and from the action of the fermentation.'

So beer didn't necessarily have to be boiled and we can't simply assume that it was. And the relationship between beer and the supply of drinkable water in the Middle Ages has also been challenged from the other side. The story we've all told ourselves is that water was unsafe to drink. But in 2013 food history blogger Jim Chevallier challenged this, presenting numerous references to water being drunk as a matter of course from Greek and Roman times, through the ages of the Franks and Gauls to classical France and Italy.

Now, I don't go as far as some in recanting my previous beliefs, and declaring that proof of the existence of clean drinking water is the same thing as disproving the idea that beer was consumed as a safer alternative to drinking water. There are plenty of stories of people dying from drinking infected water supplies.* But in pre-industrial Europe it would have been easy to find springs and rivers that contained water that was safe to drink. And techniques for purifying water without brewing it into beer were well understood by the Middle Ages. Rather than turning water into beer because the process involved boiling and sterilisation, why not just boil the water? People didn't drink beer because it was the only safe option. They drank it because they wanted to drink beer instead of water. As Jim Chevallier concludes on his blog "Les Leftovers":

> *Did people in the time prefer alcoholic drinks? Probably, and for the same reason most people today drink liquids other than water: variety and flavor. A young man in a tenth century Saxon colloquy is asked what he drinks and answers: "Beer if I have it or water if I have no beer."*

This is a curious quirk of history: it seems trivial to say that our ancestors did something for the same reasons we do, because some part of us feels that our drinking behaviour invites disapproval, and that this disapproval

---

* In the 1850s, John Snow famously proved that cholera was a water-based bacterium by mapping cases in London and noticing that they clustered around a particular well, which was found to be contaminated. Cholera bacteria are destroyed by boiling, so beer that had been made from the same well but boiled in production would not have spread the disease.

is justified. We drank beer because we liked the taste of it, and because we liked how it made us feel. And we drank a lot of it because – well – because we could, and because beer invites you to drink more in a way no other drink does. We drink water because we're thirsty, and when we're no longer thirsty we stop drinking it. In other words, the act of drinking water brings us to a state where we no longer feel the need to drink water. But if you drink beer, and it's good beer, the sign of its quality is that you immediately want a second, and a third.

So – we never really had to brew beer as an alternative to an essential supply of clean water on the grounds that beer was boiled and therefore sterilised in its production. And we didn't necessarily have to boil water in order to make beer anyway. So why is boiling almost universally regarded as an essential part of the brewing process? It undoubtedly is now, and has been for centuries, but in all the research I've done on beer, in all the key textbooks and most dependable sources on the history of beer and brewing, I've been unable to find any discussion of when boiling became common-place in beer-making, or why.

Probably longevity had something to do with it. If containers could be kept sterile and sealed, people must have felt better that the beer going into the barrels was definitely sterile when it was packaged, and would remain so after fermentation was complete. But if the beer was open to the elements in any way, boiling the beer during production wouldn't stop it from spoiling later.

No, to my mind, we began to boil beer, and expend all that energy doing so, for the same reason we boil or simmer any pot or pan on a flame: to cause reactions that start to break down the other ingredients in the pot. Brewing is cooking, and, just as in any other form of cooking, water isn't just the medium that brings the other ingredients together; it's also the medium that transforms them. Today we know where our water comes from. We know exactly what's in it, because we can analyse it and change its composition if it's not quite right, and yet we still boil it during brewing. And the main reason we spend a great deal of energy and money doing so is because of the effect it has on beer's superstar ingredient. We started boiling beer directly after, and because of, the introduction of hops. It's time to finally allow beer's superstar ingredient to take the stage.

– FOUR –

Hops

'Everything else is just a plant.'

DR PETER DARBY, hop breeder

1. The Beer Army

If you could hear the tune I'm hearing now, and if you're English, you'd probably identify it as the cheesy, you-kind-of-had-to-be-there, Cockney knees-up standard, 'Roll out the Barrel'. Also known as the 'Beer Barrel Polka', in the mid-twentieth century it was a hit for artists including Glen Miller, Benny Goodman, Bobby Vinton, Billie Holiday and the Andrews Sisters. If you've ever been to Oktoberfest and stayed sober enough to remember any of it, you might say, 'Ah, no. Before it was anglicised it was an old German drinking song called "Rosamunde",' still a favourite staple of the Bavarian 'oompah' bands, which can attain an almost rave-like groove in the hands of the right *Festkapelle*. But now, as the lusty hurdy-gurdy tune bounces off every surface in the central square of the Czech town of Žatec, someone is bellowing in my ear that it is in fact Czech in origin.

Of course it is, mate. Right now, right here, the only things that matter anywhere in the whole world are the products of Czech ingenuity, so it must be. You have to say that, my red-faced friend.

But it turns out that my companion is right: the Beer Barrel Polka was composed by Czech musician Jaromír Vejvoda, surprisingly recently, in 1927. It quickly became popular around the world, especially during the Second World War, when Germany occupied the former Czechoslovakia and modified the song to 'Rosamunde'. The combination of Czechs fleeing their homeland and soldiers from many countries fighting in Europe led to a diaspora of different versions making their way around the world.

In this respect, the story of the most famous Czech drinking song closely resembles the history of Czech beer itself.

As the enduring, jaunty European drinking song completes its latest mutation into a full-blooded werewolf of a hard-rock anthem, a parade begins to assemble beneath the pretty pastel-coloured buildings of the town square. Girls in brightly coloured costumes, wielding dangerous looking batons or less threatening pompoms, mill around near a band that seems to have far too many tubas and/or euphoniums than is healthy. There's one of those bikes where ten people can sit around a bar drinking beer while they pedal, and lots of motorbikes. Everyone is drinking beer.

It's all being organised – if that's not too strong a word – by marshals dressed in black, their big homburg-style hats garlanded with hops, black tunics with silver buttons done up tightly to the throat. Some of them have banners bearing the logo of the Beer Army – a simple tally mark familiar to anyone who has ordered beers in a Czech pub and watched the strokes accumulate on the back of a beer mat. The tally symbol doesn't just feature in the parade, but lines the entire perimeter of the square. Some people are wearing green berets, and now there seems to be more and more of them, many capping off makeshift uniforms that seem to combine a paramilitary aspect with Hawaiian-style grass skirts. Informed by my guide, I experience an *Invasion of the Body Snatchers* moment when I realise the Beer Army includes the town's mayor, the deputy mayor, the chief architect . . .

As the parade assembles into some kind of rough order and proceeds around the square, marching band music competes with endless car horns and bikes being revved. The Beer Army attempts some tightly drilled manoeuvres, but a few stumbles here and there suggest drinking started early this morning.

Women in traditional dress ride past on horses. A sports utility vehicle pulls a small steam engine. There are lots of tractors pulling trailers, most of them full of sacks with people sitting on them, drinking from large glasses of beer and yelling to friends in the crowd. Here's a group of women marching in formation, each with a pushchair containing a toddler dressed as a fat, round, miserable hop flower.

The centrepiece of the procession is a large wooden barrel on stilts on the back of a trailer. I'm going to take a wild guess and suggest it's full of beer. Behind it, an open white-and-gold carriage pulled by a team of horses contains a clergyman in opulent robes. Guarded by the Beer Army, the barrel turns around the cobbled square and comes to a stop in front of a small plot of hop bines growing in a carefully tended patch of soil. The plants are still young, having crept up to about two feet high along brown string hanging from a network of poles and wire.

The priest and several local dignitaries climb onto the trailer with the beer barrel that now forms a makeshift stage in front of the hops. They look down as a bunch of lads dressed as cavemen, all carrying phallic poles, march to the front, turn their backs and moon the crowd. Now the priest is turning his back to the crowd, too, and words can't describe the relief I feel when I realise he's doing this to say a prayer to the hop bines and sprinkle them with holy water. Then, each of the dignitaries, including the local mayor, the priest, and the Colonel of the Beer Army, takes it in turns to welcome us here to Žatec, for this year's *Chmelfest*. After their speeches everyone has one ceremonial hit of the tap being plunged into the barrel. Having tapped the beer, they fill big steins, drink deeply and toast the crowd. The lead parade marshal sings a curiously flat, monotone song, and balloons are released that are meant to represent hops. And that's when *Chmelfest*, the hop festival in the Czech town of Žatec, otherwise known by its German name Saaz, really gets into full swing, and the town's entire population heads for the bar.

Žatec has two hop festivals every year. May's *Chmelfest*, held when the hops are just beginning to climb, is the smaller of the two, attracting around 3,000 people. The September harvest festival gets over 40,000 on the streets, so this is only the rehearsal, less than a tenth of the size of what happens in the autumn. The town square is now in complete mayhem, and it's not yet even noon. But this is what hops inspire in people. This is the kind of thing hops make them do.

2. Seasoning Beer

When I do my pop quiz on the ingredients of beer, hops are the only one of the big four that most people can name. And while they may have heard of hops, most people have no idea what they are or what they do. They guess that beer is 'made from' hops the way wine is made from grapes.*

When people fall for beer in a big way, as they're doing right now in increasing numbers, it's usually hops that draw them in. I want to know

---

* I was doing an India Pale Ale (IPA) tasting event recently when a woman in the audience raised her hand and asked, 'If these beers have got so many hops in, are they still suitable for celiacs?' I replied that hops don't contain any gluten, and she nodded wisely and said, 'Ah, so they're not barley hops then?' Ironically, she could only misunderstand beer so dramatically because, compared to most people, she was better informed and more engaged.

why this is. Because out of the four main ingredients, hops are the only one that isn't strictly necessary to make beer.

Hops probably originated in China, but in various different varieties they spread around the world long before they were used for brewing. It's impossible to say when they were first used in beer. The archaeo-botanical record isn't helpful, because hops are closely related to cannabis and hemp, and the pollen from hops and hemp is identical.* Hops grow wild in hedgerows, and wild hops were being added to beer long before they were cultivated. The earliest brewing records show many different flavourings being added to beer to improve what would have been a sweet, perhaps even cloying beverage without them.

Some of these additives did more than flavour the beer: *Hyoscyamus niger*, commonly know as henbane, is a poisonous plant with a long history of being used, in small doses, to induce altered states of consciousness. Even the smell of it can make you giddy, and evidence of it being used in beer 5,000 years ago was discovered at an archaeological dig near Skara Brae in Orkney in 1929, along with evidence of *Atropa belladonna*, or deadly nightshade, and *Conium maculatum*, or hemlock. Some plant drugs, such as opium, need alcohol as a solvent to unlock their powerful chemistry. Hops may be worshipped by the modern craft beer geek, but their forebears granted drinkers an entrance to different planes.

Surviving written records of brewing in Europe date back to the eighth, ninth and tenth centuries CE, and show that before the use of hops became widespread a cocktail of hedgerow herbs known collectively as *gruit* was in common use throughout Europe. The Emperor Charlemagne's ninth-century reign across an empire that stretched from Spain through France and the Low Countries into most of Germany provides the first really detailed records of how large estates were run. Charlemagne was clearly a control freak and perfectionist, who gave detailed instructions on everything, including the range of alcoholic drinks any self-respecting noble should have, and how they should be produced. *Gruit* could contain bog myrtle (also known as sweetgale or myrica gale), wild rosemary or yarrow. These were picked and dried before use, and apparently provided a 'sharp

---

* No, you can't get high from smoking hops. And it's not a pleasant experience attempting to do so.

taste', which may possibly have been good but strikes me as euphemistic*. Different recipes of *gruit* across the Continent later included laurel leaves, marjoram, mint, sage, acorns, caraway, wormwood and tree bark. Looking back now, medieval beer starts to make even the most adventurous contemporary Hackney craft brewery look cautious.

Given that beer contained pretty much anything that could be found growing in a hedgerow, it's likely that hops first entered beer as one component of this eclectic potpourri. But eventually hops emerged as a single flavouring, set apart and defined differently from *gruit*. Whenever hops became dominant, it's likely that their initial appeal didn't have much to do with the flavour they imparted. Like so much innovation in food and drink, it was more about the hop's preservative properties. Once these were discovered, rather than being foraged in the wild like everything else, hops began to be cultivated. One of the earliest references to this is in *Physica*, written by Hildegaard von Bingen, a German Benedictine abbess, writer, composer, philosopher and mystic whose work spanned everything from drama and songs to theological and medicinal texts. *Physica*, written sometime between 1150 and 1160, consists of nine books that attempt to give a comprehensive review of the scientific and medicinal properties of various plants, stones, fish, reptiles and mammals. In it, she wrote of the hop:

> *If thou desirest to make beer from oats and hops, boil it also with the addition of 'gruz' and several ash-leaves, as such a beer purges the stomach of the drinker and eases his chest . . . Its bitterness, though, when added to beverages, prevents in the latter putrefication [sic] and gives to them a longer durability.*

This is one of the earliest references to beer being boiled in its production, and suggests that brewers started to boil wort because of something to do with the character of the hops.

Like most plants, hops are made of water, cellulose and a variety of proteins. But hops differ from most in that they also contain sacs full of alpha acids, beta acids and essential oils. When hops are boiled, these

---

* Bog myrtle is still used today as a botanical in schnapps in Denmark and Sweden.

essential oils flash off, meaning that if you're carefully positioned in the brewery you can get an amazing aromatherapy steam infusion, but this is at the expense of flavour compounds that are lost to the finished beer. Boiling also causes the alpha acids, or humulones, in the hop to undergo a process known as isomerisation, in which they convert to iso-alpha acids. These acids prevent bacteria from reproducing, therefore helping keep beer in good condition for longer. Before the discovery of the preservative properties of the hop, the only way to make beer last was to make it stronger in alcohol, which is fatally poisonous to many microorganisms. Once the properties of the hop were understood, brewers could make beer that was lower in alcohol, meaning it didn't require as much fermentable material, meaning it was cheaper to make. People could also drink more of it before they fell over. It seems likely, then, that the spread of hops wasn't driven at first by a hankering for bitterness, but by commercial and pragmatic reasons.

There is also another possible motive. In *Sacred and Herbal Healing Beers*, Stephen Buhner celebrates when beer was more than just a refreshing drink shared at the end of the day. He recalls the age of beers similar to Orkney henbane beer, and the likely use of such beverages for their mind-altering effects, and suggests that, as social hierarchies became more rigid, and spiritual enlightenment came through the monotheistic church and anything not belonging to that church's teachings was witchcraft, there was an authoritarian urge to have beer calm people rather than excite them:

> *It is important to keep in mind the properties of gruit ale: It is highly intoxicating – narcotic, aphrodisiacal, and psychotropic when consumed in sufficient quantity. Gruit ale stimulates the mind, creates euphoria, and enhances sexual drive. The hopped ale that took its place is quite different. Its effects are sedating and anaphrodisiacal. In other words, it puts the drinker to sleep and dulls sexual desire.*

It's true that, among their many other attributes, hops have a sedative effect, which is why hop and valerian herbal tablets and hop pillows are proven to help alleviate the suffering of insomniacs. But while it's an appealing idea that medieval beer drinkers were free spirits, communing with God and making free love until The Man shut them down with hopped beer, there's little evidence that the *gruit* ales of the Middle Ages had narcotic effects, or that the authorities were troubled by them if they did

The simplest explanation for the spread of hops is the most likely one: their significant practical and economic benefits. The adoption of hops was uneven, and not without resistance. But, eventually, cultivated hops caught on, and drinkers began to appreciate hops for their flavour and aroma as well as their pragmatic advantages. In fact, 'appreciate' is a colossal understatement. Today, drinkers and brewers across the world are fanatical about hops, and that passion is driving a global revolution in the appreciation of craft beer. In an ironic switch of Buhner's narrative, hops now inspire the kind of euphoria he claims they killed off. When she talks about hops in public presentations, Dr Christina Schönberger, Innovations Technical Manager at global hop merchants Barth-Haas, says simply, 'Hops are a religion.'

While brewing, like the three main monotheistic religions, may have been born in the Middle East, the worship of hops began in Bohemia, now part of the Czech Republic. And its Mecca was the town of Žatec, near the western border that artificially divides Bohemia from its beery other half, the southern German region of Bavaria.

3. Lager's Greatest Hits

King Charles IV of Bohemia was originally named Wenceslaus, or Václav, after his maternal grandfather King Wenceslaus II.* He chose the name Charles when he was made King of Bohemia in 1347 following his father's death the year before. A few months later he was also elected Holy Roman

---

* The problem with having (a) much higher standards as a writer than I once did and (b) having searchable access to the world's entire store of historical knowledge, is that where I once let a good yarn go, I now have to go back and check it. In doing so, I often find the most wonderful stories about the history of beer to be untrue or, at best, unprovable. I've previously written that the Good King Wenceslas of the famous Christmas carol was the Václav otherwise known as Emperor Charles IV. It wasn't. It wasn't even his grandfather, though Wenceslaus II is notable for having founded the city of Plzeň in 1295, and the world of beer owes him a significant debt for that. No, the famous Good King Wenceslas was St Wenceslas I, Duke of Bohemia, who was canonised and posthumously declared king after being murdered by his younger brother. After his death, legends of his great charity and piety grew, and he became a cult figure and patron saint of Bohemia.

Emperor, the first Bohemian king to rule the empire that spanned most of Central Europe and northern Italy.

Charles IV's reign is remembered as the Golden Age of Bohemia, a time of peace in which Prague became the Empire's capital. The Emperor also seems to have been something of a gastronome. He brought grape cultivation and the appreciation of wine to Bohemia, but this by no means implied a neglect of beer. Records of hops being grown in Bohemia stretch back to 859, and the earliest record of hops being grown in and around the town of Žatec is a bill of sale dated 1348, the second year of Charles's reign. The Emperor promoted the growing of hops by royal decree, and is famous for imposing severe penalties, including death, for the exportation of prized Bohemian varieties. This is not the reason why he has been known as *Pater Patriae*, the 'father of the country', ever since the term was used at his funeral, but for many Czechs today it might as well be.

Charles's actions tell us that, by the time of his reign, hops were being widely cultivated and that certain varieties from particular locations could be identified as being superior to others. For this reason, in 1538 the Prince-Bishop of Eichstätt, a small principality in Bavaria, also part of the Holy Roman Empire, granted the world's first ever hop seal to the district of Spalt, just south of Nuremberg. Other areas around Nuremberg, and parts of Bohemia including Žatec, were quickly granted hop seals of their own. These seals guaranteed that the hops genuinely came from the region they were alleged to be from, and form one of the world's earliest known examples of modern branding.

Both Bohemia and the Nuremberg area were revered across Europe for the quality of their hops. But when the Thirty Years' War devastated Central Europe, hop cultivation dispersed to France, England and other parts of Germany. Bohemia regained its reputation when peace broke out, and by the eighteenth century it was regarded as the world centre of hops, the standard by which others were judged. That reputation went stratospheric in 1842 when the burghers of the town of Plzeň recruited one of the most brilliant brewers from Germany, combined freshly perfected pale malt with soft local water, Žatec hops and German lager yeast and fermentation techniques to create 'the original Pilsner beer', or 'Pilsner Urquell' as it's known today. Pilsner Urquell claims to have been the world's first golden beer, which, assuming you're reading this book chapter by chapter, we already know cannot be true. But whatever it was, pilsner beer created a sensation across what was by then the Austro-Hungarian Empire. The twin innovations of railways and refrigeration allowed the beer to travel fast and far, and by the dawn of the twentieth century pilsner-style beers had already become the world's favourite.

You wouldn't know from tasting most commercial lagers that dare to call themselves pilsners today, but a true Czech or German pilsner has quite an assertive hop character – not the aggressively *AWESOME* hop profile craft beer drinkers have learned to expect today, but an arresting, nagging, teasing bastard of a beer that won't let you go, that compels you to have another, and sometimes alarms you with the speed with which it transfers from the glass to your throat. The Czechs drink more beer per capita than any other nation in the world. That's partly their culture, and partly because Czech brewers are obsessed with 'drinkability'. The good ones micro-manage every aspect of the beer to leave you wanting more, not for its alcohol hit, and not quite, or not only, for its flavour: drinkability is more than that. And the character of the Žatec hop is at its heart.

Zatecky Chmel, as the Czechs call the Žatec hop, has a low concentration of the alpha acids that give beer its bitterness, and moderate levels of aroma compounds that create a soft, delicate flavour that's perfect for a light beer such as pilsner. But 'soft and delicate' shouldn't be read as a euphemism for 'lacking in flavour', a weasel dodge performed by many big lager brands today as they seek to offend no one with their insipid beer. Žatec hops certainly make their presence felt, with agreeable aromas of herbs, spice, grass and freshly cut hay.

This polite, refined character inspired one brewer to describe them as 'noble'. The Noble Hops are Žatec from Bohemia, and Hallertauer Mittelfrüh, Spalter and Tettnanger from southern Germany. They're all characterised by a similar light bitterness and gentle yet assertive aromas. Recent genetic research suggests they're all closely related, and may even all have descended from the same early Žatec hop. All define the character of the lager beers of Bohemia and Bavaria. 'Noble Hops' is the perfect summation of their personality and heritage, so it's a bit of a shame that the term was only coined in the 1980s. And in America at that.

Like barley and grapes, hops are a product of their *terroir*. The Žatec region is protected by mountain ranges that dull the wind and create a rain shadow that provides the perfect amount of rainfall at the right time. The soil is Permian Red, full of sandstone, clay and shale, with a bit of sandy marl mixed in. The height and direction of the slopes are ideal. While sheltered, the valleys are wide and open, with gentle breezes. It's a unique combination, just like the composition of the soil beneath Burton upon Trent that produces such perfect ale-brewing water.

Like Burton's water, the *terroir* of the Žatec region wouldn't be perfect for all characters of hops, but the local beer style has evolved with it, so Žatec hops are perfect for pilsner-style lagers, and pilsner-style lagers are the perfect use of Žatec hops. What seems like a miraculous coincidence is more likely the product of evolution over the centuries, the nature of the local ingredients gently encouraging the emergence of a beer style that suited them ideally and brought out their best qualities.

By the late nineteenth century, Žatec was the hop capital of the world. In 1877, P. L. Simmonds, in an analysis of international hop cultivation, effused that the hops from 'Saatz in Austria' were 'the finest and most aromatic hops grown. These products are of a high reputation, and are the Chateau Lafitte, the Clos de Vougent, and the Johannisberg, as it were, of hops of continental growths.' Even though hop cultivation was expanding in Germany, England and the United States, Bohemian hops were the benchmark for determining the quality and price of hops across Europe.

The high point of hop cultivation was probably just after the First World War, when then-Czechoslovakia gained its independence from the Austro-Hungarian Empire. The Second World War sent the region's fortunes spiralling the other way. Žatec wasn't just a world centre of hop growing, it was also a hub of hop trading. Most of the hop merchants were Jewish, and when Žatec was liberated in 1945 those merchants and their families had disappeared, exterminated by the Nazis. What had once been the most prosperous town in Czechoslovakia was almost empty, and was used by its new Soviet rulers as a dormitory to house gypsies. Hop cultivation continued but went into decline. In the centralised, state-run economy, Bohemia was designated as the area that brewed beer for the whole of the Eastern European bloc. But the priority was quantity rather than quality, and the Communists didn't invest in the industry or in research and development. When the Czech Republic emerged after the Velvet Revolution, its brewing and hop industries were busy, but antiquated.

When I first visited Žatec for *Chmelfest* in 2007, many of the buildings were ramshackle, and the acreage of Žatec hops was in steady decline. At this point, the giant brewers of global lager brands dictated the hop market. The multinationals have little interest in the qualities of one region's aroma hops over another, and buy hops simply for their alpha acid content – the rest is superfluous. The giant hop fields of Tettnang and Hallertau provide the required bitterness units by growing varieties that have been bred for their high alpha acid content rather than their aroma: if hop variety A contains twice as much alpha acid as hop variety B, you only need to buy half as many hops. Žatec, still revered by connoisseurs, has a rubbish alpha acid content by modern standards, if alpha acid is what you're after. In 2007, it catered only to a niche of true pilsner aficionados. But change was just starting to become visible.

As well as being the name of a region, a town and the world's most famous hop variety, Žatec is also the name of a brewery and a beer. Žatecký Pivovar is the love child of international entrepreneur Rolf Munding. In 2001, he bought the main brewery in Žatec with a view to making proper Czech lager like it used to be. The place was bankrupt and falling apart, but that suited Rolf just fine. 'I wanted to make Czech beer in the traditional way, so I didn't want to have to rip out modern kit that we didn't need,' he told me. But the place was full of junk. The beer tasted foul and had a shelf life of a week. Rolf re-employed the workforce full time (they'd only been brewing one day a week) and they spent the first three months doing nothing but cleaning.

Rolf hired Tomas Lejsek, who had been a brewer and then technical adviser to breweries within the Communist bloc, to brew a traditional pilsner-style beer, with Žatec hops, in traditional open fermenters.

The first time I tasted Žatec beer I described it as lager's greatest hits, all in one neat package: the dryness, the fruitiness mid-mouth, the nice, crisp finish, and the gentle, insistent buzz that makes you want another. It goes down absurdly quickly.

As well as spending a lot of money on the brewery, Rolf was also investing in the town's main hotel, a dilapidated building that still bore faded memories of its grandeur a century before. 'This town has had no love for fifty years,' said Rolf. 'Now, we're giving it some love.'

I've always wanted to return to Žatec, but it's 2016 by the time I manage it. Much has changed in the intervening decade. The façades of all the large, important buildings are fresh and clean, renovated in bright pastel shades. The Žatec Brewery is gleaming and busy. The brewhouse – the collection of vessels where the beer is actually made – is brightly polished copper, but it will always bear the scars from when it was cut into pieces during the Second World War and hidden in the cellars of a nearby house. It was welded back together and reinstalled in 1946, and is in daily use today.

The windows are made of pretty stained glass featuring the brewery's 'Ž' logo. All the buildings have been repaired and the cobbled yard is now in the process of being carefully restored. It strikes me that the whole place is more beautiful than it needs to be, that a lot of this work is not strictly necessary, and that makes it even more appealing. 'After all their effort, it honours previous generations by keeping it so beautiful,' says Martin Kec.

Martin is the Managing Director of Žatecký Pivovar, and has worked with Rolf for years. Like every other important man in the town of Žatec, he's also a member of the Beer Army that officiates at *Chmelfest*. 'The Beer Army was formed in 1999 because we wanted an excuse for drinking,' he says levelly. 'At the Monday meeting, everyone gets drunk: the town architect, the head of the local energy supplier, the ex-mayor, as well as local labourers.'

They have a lot to celebrate. The hop museum – sorry – 'Hop and Beer Temple' – in the centre of town, which reopened on the day I was here in 2007, has now been dramatically expanded. Its centrepiece is an astonishingly tall tower coated in plates of fine mesh, with openings here and there offering views across the valley. Four thick white masts at its peak, skewed at different angles to represent hop poles, give it the air of a cross between a Manhattan skyscraper and a pagan fort, a castle reinvented to protect the inhabitants of a dystopian future. The building below contains 4,000 square feet of hop-related exhibits, plus a restaurant with its own microbrewery. As Martin and I arrive for lunch, the stomach-rumbling smell of mashing wort fills the room – an inspired touch for a place serving typical Czech, carb-heavy food.

This sense of confidence and renewal in the town carries through to the broader hop industry. Until around 2010, the acreage of Žatec hops was shrinking by around 5 per cent a year. But that year seems in retrospect to have been the pivot of change for the global hop industry in many ways. That's when the notion of craft beer went mainstream – and global. Brewers and drinkers began asking for hops with different aromatic properties, and to take an interest in specific varieties and where they come from. Žatec – or Saaz to most people – is one of the most well-known and romanticised hops in the world, a ready link with noble brewing tradition. At the time of writing, if you want to brew with Žatec hops and you haven't already got a forward contract for them, you're going to have to wait until 2021 before you can get your hands on some. 'Lots of new hops fields are being planted,' says Martin, 'but they can't come quick enough.'

The passion for hops here goes beyond their commercial potential. Ever since pagan times, in what is now the Czech Republic, hops were thought to have a mischievous and lascivious character, which led to the loss of chastity and virginity. Unsurprisingly, then, they've always been a symbol of fertility, and newlyweds were covered with hops to help them bear many children. Even today, people still refer to the hop as 'Czech gold'.

When I read this, the antics back at *Chmelfest* in May make more sense.

As the day progresses, a sense of abandon pervades the proceedings that feels like more than mere drunkenness. As the parade through the centre of Žatec disintegrates, the games start in the town square. Most of the men here now seem to be in drag. We fight our way through them to watch a beer barrel-throwing contest, which uses full barrels. A man wearing a miniskirt, his hair tied in bunches, doesn't do very well. The keg throwing is followed by a competition to see who can carry a barrel along a log without falling off, and time trials to determine who can run with it around the square quickest. If you don't have much, as Žatec didn't under Communism, it's amazing how much fun you can have with a beer barrel without even opening it. But I'd rather stick to drinking the contents.

'Cheaper beer is good on the first sip,' says Martin Kec. 'But with a great beer, as soon as you finish it you want another. That's what Czech beer is all about – the lure of drinkability!' I witness this national philosophy in action at *Chmelfest*. And it's impossible to witness something like this without joining in.

4. The Garden of England

Elsewhere, at the same point in the year that Žatec celebrates *Chmelfest*, it's a bleary-eyed morning as we gather at the Hackney Brewery in east London, scrappily seeking out coffee and bacon rolls from nearby shops, pointedly not mentioning the general election that kept everyone up the night before.

The invisible fog of a collective hangover shrouds the air between us. We're dressed in that nondescript kind of clothing that English people have to wear in May, embellished by the uncertain sartorial twist of city folk not quite knowing how to dress for a rare day out in the country. Some of us are wearing Wellington boots, others walking shoes. We sport a mix of hoodies, baggy sweaters and, in some cases, what look like pyjama bottoms, prepared – or not – for both mud and sunshine as well as the dejected dreich in between.

We pile onto a minibus with the same good humour and bad jokes that are mandatory for any day trip on a minibus from anywhere to anywhere in England, and soon we're out of London and into Kent, talking too loudly as we speed down narrow country lanes in the opposite direction to the commuters flowing into London.

Henry VIII named Kent 'the Garden of England' after tasting cherries grown here, and it was in this garden that the cultivation of hops in Britain first seriously took root – much to Henry's dislike.

In 1970, a curious find in Kent confused the picture of the history of hops in Britain. Wild hops are indigenous here, and archaeological evidence discovered in Cambridgeshire dates them back to at least 3000 BCE. But British brewers didn't adopt hops for widespread use until relatively recently. Documentary evidence clearly shows that, in the Middle Ages, English *ale* was quite distinct from continental *beer*: the latter contained hops as its primary flavouring and preservative, the former did not. We called it ale rather than *gruit*, and perhaps the flavourings were different, but here the schism between two entirely different styles of what we now call beer persisted much later than in Central Europe, where hopped beer had largely taken over from *gruit* ale by the thirteenth century.

So it's odd that when an Anglo-Saxon clinker-built boat was discovered under two feet of soil during improvement works to drainage channels in the village of Graveney, near Faversham, it was found to contain a cargo of hops, and was carbon-dated to the late tenth century. The ratio of hop flowers to other vegetal material showed it was a harvest of hops, dating two hundred years before Hildegaard von Bingen wrote of their use in brewing. We don't know if they were being exported or imported, and we can't be certain they were used for brewing, but the Graveney boat is a strange anomaly in the history of British hopped beer, the official story of which starts in the sixteenth century, when thousands of Protestant Flemish weavers fled to Britain to escape religious persecution from the Catholic Spanish who had occupied the Low Countries.

Flemish and Dutch immigrants had been popular arrivals in Britain for two hundred years thanks to their superb fabrics, particularly silks. But their beer didn't go down nearly so well. Hopped beers are first documented in England in the fifteenth century, when they were imported into East Anglia from Holland and Zeeland. These first imports were for Dutch workers who weren't great fans of sweet, old English ale. As Flemings and Dutch fleeing persecution settled in England in greater numbers, they began brewing hopped beer for themselves that was so good it was exported back to continental Europe.

Flemish brewers also settled in Southwark, which would become Britain's central hop market. Excluded from the City of London by the powerful trades guilds, the Flemings set up business just outside the city walls and soon became celebrated for the quality of their beer. There were, of course, those who opposed this trend, and some of the protests against these brewers bordered on xenophobia. Andrew Boorde, one of history's most hilariously miserable writers, moaned in his 1542 tract *A Compendyous Regyment or Dyetary of Healthe*:

> *Ale is made of malte and water ... Ale for an Englyssheman is a*
> *naturall drynke ... Beere is made of malte, of hoppes, and water. It is*
> *a naturall drynke for a doche [Dutch] man. And nowe of lete dayes it*
> *is moche used in England to the detryment of many Englysshe men:*
> *specyally it kylleth them the whiche be troubled with the Colyke and*
> *the stone, and the strayne coylyon; for the drynke is a cold drynke yet*
> *it doth make a man fatte, and doth inflate the bely, as it doth appere*
> *by the doche mennes faces and belyes.*

But, as Boorde concedes, by the 1540s hopped beer was becoming increasingly popular in England. London's ale brewers harassed and disparaged the immigrants they felt were coming over here and taking their jobs, which led to a writ being issued by the Sheriffs of London proclaiming:

All brewers of beer should continue their art in spite of malevolent attempts made to prevent natives of Holland and Zeeland and others from making beer, on the grounds that it was poisonous and not fit to drink and caused drunkenness, whereas it is a wholesome drink, especially in summer.

While rumours of Henry VIII banning hops aren't quite true (he forbade their use in ale brewed at several of his royal palaces), their cultivation was banned in Norwich in 1471, in Shrewsbury in 1519 and Leicester in 1523. These restrictions were not necessarily about getting rid of hopped beer: rather, they sought to maintain a clear difference between English ale and continental beer.

The bitter flavour of hopped beer may have divided opinion, but no one could argue with its superior keeping qualities. Gradually, the distinction between ale and beer disappeared, and by the seventeenth century hops became commonplace in British beer. For a while, hops were a popular and much-prized crop farmed across most of England. In a good year, a single acre of good hops could be more profitable than fifty acres of arable land. But growing them was a risk for farmers. Even today, hops still require a more intensive investment of time, labour and overheads than any other crop, and their yields can be erratic, suffering from both drought and heavy rain, as well as being particularly susceptible to mildew. During the nine-teenth century, hop cultivation began to focus on the areas that had not only the best *terroir*, but also the best expertise and access to equipment. Specialisation became self-fulfilling. By 1900, hops were only being grown in Sussex, Surrey, Hampshire, Worcestershire, Herefordshire and Kent, with Henry VIII's Garden of England growing as much as the other five counties combined.

✿ ✿ ✿

At about 10.30, we stop and pull into a flat field bounded by thick, high hedges. Old trees rear high above us wearing new finery, their fresh leaves almost fully out. I decide that 'green' is a smell as well as a colour. A cuckoo calls nearby, and my heart is lifted for the first time since last night's exit poll.

The hop field – sorry, hop *garden* here in Kent, or hop *yard* over to the west in Hereford – at Hoads Farm just outside Sandhurst on the Kentish

Weald is approximately a hundred yards wide by three hundred yards long. Green plants a foot high run in strict lines along its length. But at this stage it's not the plants you notice; it's the extraordinary structure that's been put in place to support their rapid growth over the coming months.

Hops are, by nature, hedgerow plants. Like ivy or vine, the hop is a climbing plant that doesn't support itself, but clings to something else and grows around it, along it or up it. It's tempting to refer to hops as vines, but they are in fact *bines*. I assumed for a long time that this was simply the brewing world changing the common word for something to sound more important, because that's what brewers do with everything. But a vine uses tendrils or suckers that it shoots out from its main stem to attach itself to its host, whereas a bine has a stronger stem with stiff hairs along it, which help the stem itself do the binding. Some species of bean also grow on bines, as do honeysuckle and bindweed, but hops are the bines that have had the most specialised attention given to how they can best be grown.

The classical name for the hop is *Humulus lupulus*. The origin of the name is unknown, but is commonly – and incorrectly – attributed to Pliny and his *Natural History*. Whoever came up with it, the *lupulus* part likely derives from the Latin *lupus*, 'wolf', and the idea of the hop as a wolf among sheep, growing wild among the other plants and sometimes bringing them down with its weight, is a powerful and poetic image that has endured for centuries. Hops can smother trees and snuggle their way into hedgerows – and they grow at an astonishing rate if given a custom-built framework tailored to their every quirk and need.

A hop field in spring disorientates you for a few seconds before you work out what you're looking at. It's as if someone has built a rustic, analogue approximation of the movie *Tron*, rendering the countryside in analogue 3D wireframe, like a cargo cult that once saw such an image on a computer screen and is now trying to summon it back with the materials they have to hand.

Rusty lines hang across your entire field of vision, the skeleton of a phantom building, distorting your senses and pulling your eyes out of focus wherever you look. Eventually you adjust and the picture resolves itself. The field is defined by long lines of tall, straight, wooden poles about twenty feet high. The poles at the end of each row also sport wooden crosspieces, making them look like shorn rugby goalposts or a weird wooden henge.

Running across the tops of the poles is a grid of wire cables, like the skeleton of a roof that pretends to cover the whole field. Each wire is held taut at the ends, functioning the way guy ropes on tents do, slanting down to – and under – the ground. They go about six feet down, where they're held fast by heavy wooden sleepers referred to affectionately as 'dead men'. Thanks to the guys and the dead men, the wire skeleton will remain taut even when it carries a great weight.

The wire-frame hop garden was a nineteenth-century invention that allowed a huge increase in the amount of hops that could be grown per acre. But it's a complicated and labour-intensive system. The outline structure of poles, wire skeleton, guy ropes and dead men is permanent and sturdy, and costs £10,000 per acre to put in.

In spring, workers move along each row, and at the base of every still-dormant plant they run lines of coconut fibre, three or four strings to each plant, in a slight diagonal from the earth to the wires high above. Each string must be hooked and tied manually to the wires.

Hops have a few brief months of glory and magnificence, but the work involved in making that happen lasts all year. Once the strings are in place, the hops must be manually trained up them. Hops will grow clockwise around anything they can get their hairs on. In the early weeks a strong wind can blow them off again and they have to be retrained, one by one, by hand. As they start to grow in late spring, the plants are vulnerable to pests and disease, and have to be inspected daily and sprayed frequently. It's vital that as much of the goodness in the soil goes into the hop plants as possible, so anything else that wants to grow at this time of year – and everything does – needs to be removed. In June the aphids strike, so there's more spraying, and by this time the heads of the hops are out of human reach, crawling up the strings towards the sun. If they blow off the string at this point, it takes either exceptional skill or a tractor fitted with a plat-form to retrain them by hand. July is peak danger time for wilt – a serious bacterial or fungal disease rather than just a feeling of limpness – and if it's particularly warm you have to watch out for red spider mites. From now until harvest every plant must be closely inspected at least once a week. Harvest must happen at just the right time, spanning late August and most of September, depending on the particular hop variety, meaning that when the hops are ready the working days are long. Once the harvest is done, the remnants of the bines need to be cut right back to the ground, and the wheel marks of the tractor have to be ploughed through to loosen up the soil for the roots. More ploughing and spraying takes place over the winter months, not to mention essential repairs to the poles and wirework. And then there's weeding, always weeding.

So when a group of people ask if they can come along and pick any hop shoots that haven't been trained, the farmer gets one of about a billion essential tasks done for free, and he doesn't have to worry about it – assuming he trusts the competence of the pickers.

The hop plants are spaced about two feet apart. They are close relatives of the stinging nettle, and from a distance that's what they resemble this early in the season, with broad, fanned leaves that look like they could cause some discomfort. Closer, you can see that, above the leaves, each plant is sprawling with a number of long green shoots. The green stems are shaded purple-brown a bit further down, and the long, spear-like shoot is similarly green with a purple blush. The lead shoots – the healthiest and most vigorous – have been trained around the coconut-fibre strings. Every plant has four strings, and those strings carry three and three and two and two shoots respectively – a total of ten shoots per plant. But each plant erupts with many more than ten shoots, and that's why we're here.

Any sort of agriculture comes down to a focus on maximising yield, which means maximising the nutrients that go into the plants you want to cultivate, which in turn means eliminating any competition for those nutrients. There's no room for sentimentality or compassion: you select the strongest and nurture and cosset them, and destroy the weak. Here, the ten chosen hop shoots from each plant need to be fed as much as possible, which means the shoots still trailing along the ground are surplus to requirements, a drain on the food source of the rich and powerful, and must be destroyed.

Some hop growers do this with chemicals. Others bring sheep through the hop garden to graze on the low-lying shoots once the chosen ones have grown a few feet up the strings. Very few hop farmers go through the field removing surplus hop shoots by hand, because that would be a complete pain in the arse.

Peter Haydon, author of a couple of books about beer and pubs and now the owner of the Florence Brewery, a small operation under the pub of the same name in south London,* has persuaded a group of us to come here and go through the field removing surplus hop shoots by hand.

'Hop shoots are edible,' he says. 'We eat exotic foods from all over the world and these grow on our doorstep and get thrown away. People would definitely have eaten them in the past, and hop shoots are a delicacy in Italy, where they're called "poor man's asparagus".'

My first hop shoot run is the fourth that Peter has organised. At first, he struggled to find a farmer who would agree to delay spraying until they picked. Now, the 'London Hop Shoot Festival' includes up to thirty kitchens in the capital, all cooking with freshly picked hop shoots over the first weekend in May.

The hop we're picking today is called Epic. Chris Nicholas, who owns Bourne Farm, just a short distance from where we are now, found it growing by chance in a hedgerow next to a hop field in 1987, and noticed that it was different from the variety being grown in the field. With wild hops, you can never quite tell if it's a hop that's never been domesticated, or the bastard child of cultivated hops that's run away to join nature's circus. The best genetic guess is that Epic is probably a hybrid descendant of a hop called Alliance, which had been grown in the field previously. It grew vigorously and had a heavy yield that gave it an appealing look, so it was originally cultivated mainly as an ornamental plant. But when the American craft beer explosion caused everyone to examine the aromatic character of hop varieties more closely, its berry and lemongrass character encouraged hop breeders to trial it as a commercial variety. It's been in test plantings for about a decade, and was planted for the first time more widely in the winter of 2014–15. We're looking at part of the first commercial scale crop.

With a motley assortment of plastic bags in hand, we spread out across the field and bend to our task. The top of the hop shoot snaps off easily a few inches down, just around the first pair of leaves, after which the stem gets a bit woody. The furry stem carves delicate scratches in the skin, and soon my hands are sticky with sap and pungent with a peppery, grassy perfume.

---

* Peter later quit brewing when the pub closed for refurbishment. After an enjoyable few years, 'the time felt right to move on to other things'.

The work is steady and pleasantly monotonous, allowing me time to zone out as I find my technique and get quicker at picking, snapping off three or four at a time and pushing them deep into my carrier bag. My mind drifts.

Peter Haydon had no trouble whatsoever finding enough bodies to sacrifice a working day to come and pick hop shoots. People seem to leap at the chance just to be anywhere near hops. In *The Encircling Hop: A History of Hops and Brewing*, Kent native Margaret Lawrence wrote in 1990 that hops are 'emotive', with a 'soul' that has encircled the lives of Kentish people. That hasn't happened only to the Kentish: half the people picking this morning have T-shirts or baseball caps with stylised pictures of hops on them. I know one brewer who has a rare, experimental hop tattooed on the inside of his wrist, another who has the chemical structure of his favourite essential hop oil tattooed on his leg. I wonder how many chefs have tattoos of the chemical composition of salt, or illustrations of tarragon or cuts of beef?

After ninety minutes, we've cleared the field of surplus hop shoots. I think everyone's surprised by the amount we've collected: about thirty supermarket carrier bags in a big pile. There's a bag for each of the restaurant and pub kitchens that have asked for them, and plenty more left over. It would be a shame to go to all this effort and not try them for ourselves.

Adrian Grecu, sous chef at the Bull, a brilliant foodie pub in Highgate, north London, unveils a mobile kitchen and sautées hop shoots and wild garlic, and serves them with prawns in chilli butter, and with bavette steak in wraps. They taste sweet and fresh and juicy with just a hint of bitterness. Out here in the field, looking at the plants we just picked our food from, it's one of the best meals I've ever had.

But we've hardly made a dent in our stash. Adrian tells me that hop shoots are also delicious pickled with white wine vinegar, garlic, thyme and sugar, boiled up and left to cool.

We're much quieter on the way back to London. We've had a bit of beer and it's a sleepy, sunny spring afternoon. But even though the hop flowers haven't even formed yet, we still have the smell of hops on our hands, and I wonder if the soporific effects of their essential oils still work their magic through the stems, leaves and shoots.

I end up back home with more hop shoots than I can possibly ever use, and I feel like I've stolen something that was offered for free, found gold in the street, been gifted a key that unlocks a magical gate. The hop shoot and wild garlic pesto I make that evening tastes phenomenal. How could it possibly not?

5. The Hop Man

Dr Peter Darby is not a man most people would consider a celebrity. But after a few months studying hops, the chance to sit in a pub for an entire afternoon with someone who has worked with hops for over thirty years, bred and introduced some of our most popular modern varieties, and is widely regarded as one of if not *the* most prominent hop breeders in the world, fills me with the kind of giddy excitement I might normally reserve for having a beer with my favourite band of all time.

We meet in the Sun, an old inn in the centre of Faversham, Kent. The town is home to Shepherd Neame, arguably the oldest surviving brewery in Britain, dating back to 1698, and the brewer has a deep, intimate relationship with hop growing. When government funding was pulled from the UK's hop research programme, Shepherd Neame stepped in to help fund and house part of the National Hop Collection at Queen Court Farm. The brewery's PR manager, John Humphreys, arranged this meeting for me, and he sits here now the way PRs do when their clients are being interviewed, except that he's not here to make sure Peter doesn't say anything out of turn: he's here to listen to a conversation he's heard before, but always finds fascinating.

Shepherd Neame is typical of the medium-sized regional family brewers who sit between the global lager giants and the new wave of microbreweries now springing up in Britain at the rate of two or three every week. They represent a brewing tradition that is seen by many beery neophytes as old-fashioned and boring compared to the Technicolor delights of the new wave of American-inspired craft beer. But it was brewers like Shepherd Neame who first inspired the originators of American craft beer.

The difference in beer between English tradition and US-inspired modernism is in the hops. American hops are widescreen and loud, occasionally brash and overbearing, but always exciting. The aroma and flavour they give to beer points to the horizon and encourages brewers and drinkers to go bigger, to reach for more. By contrast, European hops are more reserved. Central European Noble Hops are elegant and refined, while English ale hops such as Fuggles and Goldings are earthy and rustic, redolent of rainy autumn rather than stunning fall, the smell of loam and damp country lanes overhung by dripping trees. These are the hops Peter Darby presides over.

Peter was always interested in breeding plants for disease resistance. After gaining his PhD, he was looking for a job that would allow him to combine plant breeding and plant pathology – the study of diseases – and in 1981 the Hops Marketing Board offered him a job doing just that.

'The industry was stable but anxious back then, down quite a bit from a hundred years previously. It was all about the alpha acid. There was no discussion at all about flavour. We were looking for stuff that was wilt-resistant and had high alpha. So I was breeding new varieties with that as a brief. We didn't want hops that differed in flavour from existing varieties. It was all about yield, processing and storability – hops were simply alpha acid that stored well.'

This started to change early in the new millennium. American craft brewers were still mostly confined to their home market at this point, but some came and talked to Peter because they were keen to know more about hops generally, and were looking for varieties that were aphid-resistant. Soon, though, their beers were starting to be noticed internationally, and British brewers began importing hops that had a different character from traditional English ale hops. In 2002, the British hop industry began developing hops to compete against the imports, looking for home-grown varieties that could rival the flavours of Žatec and North America's Cascade. Peter Darby's job was turned on its head. From flavour being irrelevant, it quickly became an obsession.

'It's tricky commercially,' he says, 'because often brewers don't really know what they want. Ask them and they'll say, "something different, something new." It doesn't matter if it has notes of raspberry, cherry or grapefruit – it's the intensity and variety that matter.'

I'm surprised by how recent and how dramatic the change has been. A few months before this meeting I was speaking to Richard Westwood, Director of Brewing and now Managing Director of Marston's. 'I've learned more about hops and how we use them in the last five years than I did in the previous thirty,' he said. 'You can do so much more with hops now than you could ten years ago, not just with the arrival of New World hops, but also with a broader range of historic English varieties. We're now using hops like a range of herbs and spices, whereas before we were just using them like chilli, if you substitute bitterness for heat.' Marston's began an experimental programme of single-hop beers, using the same base beer but brewing with a different hop each month, which educated the brewers about the astonishing variations hops can produce.*

But how do hops gain this astonishing variety, this range of different flavour notes?

'We have a technology now called gas chromatography, and with that we've identified over four hundred different essential oils,' says Peter Darby as we get our second pints of Shepherd Neame's new Spitfire Gold, purely for illustrative purposes. 'Almost all of them can be found in other crops. But finding them all in one plant, and the way they interact, that's what makes hops unique.'

And that's just the start of it. 'On top of that, hops are safe – many bittering plants are poisonous. Add that to the economic and preservative qualities that first saw hops gain precedence, and you've got an extraordinarily talented plant. But there's even more.

'The botanical properties of hops interact with alcohol. They were probably first used as tinctures, mixed into an alcohol base and used medicinally, before they were used for brewing. Used in a herbal sense, because of their anti-bacterial and anti-fungal properties, they've treated diseases such as leprosy and TB. They're high in oestrogen, and can be used to alleviate the symptoms of menopause. And they're soporific: hops were used to send "Mad King George" to sleep.'

This is all so interesting that I'm in danger of not interviewing Peter Darby, but merely transcribing him. This is his patter, the stuff he says at conferences around the world. Can I get beneath his skin and ask the question no one else has asked?

'Why hops?'†

---

* This was a great thing for the brewer to do. Though it should be noted that Barnsley brewer Acorn started a similar programme several years before, and has now brewed a base 5 per cent IPA with hundreds of different hop varieties.

† That'll be a 'no' then.

'Why do you have your taste in music?' he fires back. 'It's a speciality crop, a premium product. If you're a farmer, it gives you a personal speciality, something distinctive. It's a community. It's a product of the local land. And for every hop grower working in Britain now, it's a conscious decision to stay in the industry. Because there's also the social history, the romanticism, a lot of which is all about their aroma. Hops are like vines: they have a connection with the whole of the culture. Everything else is just a plant.'

The British hop industry is still going through uncertain times, and the hop acreage in England has gone through a long period of decline. In 1962, 20,000 acres of hops were grown in Britain. By 2007, it was no more than 2,400. Climate change has randomised any expectations of what the harvest might be like. British brewers are now buying more American hops than British, and the British Hop Association has launched a new marketing campaign to promote the great British hop. But Peter is more optimistic than most people around the industry whom I speak to.

'We can't compete with Germany for providing the basic bittering hops that global brewers need,' he says. 'But we need to think of British Fuggles and Goldings hops as a premium, speciality product, and that's a product you can charge more for. Half our crop of these hops is now going to the United States, where they're trying to brew more sessionable beers. British oast houses are now at capacity. We're actually looking at an imminent global hop shortage, and British hops will be no exception.'

The difference between beer now and beer when the Kent hop fields were in their prime is that the brewing traditions of Britain, Belgium, the Czech Republic and Germany, previously discrete from the drinker's point of view, are now all part of the global craft beer scene, with long-established styles cross-fertilising and the demand for novelty seemingly endless. But behind the scenes, hops have always travelled. And, just like people, when they land in a new place they adapt to suit their new environment.

6. Pig Fat Done Two Ways

They say travel broadens the mind. I say that's a polite way of expressing the realisation that travel makes you confront your own ignorance.

In the departure lounge for a flight to Ljubljana, I try once again to burn into my mind that Slovakia and Slovenia are two different countries, in different places, and that Ljubljana is the capital of Slovenia.* Neither country existed as a separate state until after I graduated from university. Coincidentally, both are high in the league table when countries are ranked according to their consumption of beer per head of population. Both are well ahead of the UK, and Slovenia beats the United States, narrowly missing out on the top ten. It may not be Germany or the Czech Republic, but Slovenia is a country with beer in its soul. And I know absolutely nothing about it.

A passion for beer does not guarantee a perfect place to grow hops. But many other characteristics of Slovenia do. As we come in to land, the first thing that surprises me about Slovenia is its beauty. For anyone who grew up in the West in the 1980s, any former Soviet Bloc country remains grim and grey in the imagination. Such preconceptions have been instantly blown away for anyone who has holidayed in places like Montenegro or Croatia and found a relatively unspoilt Mediterranean paradise, but I never have.

Slovenia has only the tiniest strip of coastline, thanks to the Italian border creeping along and stealing a narrow, questing sliver that seems to tell a story of blatant and shameless land-grabbing when you look at it on the map. But Slovenia doesn't need the sea: it sits just south of the Alps, and much of it is mountainous and forested, dotted with lakes, fairy-tale castles and breathtaking views that rival any other Alpine tourism hotspot. In photographs, the whole country seems tinged with an ozone-rich, azure freshness. These mountain ranges are dense with rivers running through broad, pretty valleys that are perfect for either agriculture or sitting back and gazing at with a cold beer in your hand.

Located as it is with the Alps to the north, Italy to the west, the Mediterranean to the south and the bulk of Central Europe to the east, what is now the small Republic of Slovenia – about half the size of Switzerland – has always been caught in the unfortunate double bind of being both strategically important to anyone who wants to rule Europe, and completely incapable of defending itself. It's been annexed by every significant empire that has waged war across the Continent, and its borders have always been

---

* The capital of Slovakia is, of course . . . hang on, I know this. . .

subject to change. About a third of modern-day Slovenia was for centuries part of the Duchy of Styria, a territory within the Holy Roman Empire split across what are now Slovenia and Austria. And Styria is a name that should cause the ears of any brewer to prick up.

The Styrian Golding hop is popular in ale brewing, especially in the UK and Belgium. It's a friendly, no-nonsense hop, low in bitterness, and it gives beer a light spiciness. When British ale brewer Greene King launched a new blonde beer, head brewer John Bexon thought it might be just right. Although they do business through hop merchants, many brewers like to develop direct relationships with the farms they buy from, and John comes out here regularly to see his hops as they're growing. This time, Greene King's press department decided to bring along a few writers for the ride.

After a couple of hours' drive under huge blue skies, surrounded by mountains that always seem to keep their distance, we arrive at the *Institut za Hmeljarvsto in Pivovarstvo Slovenje* (IHPS), or Slovenian Institute of Hop Research and Brewing. The institute was founded in 1952 as a collective of local hop growers to help answer the most important questions in hop growing, concerning issues such as soil, fertiliser and climate. The main building looks more like a ski hotel than a scientific institute, apart from a fresco on the wall facing the road that shows families at work in the hop fields. In those fields now, long lines of hop plants run away to wooded mountains in the distance. The inscription on the fresco, repeated in the introduction to the institute's website, reads, 'When hops scratch you just once, they scratch you forever.'

The president of the institute is Martina Zupančič, a Knight of the Order of the Hop, as presented by the International Hop Growers Bureau. In her office she tell us that the main focus of the institute is cross-breeding hops, not necessarily for flavour but to make them more robust and resistant to disease. Hops are fickle, fragile plants and they need toughening up. 'There has been quite a lot of rain so far this year,' says Martina. 'This is good for the wheat, but it means the hops are late – they're only just flowering now. Man-made climate change is a fact, and it is really disturbing the growing season.'

Climate, and the hop's reaction to it, are the reasons we're here. Hop cultivation in Slovenia has been traced back to the eleventh century, when they were grown by the monks who were the first to brew beer on a large scale. The first industrial-scale hop gardens in Slovenia were planted near here 150 years ago. The first commercial varieties, imported from Germany and the former Czechoslovakia, proved vulnerable to disease. But English varieties fared much better.

Not every hop prefers the Slovenian climate to that of its native country, but once they had taken to their new surroundings the English immigrants prospered. They started winning international competitions, and some were hailed as the best in the world. In 1926, an outbreak of mildew caused widespread destruction across the hop fields, but the Styrian (or Savinjski) Golding survived and prospered. It seems obvious from its name that the Styrian Golding is a descendant – an ecotype – of the English Golding's hop that was exported here in the nineteenth century. Obvious, but wrong. It's actually an ecotype of Golding's relative, the Fuggle. Now praised for its noble qualities – low bitterness and high, refined aroma – it's regarded as a traditional Slovenian variety, accounts for 20 per cent of the country's total crop and is one of the most important export varieties. Incredibly for such a small country, Slovenia is now the sixth largest hop grower in the world, with around 3,000 acres under cultivation. Even such enthusiastic drinkers as the Slovenians find themselves with a surplus, and 90 per cent of the crop is exported.

As I sit taking studious notes in Martina Zupančič's office, the story of how an English import became a Slovenian export slowly reveals more of the magic of the hop. The reason English varieties thrived in the lower Savinja river valley is that they loved the climate. Here on the south side of the Alps, the mountains protect the fertile soil around the river networks. The amount of rainfall during the growing season is usually just right – about 800 millimetres – and the climate is sunny and pleasant without exceeding 30 degrees Celsius (86 degrees Fahrenheit), which would start growth too early. Essentially, the valley's microclimate is pretty similar to that in the English hop gardens of Kent and Herefordshire, but more stable and predictable. Those rare months in England when everything fits just right and you are reminded of the endless summers of childhood are more regular and reliable here – at least until now, and the climate change that's worrying Martina.

But what makes these hops Slovenian, as opposed to successful English expats, is their reaction to the climate. Here at the institute they carry out a chromatographic plot of the essential oils in each hop. They measure over 300 different components, and when they're all presented together they create a graph with 300 points, spiky and stark, like the remains of a petrified forest. Each different hop variety has its own plot, as unique as a fingerprint. Among other things, the institute uses these chromatographic plots to tell if a hop is genuine – it's surprisingly common for people to try to pass off a lesser hop as a more noble variety. But when hops are planted in a different climate, the variations in soil, rainfall and temperature cause this chromatographic plot to change. Imagine if moving to another country caused your personality, even your fingerprints, to change, and you understand how an English Fuggle can become a Savinjski Golding. The Fuggle is noted for its earthy, spicy, herbal notes, with little fruit. A century after it came to Slovenia, John Bexon has come in pursuit of what he calls the 'lemon and tinned peach aroma' of the Styrian Savinjski Golding.

✿ ✿ ✿

It's high time we saw some of these hops up close, so we pile back onto our minibus and head to one of the farms which is a member of the Hop Institute, just a short drive a little further up the valley.

Before we go to look at the hops, we are invited to sit down at a shady table to have a little snack. Four people are involved with the farm and they seem delighted to see us, so about twelve of us sit around a table with ice buckets full of local beers, and the biggest plate of salami I've ever seen in my life sweating slightly and shimmering in the sun. There are plates of bread and cheese, similar in bulk, echoing the peaks that sit behind us.

I dig in, alternating salami, cheese and beer while the business part of the meeting is discussed somewhere else, further up the table. Finally I sit back, pleasantly stuffed. Our hosts look up, look at us. Look at me. Look hurt. Our guide explains that it would be polite for us to finish the plate of salami, and we've hardly touched it. Politeness – that scourge of English health both mentally and physically – kicks in.

Last night we were taken to a brewpub and pizzeria on the outskirts of Ljubljana where we were treated to fantastic beer and sausage, deer goulash, pork ribs and calf's liver and roast pork and horseradish and dumplings. I had thought I had escaped dumplings when I last left the Czech Republic, but you can never escape dumplings. I accept that now. And most memorably of all, there was 'minced lard with soft pork crackling' – something a British celebrity chef might rename 'two ways with pig fat'. It was grease as an art form, soft and shiny, juicy flecks of meat contrasting with hard, chewy rind. The brewpub's pilsner harmonised with it beautifully, cleansing greasy, shiny lips and suggesting more lard might be a good idea.

The following lunchtime I'm still reliving the experience. But the insistence of our hosts seems to have gone beyond good-natured japery and become quite serious. It seems we will genuinely cause offence if we don't clear the mountain of home-made salami before us. One by one people drop out until it's just John Bexon and me, two big blokes among slim female journalists and PRs, tackling endless sweaty fat-flecked disks. Pig fat starts to ooze from my pores and sizzle under a high sun that has swung from behind the farmhouse to look down on us and mock. Again and again comes the repeated demand, 'Eat, eat!' We know we will not be taken to see the hop fields unless we can complete this endurance test, this initiation rite.

Finally, after what seems like hours, after a combination of cool, refreshing beer and mental exercises that take my brain to a faraway happy place where I'm an eighteen-year-old, one-hundred-fifty-pound vegan, Bexon and I manage to clear the plate. Our hosts cheer and clap. My fellow journalists and the PRs from Greene King look at us as if we are titans from Greek myth. We have bested great beasts here, just as Hercules triumphed in his many labours. Now, finally, we'll get a tour of the hop fields.

Or at least, we will when we've cleared the other plate.

What other plate?

One of the farmers leans back: Bexon and I are at one corner at the bottom of a table around which a dozen people are seated. We didn't think that one measly plate was for the whole table, did we? At the top end sits another Matterhorn of meat, one more peak of pork, at least equal in size to the one we just bested.

I've often found that whining like a caged animal is a good way of cutting through potential cultural barriers. After no more than a quarter, maybe a third, of the second plate, Bexon and I are slid from our seats, our greased skins compensating for our dramatically increased bulk. Amazed that I can still walk, disoriented by the sun and feeling quite unusual, I follow the rest of the party out towards the hop fields, unaware that my day's polite intake of pig fat has only just begun.

Hops

The hop fields are neatly ordered on dry, rocky soil, long lines running straight across the valley floor right to the foothills of the mountains in the distance. At their growing peak in June, the shoots that have been trained around the network of strings can grow as fast as an inch every hour, constantly twining around the string, climbing up towards the sun. Hops grow best between latitudes of 35 and 55 degrees because of a balance of factors. They need around thirteen hours of sunshine a day at their peak – closer to the equator, where there's less variance between the length of day and night, there's not enough sun. The sun almost seems to pull them up, stretching them from the ground, and on Midsummer's day they reach their zenith. At first I assumed this was a romantic notion, a grower's superstition, but it's true, to the precise date. But day length isn't the only factor: it's also about *relative* day length, the speed with which day length changes. The further north you go, the faster that change is. When the change is quicker, you get fewer, bigger cones. Here, 700 miles south of the UK, where the summer days are slightly shorter, the bines grow two or three feet higher. Looking up, the deep green against the clear deep blue again reminds me of the British on holiday, luxuriating in the easy-going warmth.

Until Midsummer's day the plants throw out a lot of vegetation, bulking up in volume to create as much potential as they can for a big harvest. Whatever latitude they grow at, when day length begins to shorten, the hops immediately switch from vegetation to flowering, throwing out laterals that produce the flowers that will grow into hop cones.

Now, in early August, the hops are growing heavy. They look magnificent, the pale, bright green of the hop cones standing vividly against the lush, dark green of the leaves. The sight of them is joyful. There are still weeks to go until the harvest, but we can all see that it's going to be a good one. I feel privileged to be here.

But we have to move on, and, as we do so, the afternoon begins to unravel. Greene King doesn't buy its hops from just one supplier, and it seems we can't show favouritism. At a time when it feels like the whole world should be enjoying a siesta, we arrive at a second hop farm, a little smaller than the last. As we step off the minibus, we're urged to come and look at a horse. It stretches its head out of a stable window and gives us a wide grin. Then we're led to a shady outdoor table, piled high with heaving plates of salami, cheese, bread, salami, chicken and salami. We stare at the table in horror, and then I begin to giggle uncontrollably, and someone presses a glass of cherry schnapps into my hand, explaining that it is good for me. I knock it back, straighten up and immediately decide I'd like to be a polar explorer or a lion tamer. A full crate of beer appears, then three or four bottles containing something murky and home-distilled. We eat and drink and laugh, hard, at things we don't understand. We're dragged from our seats to see a sculpture of an old man carved into a massive tree trunk. We make admiring noises while a dog in a cage pirouettes, barking madly, and then we're back on the minibus, off to see more hop fields.

I feel changed. If I stayed here, I think I'd become a different person. When it came to Slovenia, the earthy, spicy Fuggle became the fruity Styrian Golding. I worry that the transformation the country might subject me to might be fun for a while, but wouldn't last anywhere near as long or be in any way as successful.

7. Hopper's Morning

Mist fills the low troughs of the Kentish Weald, and from the perspective of the road that runs along the top of the high ridge, the hop fields are hidden by dense clouds, even though the sky above is a spotless blue. This is perfect weather for hop picking, and Robert Wicks, a former investment banker who opened the Westerham Brewery in Kent in 2004, is brimming with excitement. I've known Robert for years and his authoritative, forceful bearing has always reminded me of an army brigadier. Today, as he picks me up from the station after a painfully early train, he's more like a small boy on Christmas Day.

This is the second day of hop picking at Little Scotney Farm. Yesterday, the first day, was wet and horrible, so this is already looking like a vast improvement. 'Wet weather affects the hops,' explains Robert. 'The colours fade. It's not a problem, but the aesthetic isn't as good, so we sometimes leave them on the vine and wait for better weather. Today, this – *this* – is a hopper's morning.'

Robert and Westerham have an intimate relationship with the hop garden at Little Scotney Farm. In the heart of the Weald on the border of Kent and Sussex, the farm is part of the Scotney Castle Estate, near Lamberhurst, which is owned by the National Trust. Ian Strang has been a tenant farmer on the estate since 1990. In 2005, Robert partnered with Ian to launch Little Scotney Ale, a beer marketed by the National Trust to promote the farm as a living, going concern rather than a museum. It's a wonderful beer, dry and crisp, and always reminds me that hops can have a distinctive character without having to punch you in the face. Robert and Ian are now firm friends as well as business partners, united by – in a theme that's becoming a constant on my journey through beer's ingredients – a passion for their product that goes way beyond professional interest.

The mist has burned off now and the sun is blazing down. It's turning into a perfect late English summer's day, with Battle of Britain skies and a cock crowing somewhere in the distance. The hop garden at Scotney sits in the gentle bowl of a green valley. The Scotney Estate gardens were designed in the Picturesque style, which emerged as a trade-off between two different ideas of nature: the beautiful and the sublime. Sublime is all about greatness and majesty, nature as something to be admired or even feared, while the notion of the beautiful in this comparison is smaller, manicured and controllable. Blend the two ideas, and a hop garden is a perfect addition to the estate.

I'm struck, again, by the fact that, in Kent, people refer to these places as *gardens*. There's nothing ornamental about a hop garden (although sometimes hops are grown purely for decorative purposes) but the symmetry of the hanging bines, bowing like gathered curtains framing long aisles, suggests a cosmetic, artistic motivation even if there isn't one. And then there's the smell: as soon as the harvest starts, the air fills with resiny, floral perfume. Growing and harvesting hops is an aesthetic experience, bringing joy to the senses in a way that growing, say, potatoes never could.

Close up, the bines are now thick cords, two or three wrapped tightly around each string to form heavy green ropes. The first vegetation thrown off by these stalks doesn't start happening until at least three feet up, and the main action is really at the top, on the wires eighteen to twenty feet above ground, where they've thrown off a lot of laterals that hang heavy with flowers. It's going to be a good crop this year – in Kent at least.

When it's time to pick, the working day lasts from 7 a.m. to 5 p.m. Just like barley, hops have to be picked at exactly the right moment. You want them to be as ripe as possible, full of their precious essential oils and alpha acids, but if you leave it too late you get petalling – just as barley grains will detach from the ear, so hops reach a point where they fall apart.

The days of fully manual hop picking are long gone. Now, tiny, narrow tractors squeeze up and down the hop-lined avenues, each pulling a long wooden trailer. At one front corner of the trailer there's a big wheel that spins on its side, armed with a blade that cuts the strings holding the bines and gently pulls them from the wires above. The fat, heavy bines cling for a second before letting go and falling softly to be caught by the trailer as the tractor moves slowly forward. One or two people stand on the trailer, guiding the bines down to lie flat, and in this way the rows are stripped and left naked. Behind the first tractor, another vehicle with a crow's nest goes along to collect any bines that don't fall. It doesn't look like a great job, but it's better than the job on stilts that the crow's nest replaced.

'Do you want a go?' asks Robert.

I'm relieved that he means a go on the back of the tractor rather than in the crow's nest. The fleece I brought is forgotten in the back of Robert's van thanks to the clear blue sky and bright, hot sun, and it feels good to hoist myself up on the trailer in my polo shirt, shades and thick leather gloves. I'm not a very physical person, but I feel a rare confidence as I grip the thick ropes of twisted bines and coconut string and pull them away from the wires above. As the tractor moves forward, they fall naturally along the trailer, and we just have to guide them slightly, press them gently down to be ready for the next one and here it comes, trailing through my hair as its stem is cut and it hangs loose from the wire. I get into the flow and the trailer fills quickly and I imagine I could really go for doing a week or two of this work, physical without being exhausting, fast and all-consuming without being difficult or hectic. We've filled the trailer already. I jump off and am ready to do the next one, when I notice several hop-pickers laughing at me.

What have I done wrong?

'You haven't told him, have you?' says one of them to Robert.

'Told him what?' replies Robert, seeming genuinely nonplussed.

'Look at your arms, mate.'

I look down, and suddenly realise why everyone else working here is dressed in thick sweatshirts, hoodies, hats and scarves, despite the weather. I suppress the urge to scream.

Hops

I mentioned earlier that what differentiates a bine from a vine is that it climbs up a supporting structure by gripping it with thousands of tiny hairs. Those hairs are tough and strong, and today we're picking Target hops, which have a particularly thick and strong stem. The hairs on those stems have covered my arms in a network of cuts, scratches, welts and grazes. Half the skin is bright red and angry-looking. Some of the welts are quite impressively inflamed. There are a few drops of blood. And now, the oils and resins from the traumatised hops are working their way into the cuts, and a gentle stinging is building on my forearms.

Hops are frail and insecure. They can't even stand on their own, and a strong wind or heavy rainfall can destroy an entire crop. On the ground they're prone to mildew and rot, and bugs love tearing them apart. But try to harvest this weak and feeble plant and that's when it finally decides to fight back. George Orwell harvested hops in 1931, and in the diary he kept of his experiences, later written up as an article for the *New Statesman*, he described the 'spiny stems [that] cut the palms of one's hands to pieces'. Orwell obviously didn't have the thick leather gloves we have now, adding, 'in the early morning, before the cuts have reopened, it is painful work'.

When the trailers are full, the tractors pick up speed and head off to the big hop shed. Three tractors cross each other, careful and patient with their precious cargo.

In the shed, half a dozen people dressed, like the pickers, in multiple layers of long sleeves, hats and gloves, give the place a gloomy air, evoking midwinter on such a bright, warm day. The bines are resting on some kind of long, flat board on the trailer with a chain attached to the back. This gets attached to another chain by a big hook, and the tractor drives slowly away, the board sliding in place until it drops to the floor of the shed and leaves the hops there with as little disturbance as possible. 'They're frail and need looking after,' says Ian Strang. 'Harvest traumatises them, and they have to be kept safe.'

The workers – mostly women – take a bine at a time from the pile and twist it around a hook on an overhead chain, which runs like a rollercoaster above our heads and swoops down lower than head height when it reaches the point where the hops have been deposited on the floor. 'A wife can beat her husband in an arm wrestle after doing this for a while,' says Dawn, a middle-aged Kentish woman who has been sorting hops since she was fifteen years old and still comes back every year.

When I was very small, children's programmes such as *Play School* used to be obsessed with showing how things were made. Perhaps preparing a generation of children for a lifetime in manufacturing jobs that would have largely disappeared by the time we were old enough to drink, they lulled us into a stupor with the repetitive clunks, whumps and clackers of big, shiny pieces of machinery, made the people in white coats or brown overalls monitoring the endless conveyor belt flows look very important and gave us the satisfaction of guessing what the finished product was going to be as it slowly took shape. But they never showed anything as big, as thrilling or as gloriously fucked up as a hop-picking machine. If they had, the children of the 1970s would have been clamouring for jobs on hop farms.

It makes a terrific roar. The thick chain carries the hop bines, dangling uselessly, up into the air, on a curve around the perimeter of the shed and up further, into the belly of the beast. First, a set of rollers with long, metal teeth strips all the vegetation from the tough bines, and separates the bines from the coconut string. A conveyor belt carries hop flowers and leaves over an assault course of different sieves, shakers and threshers and filters, up and round and through and down and up again, until eventually only the hops remain, a seam of vivid pale green that's carried up to the first floor, a wooden, barnlike platform which opens out into the kilns adjacent to the shed. Out the back of the building, all the vegetation that isn't hop flowers is minced and shot out of a long pipe into the air, where it falls in a thick snow of green flakes onto a composting pile, to be dug back into the soil.

This is the machinery that replaced armies of manual hop-pickers in the 1960s and 1970s. It's a compromise between traumatising the hops and picking and processing them in a way that's economically viable. Machines like this are like Roger Coe's combine harvester, only on a grander scale, costing far more to install, and used for a much more specific function for just a few weeks a year. From a strictly business point of view, it doesn't stack up. 'It costs £3,000 an acre to grow hops before you even think about the investment in machinery and infrastructure,' says Ian. 'This is the first generation of hop machine, sixty years old now. Everyone who installed these machines is now retired or dead. The spares are getting rarer, and we should be investing in new kit now but the business just doesn't generate enough money for that to be viable.'

One man here is employed full-time just to keep the machine going. Watching him at work, and watching Ian's reaction to him, this seems to involve a combination of extraordinary mechanical skill, empathy with the machine and magic. 'I don't know what we'd do if anything happened to him,' says Ian. 'All the hop growers around here tend to be in their late fifties or older. You have to be born into it. Will anyone take over from us when we go?'

When the hops are picked and separated like this, they're fresh and moist, plump and soft and shiny. They're beautiful to look at and wonderfully aromatic, but if we just kept them in this state they'd begin to break down and compost before the day was out. Unless they're going immediately into the brewhouse, they need to be dried.

The traditional oast house is the architectural feature that gives Kent its identity. It's a circular, brick building with a tall, conical peak that resembles a wizard's hat, with a white wooden cowl that turns so the opening that allows the heat to escape is always facing out of the wind. Modern techniques of industrialised hop drying made oast houses like these obsolete, and while the buildings are still everywhere you look in Kent, most of them have been converted into attractive residential spaces. Here at Scotney they're still used to dry hops the traditional way, and four of them huddle in a group, each enjoying its few weeks of intensive use.

Within each circular space, sackcloth is laid across the floor in a careful sequence which will mean the hops are treated as gently as possible. 'Years ago hops were treated with such reverence,' says Ian. 'If you trod on one it was sacrilege. Drying them in these kilns involved enormous attention to detail. In a big industrial operation now you see them getting thrown around and damaged, and that has a massive impact on quality.'

Now, men carry in sacks of hops one at a time, loaded just minutes ago from the picking machine, and carefully spread them on the sackcloth-covered floor. Hop merchants and brewers want to buy whole hops, so the idea is to dry them without them breaking up. They're gently raked flat, until the whole kiln is full up to a level of three feet, a board across the bottom of the doorway stopping them from spilling out as well as measuring the correct depth.

While one oast house is being filled, the one next to it is already warm. The 'reek' – the first blast of moisture that comes off when the heat hits – is sweet, grassy and resinous, uplifting and enlivening, an aromatic inhalation for the soul. This is one of the parts Robert Wicks loves the most. 'Outside, at night, you can see the steam. The smell is fresh, zesty. There's almost something of the sea about it. And a sappy, fresh-cut grass.'

Unfortunately, if these volatile aroma compounds are in the air here in the oast house, they're obviously no longer in the hops and won't feature in the beer, which is a crying shame. But there's no real alternative to drying hops if we want to brew with them more than a day after they're harvested. Traditionally, oast houses like this used coal fires and natural draught to dry the hops. This took up to four days, but if you dried the hops more slowly more of the aroma compounds would be retained in the hops. Now they're dried by big gas burners, low and slow, for about eight hours, but the perfect time and temperature depends on the variety. 'You have to get to know your hops, know how they'll behave,' says Ian, who clearly has, and does.

The inside of the shed, the central loft space between the kilns, is pungent with layers of hops being dried at different times pretty much around the clock at the start of each autumn. It's deeply resiny and musky, fuggy rather than fresh, from the accumulated layers of aroma.

When the hops are dried, they're paler, almost translucent, and the level of the hops in the kiln has fallen from three feet deep to less than two. Now, the boards are removed and the dried hops are dragged gently towards a square chute in the middle of the wooden floor. This is the baling machine, customised from a piece of kit designed for the wool industry. The chute is about twenty feet deep, ending in a metal rectangle on the floor below, which now supports a burlap sack over five feet tall. The dried hops are shovelled into the chute until they're level with the floor above. Then, a hydraulic ram compresses a twenty-foot-high cylinder of dried hops into five. Hop merchants expect these bales – known as pockets – to weigh exactly sixty-five kilograms, and they do.

'Pocket' is a ridiculous name for a sixty-five-kilogram sack that's as tall as a person, but this is hops. 'They're visually nice, but they're no good at all for storage and handling,' says Ian. That doesn't matter, though: they're called pockets, and they're traditional, and they look great. I'm starting to understand that in some aspects, the aesthetics of hop farming are more important than the practical considerations.

The hop harvest in Kent was always so important, and so variable, that there was a healthy (or unhealthy, depending on your view) betting scene around what the annual yield would be. That tradition is alive and well at Scotney. There's a board fixed to one wall of the oast house on which the total number of hop pockets of each year's harvest is stencilled in black paint. The last few years read:

2011 – 486
2012 – 498
2013 – 342
2014 – 450

Throughout 2013, the weather conditions in England were pretty much the opposite of what they should have been in each season, creating havoc for British agriculture and horticulture. Ian says he's expecting that 2015 will equal 2014, but he'd make a terrible poker player: I can tell he's hoping it will be much better than that.

Beer lovers are fond of comparing hops in beer to grapes in wine. In many ways, the comparison is apt, and in some ways that's a huge problem. Hops need at least as much quality and attention to detail as you would give grapes in a vineyard, but people don't want to pay as much for their beer as they do a good-quality wine. If you're going to be brutal about it, there doesn't seem to be an economic case for people like Ian Strang to continue growing hops. I've never been happier that, for some people, it's not all about the money.

8. The Pursuit of Hoppiness

'That's an interesting haircut you have. Are you a university professor?'
'No, I'm a writer.'
'What brings you to America?'
'I'm writing about hops.'
'Hops?'
'Yes.'
'You're dressed a lot smarter than most people.'

'I had to give a big presentation right before I went to the airport.'

'Are you a university professor?'

'No.'

'Well, you seem to have been to America a few times and everyone else has seemed happy to let you in. On you go.'

Getting through US customs is an interesting experience, always best appreciated when you've been awake and dressed for twenty-four hours. It seems designed to intimidate, to make you crack and say, 'OK you got me, I was going to try to start a Communist revolution but you've foiled my plans.' Instead, it makes me want to say, 'Get over yourself, your country's not that special.'

But that wouldn't be true. If I go more than two years without a visit to America, I start to get scratchy and fretful, like I'm missing something important. Just don't tell the Americans I said that, OK?

It's about a two-hour drive from Seattle to Yakima. You spend the first hour climbing up through misty rainforests of Douglas firs that will be familiar to anyone who watched *Twin Peaks*, which was filmed nearby. Then, you get out of the rain shadow and the landscape changes instantly. The firs fade out into burnt grass that shines gold under the deep blue sky. It's beautiful, but also barren. This is the high desert of Washington State. There are about eight inches of rainfall a year here, compared with thirty-eight inches back in Seattle.

We crest a hill and the shining gold slopes stretch out before us. Here and there, the snow-capped peaks of (mostly) extinct volcanoes shimmer like mirages in the distance. But when we look down, the valley bottom is such a deep, dark green it feels as if we've discovered some lost paradise.

The Yakima Valley is America's fruit bowl. It's broad and flat, sheltered from the extremes of weather by the surrounding hills and mountains. At peak growing season its northerly latitude gives it an hour more sunlight than California to the south, and the high and dry altitude means there are far fewer bugs and pests here than in most temperate farming regions around the world, so the need to spray the plants with chemicals is relatively low. The volcanic soil is rich and fertile. The only problem is water: it's a desert. But in the early twentieth century, an irrigation system was put in place to channel meltwater from the snows that fall on the volcanic peaks in winter down into the valley below. Washington State grows over half of

America's crop of fruits such as cherries and apples. This one valley grows 70 per cent of America's hops, equating to 25 per cent of the global hop harvest.

Yakima has been a place of almost spiritual significance to me ever since I first discovered the joys of American-style India Pale Ale. I've seen many people fall in love in the same way since, and the best part of my job is witnessing the progression of expressions on the face of someone tasting these beers, these hops, for the first time. Sometimes you're already a beer fan. Other times you think you don't like beer, because up to now you've only been exposed to a very narrow interpretation of what beer can be. And then someone hands you a small, elegant stemmed glass of a liquid that could be pale blonde, like lager, through to darker, burnished bronze. You raise it to your nose and experience a sensory dissonance, the circuits between your olfactory bulb and brain momentarily fried because this doesn't fit: this liquid that looks like beer is assaulting your senses with an array of tropical fruit, fresh pine resin, vivid citrus and a hint of weed. You have to taste, but if the aroma set you up for some kind of sweet fruit cocktail, the palate confounds you because all the fruit flavour is there but with very little sweetness. It's balanced by the 'strong malty backbone' all those Maris Otter fans were talking about back in Norwich, and it ends with a drying, assertive bitterness that's full on the palate, challenging to some, but compels most to drink again. And again. It's love at first sip. You look up, wide-eyed, at the person who has given you this elixir, and say 'What . . . ? How . . .?' and they smile and say, 'American hops.'

And that's it: you're hooked. Sometimes people say, 'I still don't like beer, but I LOVE this.' Other times people devote themselves to craft beer and the word 'awesome' becomes the most overused in their vocabulary. Some people go on a years-long binge, seeking ever-hoppier and more extreme beers in the search to recreate that first hit.* Some are stuck in this spiral forever. Others finally come down and remember that other styles of

---

* Which happens rarely, if ever. In the fifteen years since I tasted my first American IPA, I've had maybe two beers that match up to that first experience. And when I go back to that first beer and taste it again, it's a pale shadow of what I remember. The beer hasn't changed, but my palate has. *The beer changed me*, permanently opening doors of flavour perception which can never be closed again, and changed permanently my demands, expectations and standards for flavour experiences. You can never have a first impression a second time.

beer are available, relearn an appreciation of balance as well as intensity, or seek similar highs in other flavour dimensions such as so-called 'sour beers'. And, yes, for a small minority the record playing the swirling, stirring orchestral soundtrack to these last two paragraphs scratches across the vinyl and crashes into the buffers with an 'Ugh! That's so *bitter!*'

Hoppiness is a strong, assertive flavour, and such flavours will always divide opinion. But around the world enough people like the flavour of American hops that they have turned a grassroots, small-scale cottage industry that began after the prohibition on home brewing was repealed in 1979 into the global phenomenon of craft beer. There are many, many different styles of craft beer that originate in different brewing traditions around the world and continue to expand as those traditions cross-pollinate and give birth to new ideas. But for most people who get into craft beer, and for most brewers who decide to devote themselves to the vocation of creating it, the hops grown in the Yakima Valley were the spark.

After a pleasant evening in the town of Yakima carefully sampling the beers these hops make, we stumble back onto our minibus the next morning and are joined there by Ann George, Executive Director of Hop Growers of America. I'm one of several journalists on the bus, together with a gang of people from London's Meantime Brewing, who organised the trip.

There are some rumblings about this year's hop harvest that Ann is keen to address. As interest in craft beer soars, the global demand for hops is increasing. The trouble is, as global warming continues to randomise the world's weather, the ever so delicate hop is suffering. At a British hop event a couple of weeks before we flew out here, the mood was sombre. Central Europe has had a hot, dry year. The Žatec (Saaz) hop cones are very small, and the total volume is down 25–30 per cent from where it should be. Early varieties in Slovenia were reported to be between 30 and 50 per cent down. People were expressing relief that the UK yield looks to be average, because that's so much better than anywhere else. And there were dark rumours about Washington State, which has had temperatures above 35 degrees Celsius (95 degrees Fahrenheit) since June, and no rain at all, of water supplies to hop farms being shut off.

Ann wastes no time in bringing us up to speed. The El Niño weather pattern has indeed stopped the rain here. There was a snow drought last winter, meaning the water supply from the melt is only half of what's needed. Across the valley all the water is spoken for, all carefully allocated. But there are reserves. Some growers have emergency drought wells. Others trade water with their neighbours, while others still will focus on a smaller area, leaving part of their acreage idle and focusing what water they do have on fewer fields, so it's not as if there are hops shrivelling and dying on the bine. And while the harvest of some early varieties was poor, the longer the season goes on the better it's getting. By the time all the hops are in, a few weeks from now, the United States will post a 15 per cent increase on the previous year.

Puterbaugh Farms has been growing hops for five generations, and now boasts 1,000 acres of bines carrying 120 different varieties. The bines are taller here than they were back in Kent, the wires higher. The scale of the place gives the bucolic idyll of the hop garden a slightly industrial edge that I'm never quite able to shake for the rest of the day. Thick, black rubber pipes run along the base of each row of bines. Long frames with spindly metal wheels fling water into the fields.

British hops aren't irrigated like this. The UK hop industry turns this into a boast, pointing out that doing it the natural way is far more environmentally friendly than the precisely controlled, optimal growing conditions created here. But here, this level of control is necessary. America may look fertile and verdant, but humans can't live on grass and fir trees. Cuttings and seeds brought over by the first European settlers invariably failed, and people frequently starved to death on the long treks west across the new continent. America collectively remembers what it was like to go hungry, and is terrified of going back to that. If it wasn't for irrigation, there'd be no agriculture here.

At this time of year, every daily flight from London to Seattle carries representatives of the British brewing industry. Yakima used to grow just a few hop varieties for giant lager brands, but when Anheuser-Busch was bought by the notorious cost-cutters Inbev, the recipe for Budweiser was changed and the biggest brewer in the world started sourcing cheaper hops from Germany instead. Yakima was saved when the craft beer revolution hit Europe, and brewers around the world started clamouring for American aroma hops. Ann George has worked in the American hop industry for twenty-eight years, and has seen her job change from selling a standard product to a few large customers into one where she's selling a specialist product to many small ones. If that sounds like more work, it doesn't seem to bother Ann. 'Craft may account for a small percentage of total beer volume, but it's transformed the hop industry,' she says 'The average hopping rate of American beer is 0.2 to 0.25 pounds per barrel. Last year, craft brewers were averaging 1.4 pounds per barrel. According to the American Brewers' Association and the narrow definition they use for craft beer, craft accounts for 11 per cent of market volume. But they use six times as many hops as average beers, and account for a quarter of annual hop production. With estimates of craft's share being at 20 per cent by 2020, they'll account for half the entire crop.' And that's not counting the demand from the visiting Brits.

Today, Puterbaugh is hosting some of its oldest international customers. Alastair Hook came for the first time in 1998, the year before he set up Meantime Brewing in Greenwich, and has returned here every year since. Having recently sold Meantime to global giant SABMiller for a great deal of money, Alastair can now afford a more relaxed approach to how he spends his time. I'm happy for him every time I see a Facebook status update from a cricket match in Delhi, or a picture of him knee-deep in a river somewhere in Oregon, holding a prize salmon. The frown he used to wear almost permanently while we discussed the frustrations of the British brewing industry has been replaced by a joyful grin that takes a decade off his appearance. Alastair worked tirelessly to create arguably the UK's first modern craft brewery, did a huge amount to help broaden a parochial British brewing industry's idea of what good beer can be and deserves every bit of his new-found wealth and leisure time. And yet here he is, doing what he has done every year for almost two decades, carefully examining and buying the hops Meantime will brew with over the coming year. He could choose to be anywhere in the world right now, doing whatever he likes, and he's here sniffing hops. He seems as hungry and focused today as I imagine he was in 1998. The only difference compared to previous years is that his wife, Nina, has been able to give up work and has joined him in Yakima for the first time.*

---

* Just before this visit, the unstoppable Anheuser-Busch Inbev in turn bought SABMiller. At the time of our visit, this meant the fate of Meantime was uncertain. I spent about an hour sitting next to Alastair on our minibus later in the trip, chatting away, and about a week afterwards received a panicked call from Meantime's PR people asking if Alastair had mentioned the takeover while we were talking,

With Alastair is Paul Corbett of British hop merchants Charles Faram. Paul first came to Puterbaugh in 2002, and bought ten bales of Cascade hops to sell to British brewers. Now, Faram's ship a hundred containers of hops from Yakima every year, and sell more American hops in Britain than British hops.

Alastair Hook has a theory about the dramatic change in what we're looking for in hops. 'Traditionally, the oils in beer prevented it from souring, so big bitterness and aroma go together, creating a storable product by preventing infection, and making it commercial. But now, most of us have enough money and stability not just to be utilitarian, but also to buy pretty things. We can spend money on things we appreciate aesthetically.'

The relationship between hop farm and hop merchant goes deeper than simple buying and selling. It's more of a partnership of developing and nurturing the best varieties. Yesterday Paul Corbett went through around sixty different samples. From those, there are a dozen for us to try today.

The main room in the office at Puterbaugh Farms is dominated by a large table with a stainless-steel surface. Sitting in the middle of it is a pile of a dozen parcels, tightly wrapped in brown paper, each about the size of a bag of sugar. As Paul opens each one, it feels like Christmas.

The first one we try is Cluster, an old landrace variety of unknown parentage. Cluster used to account for the majority of America's hop harvest because it's a dual-purpose hop, high enough in alpha acid to be used for bittering, but with a pleasing, earthy, fruity aroma. It was the first hop variety cultivated at Puterbaugh, and the only one grown here until the 1960s. It's the standard hop in American brewing, the equivalent of Fuggles in the UK.

The first things a hop merchant or brewer looks for when evaluating hops like this are colour, freshness and, ideally, whole flowers. 'There's a little bit of brown on these samples, which we used to frown on but increasingly it's OK, because it indicates ripeness and a fuller flavour,' says Paul. 'There's a little bit of windburn – you can see here where some cones were damaged by a wind storm.'

---

and insisting that anything he had said about it was off the record. I was happy to reply that we'd talked nothing but hops. I'm even happier that A-B Inbev decided to sell on Meantime to Asahi. The brewery may still be corporately owned now, but it's owned by a corporation that at least gives a shit about beer.

Next, Paul presses down gently on the tight bundle of hops. There's a bit of bounce in them, and the green brick springs back into shape. This means they're dried perfectly, with just a bit of moisture left. If they're too dry, you lose all the aromas, but if there's more than 12 per cent moisture, they'll start to compost. Not only does this render the hops useless, the composting process creates heat that could cause fire in the hop store.

I've rubbed hops before, but I've never been given a masterclass like this. When I break open a hop flower it spills yellow powder. I immediately think of pollen, but this is lupulin, the resinous powder that contains our alpha acids and aroma compounds, produced by glands in the centre of the flower. There are oils and resins in the leaves, too, but the most intense part is around the lupulin glands. There's a bony stem, known as the 'strig,' running up the centre of the cone. Tight leaves called 'bracts' run off the strig to give the cone its shape and walls. In the spaces between the bracts, smaller bracteoles create sheltered compartments for the lupulin glands. The whole structure is essentially a natural factory for creating these precious oils and resins. 'Currently there are about four hundred named compounds, but there are still some that the human nose can recognise that haven't yet been picked up by even the most sensitive equipment,' says Alastair.

In order to fully evaluate the aroma of the oils, brewers, hop merchants and growers like to crush hop flowers in their hands. By grinding the heels of your palms together, not only do you crush the lupulin sacs to release the aromas, your body heat also excites the oils and gets them moving. Cupping your hands then provides an aroma chamber that offers a dazzling organoleptic delight.

When we do this with the Cluster hops, I get strong aromas of lemon, blackcurrant and boiled sweets. It's much sweeter and fruitier than descriptions of its character I've seen in brewing books.

'That's because what you're smelling now are the volatile oils, and they'll flash off in brewing,' says Alastair. 'Fermentation also drives off some aromas, so what you get in the field can be quite different from what you end up with in the beer.'

Ann nods. 'Brewing is a vital part of working out the viability of a hop. It might smell like the cat peed on the Christmas tree right now, but we've thrown away varieties that would have been incredible if we'd used them to brew.'

'At Meantime we have four brewers sniffing the hops, and they always disagree,' says Alastair. 'The big, strong oils can mask some of the prettiness behind. You have to do the work in the fields to get consistency. It all starts here – you have to understand the hop here to know how it's going to turn out at the end.'

Next we rub Magnum, a German variety. Here in the field, it's much more herbal and spicier than Cluster. There's a strong aroma of lemon, with a tiny hint of onion. Magnum is higher in alpha acid, and I can feel the oils on my skin. It's mainly used as a bittering hop. Its citrus, herbal character barely gets a mention in commercial hop descriptions, but it's pronounced here.

Willamette is a classic American hop, a descendant of the Fuggle, and it retains some of the English hop's spicy, earthy character, but has gained more fruitiness in its new home. Having seen it cited regularly on the labels of craft beer bottles, I'm surprised to learn that it was the main hop in Budweiser until Anheuser-Busch Inbev switched to higher alpha hops to save money. The sample today has a dusting of brown, a nice ripeness. I find it quite delicate, with notes of blackcurrant and pepper. Willamette is the most consistent hop in transferring the aromas we get now into the finished beer, and stands up well to big bruisers like Cascade and Chinook.

Individual hop varieties have attracted their own cult followings over the last few years, with Citra in particular almost becoming a brand in its own right. Every new craft brewer in the UK seemingly wants to brew a pale ale or IPA using Citra as its single or main aroma hop, and around 2013 the market was flooded with pale beers characterised by the hop's distinctive grapefruit aroma. Used on its own, I increasingly found it dull and one-dimensional. But the reason the fashion for Citra waned had more to do with supply than demand. The price of the hop soared – where it was even available. Dark rumours began circulating that the best hops were being bought up by big brewers who sought to kill the craft beer movement by denying small brewers access to the ingredients they needed. It's a conspiracy theory Paul Corbett has heard many times. 'We buy our hops on an annual basis, like we're doing now,' he says. 'When our customers like a hop, they place forward contracts for it. With something like Citra, we buy as much of it as we can but there's only so much to go around, and so the whole harvest can be spoken for as soon as we get it. We try to keep everyone happy. But we have three new breweries opening in the UK every week now. Almost every day, a new customer we've never dealt with before will phone up on spec and ask for a load of Citra or Nelson Sauvin, because that's what everyone wants, and we just don't have it to sell to them.'

Puterbaugh Farms is big. Roy Farms, which we head on to after lunch at Puterbaugh, is even bigger. I need share only one statistic to put it in perspective: in the whole of the UK there are currently 2,400 acres under hop cultivation. Roy Farms – one family business in Yakima – has 3,200 acres of hops.

The scale of it is completely different from anything even imaginable in Kent. Apples, cherries and pears take the total size of Roy Farms to over 6,000 acres. They employ 325 people all year round, and that figure rises to between 600 and 650 during harvest time. Out in the hop fields, the rows between bines are wide enough to fit a full-size tractor. First, a bottom cutter goes along and slashes the bines about two feet from the ground, leaving them hanging loose from the wires, doing two rows at a time, one either side. Then the top cutter, which looks like a demented mechanical barber, goes along and scissors the hops from the top wires. The top cutter is seemingly fastened to a truck in front of it, pushing it along, and the bines fall into the back of the truck as they're cut.

The farm has four separate hop-processing facilities. Four of the big trucks from the field line up side by side at the edge of a vast shed. The hops are taken from their trailers and tied onto the hooks that will take them into the giant hop-picking machine. Another six trucks are queuing behind, waiting for their turn. The principle of the hop-picking machine is the same as I've seen in Kent, but the scale is, of course, much bigger and the equipment much newer and shinier – a new one would cost $25 million. There are layers and layers of hops on conveyors, shooting off in all directions. The whole thing looks like a Hollywood set designed by Terry Gilliam, and I simply can't follow the journey of the hop as it speeds along conveyors that dip into hidden spaces, belts sorting different parts, separating the precious flowers that will be dried from the vegetal bulk, the bines and leaves that will be mulched back into the soil.

The floor is covered with hops and hop detritus, and I remember Ian Strang talking about the old days when each hop flower was precious, and to tread on one would be a faux pas. We're not in that world any more, not on this scale. But that's not to say the hops aren't carefully treated. Once the threshing and sieving and sorting is completed, the fresh hop flowers are pulled off their conveyor by an automated system and poured into kilns, each one about three feet high and the size of a tennis court. A giant metal bar moves slowly along the kiln from one end to the other, pouring hops and then smoothing them to the required depth.

The burners that fire the kilns are immense, like jet engines, roaring with blue flame behind a mesh enclosure just outside the shed. In thirty days, Roy Farms spends $608,000 on fuel to power them. But this immense power is controlled with an incredible degree of finesse. The hops are dried at 125 degrees Celsius (257 degrees Fahrenheit) for between eight and twelve hours. The precise drying time is calculated taking into account variables including the amount of sunshine on the day of the harvest, the ambient temperature, the size of the cone and the presence of dew. The aim is to take the moisture content down from 70 per cent to between 8 and 10 per cent. The drying temperature used to be 140 degrees Celsius (284 degrees Fahrenheit), but this lower temperature helps preserve more of the precious oils. There are blowholes here and there on the surface of the drying hops where hot air has bubbled up and escaped.

Our guide is a giant with a moustache that hangs down below his mouth, and a beard that falls to his chest. One bare arm is a sleeve of hop tattoos. This is Jim Boyd, described memorably by local Yakima writer Brendan Monahan as being 'like Paul Bunyan got kicked out of Hogwarts and then founded a biker gang . . . Jim Boyd is not a guy who can disappear in a crowd. Jim Boyd IS a crowd.' Jim takes us to a large warehouse where hops coming off the kilns, from a conveyor that moves across the ceiling, fall whispering and shushing into piles thirty feet high. I've never seen so many hops before. And of all the emotional reactions the hop harvest provokes, right now I just want to jump into them. I'm not the only one, and someone mentions the possibility.

'Two reasons why you can't do that,' says Big Jim Boyd. 'One is, you will itch for days. Two, this is a food product and I don't want your stinky ass in my beer.'

The hops are piled into a compression plunger, 100 pounds of hops hit with a heavy *woomph*, followed by another 100 pounds on top to create 200-pound bales, each stencilled with the year, grower and plot, and taken straight to chilled storage. The delicacy and pungency of the storage facility is like nothing else I've yet experienced. Resin and tropical fruit hang thick and drowsy in the cool air. Alastair Hook is visibly delighted that once the hops are here and have been inspected by a man from the State Department, no one can do anything else to them.

At least, that's the story for the hops that will be sold whole. But about 70 per cent of the crop from Roy Farms is processed into pellets.

I think any craft beer drinker whose habits are shaped by a yearning for a natural product would be instinctively against the idea of pellets. I know I am. But many brewers would argue that this is an irrational prejudice. Rationally, brewers are split on which works best.

Hops are turned into pellets at the farm, within a few days of picking. Pelletisation involves the hops being coarsely ground at low temperatures, to preserve as much of the essential oils as possible, and then compressed in a machine that extrudes them as tiny cylinders about as long as your thumbnail and about five millimetres in diameter.

The advantages of pelletised hops are numerous. They're more compact and easier to store. They deliver all the bittering alpha acids and aromatics that whole hops do, but because they've been blitzed and blended they deliver these attributes with greater consistency. They're much easier and less messy to use in brewing and in dry-hopping – where hops are added to the keg or cask as they're filled, to put back some of the character lost in the brewing process. The blitzing smashes open every lupulin gland, releasing all the oils, which means that if pellets are left unprotected they oxidise and lose their flavour much more quickly than whole hop flowers would. But if they're stored correctly, they actually retain what's left of that precious character for longer.

Against that, many of the brewers who prefer to stick with whole hop flowers acknowledge the advantages of pellets, but excuse themselves as traditionalists. A few will go further. In the 1980s, Sierra Nevada split a batch of their Celebration Ale and hopped half with pellets and half with flowers. When they tasted the finished beer, everyone preferred the whole-hop version. Sierra Nevada, now massive by the scale of most countries' brewers, still only uses whole hops in every beer it brews.

This makes intuitive sense to me. As I follow the hop harvest, the consistent theme is that everything you do to this frail little flower from the point it is picked to the point its products end up in the finished beer results in the loss of a portion of those precious, volatile oils. Pelletising introduces another stage of processing, risking another chunk of the hop's bounty being lost. Maybe. Or maybe not. This is another point where brewing science and biochemistry still fall short of explaining and determining everything that is good and special about beer.

When I was with him in České Budějovice, Josef Tolar threw another curve ball into the debate. He explained to me that the leaves of the hop contain most of the polyphenols. These don't get much press in the current adoration of hops, but, according to Mr Tolar, they're particularly good at binding protein molecules, helping coagulation during the boil and therefore leaving a cleaner, brighter beer. They also have an effect on flavour – tannins are one class of polyphenols, and they make the beer more drinkable. 'When you separate the leaves from the other components by pelletising the hops, you lose this,' says Mr Tolar. And the thing he's focused on more than anything else, like most Czech brewers, is making his beer as drinkable as he can.

Processing can also go one stage further. Both aromatic oils and alpha acids can be extracted so you can just use the extract and not bother with the messy plant at all. There are some talented brewers who stand up for hop extracts because they help reduce the tannic bitterness of hoppy beers. Josef Tolar is not one of these people. 'There's zero polyphenol. Such beers are hoppy, but not moreish.'

Back at Roy Farms, Big Jim is taking us to the experimental hop garden. This is a cracked, bare scrap of earth planted with about 800 random hop varieties, just one plant of each. These hops are treated deliberately badly. They get no spray and no fertiliser – it's all about the survival of the fittest. 'We're looking for something that's gonna be able to yield six hundred to seven hundred pounds an acre,' says Jim, 'so get in there and see what you can find. Under these conditions, anything that's got a good crop on it is promising. Then, you're looking for hops that have a pleasing aroma. Throw away any popcorn farts.'

Popcorn farts?

'Flimsy cones that fall apart when you touch 'em. If it's flowering well and the cones are good, then you can break them apart, smell them. If you find anything you like, let me know.'

This is nothing like the hop gardens I've visited so far. It's like a hop torture garden – in fact, that's exactly what it is. Insects buzz everywhere. There's a sour fug in the air, and most of the plants look tired and deflated. But we quickly find plenty that seem to be thriving, and we break apart and rub the cones from these as we've been taught. Most of them smell strongly of onion, garlic or cheese. After a while my senses give up – my nose doesn't want to do this any more. But we're in there for about an hour. This is a treasure hunt, and the possibility of finding the new superstar variety keeps a hard core of our party going.

Finally, late afternoon catches up with us and taps us on the shoulder. A day in the Yakima hop fields has given me a thirst like I've never known before, both from the adoration of the hop and from the heat and dust. We pile back onto our minibus and drive a short distance to Bale Breaker.

Bale Breaker is an idea so wonderful it makes me want to cry. It's a brewery and pub inside a hop field. Established in 1932 – the year before Prohibition ended – B.T. Loftus Ranches is one of Yakima Valley's longest-running hop farms. In 2013, the grandchildren of the first farmers opened a brewery in Field 41 of the family's 900-acre farm. There were already several successful wineries in Yakima, showcasing the potential of the grapes grown here, so why not a brewery? Bale Breaker has been crazily busy ever since. I'm just amazed it took so long for someone to have the idea.

The farm specialises in the massive aroma hops that are still so popular here: Simcoe, Citra, Mosaic, Ahtanum, Equinox and Cascade. The brewpub stands next to the brewery out in the corner of the hop field, which grows Simcoe and Cascade, and the beer named Field 41 is hopped with these varieties. The stronger Topcutter uses Citra and Ahtanum. The brewery has grown so quickly that it now uses 2 per cent of all the hops grown on the farm. That may not sound much, but Loftus Ranches harvests over two million pounds of hops every year.

The beers are ridiculously good, the best I encounter on this trip to the United States, and I don't think that's just because we're parched and fixated after the long day. At the truck stop we paused in while coming over the mountains yesterday, even the guy behind the counter went out of his way to recommend Bale Breaker's beers from the wide selection cooling in his fridges. Field 41 has intense aromas of citrus fruit and pine, but goes easy on the bitterness and is light and easy in the mouth. Topcutter is a full-on, assertive

IPA with a thicker grapefruit, orange and pine hit from the piles of hops that are added to the brew late, to preserve as much of their magic as possible.

Another thing that makes these beers so good is that they are obviously so fresh. The fleeting delicacy of hop aromas doesn't end once the brewing process is complete. The longer the beer lives, the more its hop character will fade, which is why American craft brewers take great care to keep their beers chilled. Recently I spoke to Bob Pease, CEO of the Brewers Association (BA) and champion of its successful export programme. In the United States, brewers are committed to what Bob calls a 'cold chain infrastructure' of temperature-controlled distribution. From the moment the beer is packaged to the moment it gets into the drinker's hand, it's kept chilled at every stage. The BA recommends a temperature range of 50–55 degrees Fahrenheit (or 10–13 degrees Celsius, which also just happens to be Cask Marque's recommended cellar temperature for British-style cask ale). 'Time, sunlight, oxygen and temperature fluctuation – these are the enemies of craft beer,' says Bob.

When it comes to shipping abroad, the cost of cold chain infrastructure multiplies at the same time as the risks of spoilage. 'To keep the beer in perfect condition we have to insist on reefers [refrigerated shipping containers] which can be cost-prohibitive for many,' says Bob. 'Finding an importer who can do it is difficult, but if they want the beer, it has to be chilled.' All of which means there's probably no better place to drink a hop-forward beer than at the place it was brewed, fresh off the line.

But our tastes change over time, and the quality we currently refer to as freshness, that we invest a huge amount of money to preserve and taste, hasn't always been considered an attribute.

While I was at Guinness I had one of those rare, precious moments in a beer historian's life that's like a nerdy lottery win. Faced with a library of books and archive records, I picked up and opened a book at random, and found a gem. D. O. Williams wrote *Notes on the St James's Gate Brewery* in 1937, when he was head brewer. The book was updated in 1964 by his successor, H. S. Corran. So I'm not sure whether it was in one or both editions, but certainly in the 1960s the character of American hops was well known, but not loved:

> *The American hops have a flavour which is not entirely acceptable to the pale ale brewer. However, for the reasons given here they are quite*

suitable for our stout when blended with our supplies from England
... The flavour of roast barley masks the more delicate nuances of hop
flavour and it is not to our advantage to buy the choicer growths for
which the pale ale brewer will pay higher prices.

This was not a new prejudice. Records from Bass show that by the 1870s the demand for hops in Britain exceeded supply. Hops were imported from both Europe and America, but American hops were found to have an 'unpleasant' aroma of blackcurrant leaf – one of the aromas we've been rhapsodising over in the fields today.

And if we go to such pains to preserve those aromas today, keeping the beer cold and insisting it be drunk as quickly as possible, that's in stark contrast to the practice of deliberately ageing the beer for up to a year, as was commonplace for India Pale Ale in the 1870s. At a time when refrigeration was newly available and was used actively to ship new pilsner-style lagers, the brewers, merchants and bottlers of IPA stored it at ambient temperatures to ripen. Contemporary descriptions of nineteenth-century IPA make no mention of big hop characters, unless perhaps this is part of what they mean when they describe a beer as 'green' and not yet ready to drink.

English hops have an entirely different character from the now crazily popular American varieties. I've always attributed this to *terroir*, and I was right to do so. But hops have also been carefully bred, just like barley, for over a century now. Modern British hop breeders believe it's possible to recreate the flavours of American hops in places like Kent, and back in the UK Paul Corbett recently introduced me to Jester, a hop variety developed by Charles Faram that's full of Yakima-style citrus notes. If we can breed this character into British hops now, modern breeders like Peter Darby suspect it was deliberately bred out of Kentish hops years ago, to suit British tastes.

So where will the yearning for hops go from here? Britain may be buying more American hops than British nowadays, but the Americans are importing half the UK harvest of Fuggles and Goldings in their search for more moderate flavours and sessionable beers.

Climate change adds another variable to the mix: whatever flavour we're after, can we always guarantee we'll be able to get it, or get enough of it?

'The German crop has been decimated this year,' says Alastair Hook. 'A lot of beers will be brewed with different hops this year. You could have been using one hop in a pilsner for fifty years, but contracts have clauses in them that include things such as acts of God. People are being shorted this year, so there's lots of substitution. This presents a challenge to the idea of what brewers really need. You say you need this exact hop? Well, the nature of that hop changes from year to year anyway. This kind of thing is never a problem when it happens in wine.'

And that's what I enjoy most about Bale Breaker's beers. Up to now, specific varieties of hop have been fetishised by brewers and drinkers alike. Cascade was the big star, now it's Citra. Blending a cocktail of different hops provides an insurance policy against the randomness of the harvest and the vagaries of the market. But it also demonstrates a higher level of brewing skill. The character of a single-hop Citra pale ale is like a guitar solo, the rest of the beer providing the backdrop for the hop to strut its stuff across your palate. But the best IPAs I'm tasting now are more like a classical orchestra, still offering big flavours, but blended and balanced, richer and deeper. The brewers that can compose these symphonies in the key of lupulin will be the ones that outlive the heady infatuation with the hop.

9. 'Oppin' Dahn in Kent

'BAAAY-CONNNN BAAAAAAAPS!'

There's a twang to the Kentish accent that makes the offer of my favourite breakfast item in the world sound like a threat of imminent violence. Fortunately, there are alternatives. The streets of Faversham are lined with food stalls, offering chips, pies, pasties, burgers, ice cream and everything else we Brits love to eat by hand on a nice day out.

On the pavement outside the HSBC Bank stands a metal trailer full of hops, still clinging to bines that must have been cut in the last twenty-four hours. The back of the trailer is down and the hops are spilling onto the pavement. Two elderly women sit turning the bines into garlands, their faces fixed in grim concentration. A rickety wooden wallpaper-paste table is piled up with hop garlands, and a steady stream of people are buying and wearing them. The old women are struggling to keep up with demand.

Hops are everywhere I look: in every shop window, twined around the fast-food stalls and among the crash barriers marking off some areas of the town centre. Whether in a headpiece, corsage or garland, almost everyone on the street is wearing hops. And there are a lot of people on the streets.

As I learned in Žatec, people who like hops also seem to really love a good parade, and now, here it comes. Along the old high street of this pretty market town crawls an ancient but gleaming brewery dray, painted in the colours of Shepherd Neame, the town's local brewer. Next comes a Spitfire – the car, not the plane – although the car is decked out in the livery of Spitfire the beer, which was named after the plane, and was once memorably advertised as being 'Downed all over Kent – just like the Luftwaffe'.

Next comes Harry the Hop, a giant foam hop cone, bright green and about five feet tall, followed by stilt walkers, costumed clog dancers, and what I increasingly think of as 'good morris dancers', the type that wear facial disguises and costumes that look like they've emerged from the wild wood, carrying big, dangerous-looking sticks instead of the limp-wristed white handkerchiefs of surrender, ripping the air with throaty roars. And that's just the women.

Somewhere in the massed ranks of Morris dancers, Peter Darby is dancing away, but I can't spot him. Now here's a fully tooled-up pagan warrior pounding a set of drums, followed by a group of children whose job it is to beat hollow metal sticks together to make a menacing clang, like a cracked bell in a 'Hammer Horror' movie. They look frightened, possibly because they're being corralled by a dancing figure with a bull's head, and an elderly but stocky, strong-looking man wearing a pink tutu under a fur coat, his long white hair tied in pigtails and flowing with hops.

In the centre of the procession are the Pearly Kings and Queens, striding with more purpose and confidence than anyone else in the parade. They seem assured that they are the main event, the people we've all come to see, waving assuredly to the crowd like celebrities or the more official royal family, which is impressive given that they're competing for attention with the morris dancers, who generally have the most egocentric approach to any event they turn up at. The pearlies certainly are an impressive, if curious, sight, with smart formal suits almost entirely covered in mother-of-pearl buttons. Some of the men wear shining flat caps with the red cross of St George quartering the pearls, and trousers with lucky horseshoes or the four suits from a pack of playing cards. They look like a weird clash of 1960s mod and glam rock gone wrong, while the women's flowery bonnets give them a more Edwardian air.

The entire crew processes into the market square, home to one of five stages set up for bands, singers and dancers throughout the weekend. There's a cordoned-off area directly in front of the stage, crowded with local dignitaries. I count at least a dozen people wearing ceremonial chains of office, all of them looking around anxiously to make sure they're seen, half of them with hop garlands in their hair. They quieten down a little as we get a string of speeches, including the announcements of the winners of the shop window competition and the presentation of this year's Hop Queen, a clearly terrified twelve-year-old girl called Leanne, who mumbles into the microphone, 'Fank you for everyone coming to see me', and gets offstage as quickly as she can. The mayor tells us proudly about Faversham's royal connections, its role as one of the Cinque Ports defending Kent from French attack, and its link to the Magna Carta. A couple of Pearly Kings slouch by the edge of the stage, smoking a crafty fag. Just as I'm thinking how gloriously English this all is, the first drops of rain start to speckle the pages of my notebook. This really couldn't be any better.

The speeches move on to hops and hop picking, the reason we're here today. The Faversham Hop Festival has been running for twenty-five years now, a volunteer-run, brewery-sponsored, two-day binge of food, beer and music to commemorate the time when up to 80,000 people would travel down to Kent for the hop harvest.

And now the London Pearly Kings and Queens Society take to the stage to sing us the songs that were sung in the hop fields all those years ago.*

---

* The Pearly Kings and Queens trace their roots back to Henry Croft, an orphan street sweeper who collected money for charity and created an outfit covered in mother-of-pearl buttons inspired by the pearl-decorated trousers worn by London's costermongers at the time. He set up an organisation that installed a Pearly King and Queen in each of London's boroughs, plus one for the City of London and one for the City of Westminster. The titles are normally hereditary, but there are exceptions, and this has caused a deep rift in the ranks of the pearlies. In 2001, they split into three factions, following disagreements over finances and the question of whether or not you could marry in to a pearly dynasty. The London Pearly Kings and Queens Society in Faversham today is, in the eyes of the original association, a renegade, breakaway group. If I understand the politics correctly, we're enjoying the company of the more progressive, less militant pearlies.

Their first song is called 'Hopping Down in Kent', which manages to be both cloyingly sentimental and surprisingly shallow, full of verses about how hop picking was a complete rip-off financially and astonishingly unpleasant physically, followed by a speech of heartfelt regret over the loss of such halcyon days. It reminds me of *Father Ted*'s Mrs Doyle, reacting to the gift of a new tea maker by grumbling, 'Maybe I *like* the misery.'

They follow this up with 'Roll out the Barrel', unwittingly creating a psychic link between Faversham and Žatec. The older members of the audience join in with this one. Teenagers stare at their parents, and then at the stage, and then back at their parents, mortified, mouths open, smart-phones hanging limply, forgotten.

The next song is called 'Hold Your Hand out, Naughty Boy', and turns out to be the first in a long line of songs themed around taking a prurient interest in others' romantic lives. Ooh, I saw you with that girl. I know what you were doing. Who was she? Where do you think you were going? We all know what you've been up to!

I know how the teenagers feel. I'm drowning in someone else's nostalgia, and have to move away. But then it strikes me: the teenagers are *here*. I look around, and realise that pretty much everyone in Faversham must be out for the festival. People of all ages and social strata are on the streets: old ladies, gangs of lads, family groups, young couples, all searching for a version of the festival they can enjoy. Is this anything to do with hops particularly, or is Faversham just desperate for a good knees-up? Would the pearlies be here to entertain, educate and inform us if it had been a different crop their forebears were harvesting? There's an exhibition of hop picking in a church hall on the outskirts of town. I decide to head up there to investigate.

It's slow going at first – the streets are packed. There's hardly a shop window that isn't garlanded with hops. Many have gone further and created themed displays, and there's a hotly contested competition for which is best. There are different categories, including a special one for charity shops. The winner this year, the Hospice of Hope, is extraordinary. The whole front of the shop has been turned into a hopper's hut, with a straw-covered floor, tools leaning against the wall, and a table set for breakfast with a life-sized little-girl doll sitting down. A sign in the window displays old black-and-white photographs of hop-pickers on stilts, and women and small children sorting and bagging hops. Acknowledgements thank 'The Duke of Cumberland pub in Whitstable for loan of barrel and other items', and 'Mr Barrows for his kind loan of wooden ladder'. Are there no lengths to which these people won't go to win?

The shop window scene aims to represent the typical living conditions of the working-class East Enders who came down from London to spend their late summers in the hop gardens, and it's one I see repeated in old photographs up at the exhibition, most of them black and white, a few in blurry, washed-out, late sixties or early seventies colour. Special trains were laid on to bring them down, and some families would seemingly pack the entire house, bringing the whole kitchen, even sizeable bits of furniture with them. They lived in rude huts at the edges of the hop fields. There are still a few of these around, but they haven't been as lovingly preserved as the oast houses – they don't have quite the same appeal as living accommodation to modern tastes. And yet, these huts would be booked up by families as early as January.

There's an incredible drive to preserve the memory of hopping in written, spoken and filmed histories. The last generation of children to work in the hop gardens are now well into middle age, and there's a race to get as many accounts as possible from the time, even though they're all remarkably similar.

It was hard work. You'd get up at 6 a.m. and be at work by 7, and the whole family would take part – even the smallest children. The days were long because the crop had to be picked and dried at precisely the right time, and this was a labour-intensive process. You got paid by weight so you worked as fast as you could. And then, in the evenings, you'd either go to the pub or gather around a fire, drinking and singing songs, loving and fighting.

That's the basis of every account of hopping I've read. And yet there are scores of them. I decided to buy a locally published memoir of hopping on Amazon, and when I did so five more popped up as suggestions. There's a sweet ache to the memory, and the Mrs Doyle moment won't go away. The last verse of 'Hopping down in Kent' goes:

Now hopping is all over
All the money spent

Don't I wish I'd never done
No hopping down in Kent.
I say one, I say two,
No more hopping I shall do.

But they were back every year, looking forward to it. And those that still remember it now celebrate it in reveries that are only slightly wistful.

There were grim realities behind the romance, of course. Writing in 1889, John Bickerdyke, author of *The Curiosities of Ale and Beer*, observed:

> *If the weather be but reasonably fine, the life of these latter-day pilgrims is not a hard one, for the balmy country air, the soft turf and beautiful surroundings must seem to these poor creatures a kind of paradise after the dens of filth, disease, and darkness from which they have come...*
>
> *The high road from London to the hopfields of Kent presents a curious appearance immediately before the hop-picking season. A stranger might imagine that the poorer classes of a big city were flying before an invading army.*

Hop picking may have been hard work, but for generations of working-class people that was far better than the only alternative. And conditions were better than home: the air was cleaner, and the whole family could be together. However hard the work was, the entire experience bore that heady, slightly unreal dreaminess of a rare, exotic holiday. Vita Sackville-West, comfortable in her home at Sissinghurst Castle in the heart of Kent's hop gardens, wrote in 'The Hop-Picking Season' (*Country Notes,* 1939) that when London's hoppers left their 'slums' in Bermondsey, they ceased to be 'rather vulgar' and assumed a romantic aspect, exotic and colourful, reminding her of Neapolitan peasants getting in the harvest of Muscat grapes.

Orwell's hop-picking diary maintained that the work itself wasn't too bad – it was simple enough and the conditions were pleasant, even if the living accommodation made stables look swanky. But it was the rates paid for piecework that angered him. Not only was the typical rate of twopence per bushel appallingly low, it was more difficult to pick a bushel than it seemed. Hops are not like apples or potatoes – 'they are soft things as compressible as sponges' – and it was a common trick of the measurer to push hops down and pay less for them. Orwell then quotes one of the verses of 'Hopping down in Kent', which complains about the practice:

> *When he comes to measure*
> *He never knows where to stop;*
> *Ay, ay, get in the bin,*
> *And take the bloody lot!*

The hop-pickers Orwell spoke to never ended up making a profit from their excursion. They spoke of 'coming home five quid in pocket', but Orwell's experience was that they usually went home with less money than when they arrived. And yet, he concludes, 'there is no difficulty in getting people to do the work . . . When the season is over the pickers are heartily glad – glad to be back in London, where you do not have to sleep on straw, and you can put a penny in the gas instead of hunting the firewood, and Woolworth's is round the corner – but still, hop-picking is in the category of things that are great fun when they are over.'

Orwell fictionalised his experience in his 1935 novel, *A Clergyman's Daughter*. Dorothy, the heroine of the book's title, falls in with a gang who take her hop picking with them. She returns home penniless and exhausted. And yet:

> *Looking back, afterwards, upon her interlude of hop-picking, it was always the afternoons that Dorothy remembered. Those long, laborious hours in the strong sunlight, in the sound of forty voices singing, in the smell of hops and wood smoke, had a quality peculiar and unforgettable. As the afternoon wore on you grew almost too tired to stand, and the small green hop lice got into your hair and into your ears and worried you, and your hands, from the sulphurous juice, were as black as a Negro's except where they were bleeding. Yet you were happy, with an unreasonable happiness. The work took hold of you and absorbed you. It was stupid work, mechanical, exhausting and every day more painful to the hands, and yet you never wearied of it; when the weather was fine and the hops were good you had the feeling that you could go on picking for ever and for ever. It gave you*

a physical joy, a warm satisfied feeling inside you, to stand there hour after hour, tearing off the heavy clusters and watching the pale green pile grow higher and higher...

When Somerset Maugham's unhappy, semi-autobiographical hero Philip Carey goes hop picking in the closing chapters of *Of Human Bondage*, he finds love in the warm night and the narrow country lanes. When he believes the girl, Sally, is pregnant, he decides to marry her and settle down, accepting his lot.

Philip's experience was common, even if the ending was not. According to Peter Darby, the month of June would always see a sharp increase in the number of unwanted babies being abandoned at hospitals and orphanages across east London. 'The oestrogen in hops meant that in the hop fields, menstrual cycles got upset,' he explains. 'Lots of women came back pregnant. The surname Hopkins literally means "children of the hops", and it was given to the June babies that ended up in orphanages.'

So hops helped cause pregnancies. I believe they did so in a number of different ways. The only problem with science is that it can encourage us to discount the importance of irrational thought. We like to think of ourselves as rational beings, but that's only partly true. There's a liminality to being on holiday, a sense that normal rules don't apply and a sneaky subconscious voice whispering that actions here won't have consequences at home. Everywhere I've been on my journey with hops, I've encountered the same dreamy, dippy, blissed-out happiness, particularly in the fields, and especially at harvest. And I think a lot of that is to do with the aroma of those essential oils. As soon as the hops are jostled, they fill the air with their perfume. Smell is the most evocative of the senses, and no plant is more densely charged with heady aromas than the hop.

Orwell, as ever, says it best. I've spent weeks trying to put the magic of hops into the right form of words, to explain how they cause this 'unreasonable happiness', and, like the mysterious volatiles themselves, I've not quite been able to capture it. It's not the first time I've struggled like this and then found that Orwell nailed it, in this instance finding time amid his criticism of hop picking to observe that 'on hot days there is no pleasanter place than the shady lanes of hops, with their bitter scent – an unutterably refreshing scent, like a wind blowing from oceans of cool beer.'

How did hops become the poster ingredient for beer? Why is the only ingredient that isn't necessary for brewing beer the only one most drinkers can name? As is his wont, Orwell nails the answers to these questions in one simple sentence. The utter bastard.

10. Guardians of the Galaxy

And that's where my exploration of hops might have ended, and almost did. But I didn't want it to. The hop harvest is a few weeks long, and once it's over I miss it. I miss the hop gardens, the blue skies and the deep greens against them, those intoxicating smells and the barely contained euphoria they inspire. I can't believe I have to wait another year to be back there. And then it turns out that I don't. Because I've only told the story of half the world's hops.

Jamie Cook is one of the founders of Stone & Wood, a craft brewery in Byron Bay, New South Wales, Australia. When he learned about this book, he was concerned that I was missing out on the story of hops in the southern hemisphere. As one of that hemisphere's most decorated breweries, whose main beer is a showcase for Australia's most desired hop variety, Stone & Wood felt this wouldn't do at all, and managed to convince me that I really needed to visit when the Australian hop harvest was happening in Tasmania, in mid-March.

Just like New World wines, when it comes to hops Australia and New Zealand rival the west coast of the United States for big, bold flavours. As I write this, craft brewers around the world are desperate to get their hands on Nelson Sauvin, a rich, tropical fruit and floral hop that sounds a bit like Sauvignon Blanc because it comes from the same land as Kiwi Sauvignon. But coming up fast as its main antipodean rival is Galaxy, which originated in Tasmania and is still only grown there.

Hobart, Tasmania's capital, is on the southern tip of the island, sheltering in a round bay with a deep natural harbour. I instantly fall in love with the city. South of here, there's nothing until Antarctica. East, you can keep going for 5,400 miles before you glance off Cape Horn. The rest of the world thinks of Australia as remote. And this is the bit of it that Australians themselves regard as a bit of a hike.

But Hobart is no backwater. There's craft beer, great coffee, a modern art gallery and an award-winning distillery. Around each corner lies the smell of naggingly good pizza base being cooked, or the Pavlovian allure of fresh shellfish in garlic and butter. There's a tension between the urbane and the wilderness that adds another note to the mix, heightening the feelings and flavours of everything. The main industries of Tasmania are farming and tourism, and the green hills around Hobart are packed with farms, vineyards and orchards.

As well as thinking of Tassie as remote, most Australians also believe it's cold. Even here on the island's southern tip, we're only as far south of the equator as the Balearic Islands are to the north. To me, early autumn here in the southern hemisphere feels like a perfect English summer's day, but the team from Stone & Wood are wrapped up in layers, grimacing as if the gentle evening breeze is an Antarctic gale.

Brad Rogers is another of the founders of Stone & Wood alongside Jamie, who persuaded his partners to bring me over, along with third partner, Ross Jursich. Brad is the brewer. For him, trips like this aren't just practical hop-buying expeditions. He's taking a team picked from all areas of the brewery to a local distillery, a local cider maker and another brewery, making them think about how beer fits in with this broader gastronomic boom. He brings a different crew every year, and I soon learn that winning a place on one of these trips is Stone & Wood's equivalent to one of Willy Wonka's golden tickets.

About an hour's drive north-west from Hobart, on a road that hugs the left bank of the clear, shining Derwent River, is Bushy Park Estates, one of the oldest hop farms in Australia. Hops came out from England pretty soon after the first fleet sailed in 1788, because beer was regarded as an essential part of life, even for a penal colony, and the government paid for hops and brewing equipment to be transported. James Squire founded Australia's first commercial brewery in 1798, and claimed he first bought hops from HMS *Daedalus*, which arrived in 1790. In 1806, after three seasons of hard work, Squire cultivated the first Australian hops. He cut two bines from his plantation and presented them to the Governor, who was so pleased with their quality he 'directed a cow to be given to Mr Squire from the Government herd'.

Hops were first grown in Tasmania, then known as Van Diemen's Land, in 1822 by a Kentish farmer named William Shoobridge. He was a free settler, with access to cheap land and a convict workforce, so he tried cultivating hops in an area he named Providence Valley. But that name turned out to be inappropriate, and he struggled to produce a yield. His son, Ebenezer, moved further north and tried again, establishing the Bushy Park plantation in 1865. Thanks to a mixture of up to fifteen hours of sunlight a day, the rich alluvial soil, the river, the sheltering hills and his own business nous and enlightened attitude to his workers, it was an immediate success, and Ebenezer Shoobridge became known as 'the king of the hop growers'.

Bushy Park is now the largest hop plantation in the southern hemisphere, and I'm here for the 151st consecutive harvest. Tim Lord of Hop Products Australia (HPA) is one of the proud Australians who can trace his ancestry back to the first fleet of convict ships, and is responsible for delivering about 80 per cent of Australia's hop crop. He drives us up to a hillside from where we can see the entire 275 hectares of Bushy Park's hop gardens – or 'paddocks' as Tim calls them. The harvest is under way, machines crawling along the rows. The contrast between the dense, thick green and the blasted landscape of bare poles, which one poet referred to as 'the tattered banners of departing summer', makes the hop harvest seem particularly brutal. The smell of fresh hops reaches us even up here, half a mile away, lifted by the breeze.

'The hops we grow here are varieties we bred ourselves,' says Tim. 'We've been breeding them since the 1950s to find hops that like the conditions on these farms.'

Hop breeding began in earnest back in Kent in 1917, when E. S. Salmon of Wye College began crossing varieties to increase their alpha acid content for their greater 'keeping power'. Most modern hop varieties eventually trace their way back to Salmon's cultivars, and the drive for higher alpha dominated breeding programmes for most of the twentieth century. In the 1960s, Carlton & United Breweries (CUB), the giant that dominates Australian brewing, released Pride of Ringwood, with an alpha acid content of 10 per cent – at that time the highest anywhere in the world, more than twice that of varieties such as Žatec or Fuggles. Beer was being produced on an industrial scale, and Pride of Ringwood was the perfect industrial hop: with twice the alpha acids, you only needed half the hops. The family-owned hop fields of Tasmania collapsed. Those that survived were bought up by corporates, and the whole lot was eventually purchased by global hop giant Barth-Haas in the 1980s, and Hop Products Australia was born.

In 1995, HPA introduced Super Pride, the offspring of Pride of Ringwood, which had an even higher alpha content. Super Pride is the hop that defines Australian lagers such as Foster's. But HPA could see change coming.

'With alpha hops, you're buying a commodity. We started to move back to aroma hops,' says Tim. 'We made crosses of Saaz and Hallertau, looking for something that worked here, and in 1994 we crossed a German aroma hop with a high-alpha Australian hop and got Galaxy. We immediately fell in love with its passion fruit aromas.'

Hop breeding starts with 3,000 new seedlings. These are selected for their growing ability, then their physical and chemical characteristics, and finally their suitability for brewing. That initial 3,000 might eventually produce one or two viable new varieties if you're lucky. The whole process takes eight to ten years, and although Galaxy was born in 1994 it didn't appear commercially until much later. In 2008, Tim grew 6 tonnes of Galaxy. In 2016 that figure has grown to 500 tonnes. Hopefully, next year it'll be 750, then 900.

Three-quarters of the Tasmanian crop is exported, with half of that going to the United States. As craft beer becomes a global phenomenon, that 500 tonnes could be sold many times over. When I announced on Twitter that I was visiting Bushy Park, several brewers in the UK begged me to try to bring them back some Galaxy, even just a small amount.* Galaxy's passion fruit character is what Peter Darby says every brewer wants – something different, something interesting. Galaxy is also one of the few hops that presents in the finished beer in a very similar way to how it smells in the field, meaning it's guaranteed to inspire and excite hop heads everywhere.

---

* I did pick two Galaxy hops with a view to coming back to the UK and putting them on eBay as 'the UK's entire availability of Galaxy hops'. But I forgot about them and left them in my shirt pocket when it went into the laundry, thereby denying myself a small fortune.

Hops

We move from the hill down into the paddock where Galaxy is growing. A cooler full of beers appears from the back of the Stone & Wood–branded Land Rover. Everyone feels the sheer delight of the moment. It's unseasonably hot for this late in the summer – even the Aussies can sense that. This is it – the reason to be alive – a hot day, a fresh, cold beer, the woozy and sensuous perfume and visual delight of the hops. Everyone is infused with Orwell's unreasonable happiness. You can see it in their grins.

As if reading my mind, Brad comes close and says quietly, 'I bring people here from the brewery because I love how their faces light up. Look at them. And that passion goes back into the brewery.'

When hops are harvested, you have to dry them immediately because otherwise they'll start to rot. The only alternative is to brew with them right away. 'Green hop', 'fresh hop' or 'wet hop' beers are currently capturing imaginations around the world. Instead of drying and packing the hops, you just bag them, rush them to the brewery and throw them into the brewing copper. I know some brewers near hop fields who time a brew so it's just coming to the boil as the freshly picked hops arrive, getting them into the beer within a few hours of being picked. In Kent there's now a two-week-long green-hop beer festival, with around fifteen brewers creating these beers that can only be made once a year. It's a nice reminder of beer's seasonality. But how different is a green-hopped beer?

We're about to find out: Stone & Wood is going to use green hops in a beer. The only problem is, the green, freshly picked hops are in Hobart, Tasmania, and the brewery is in Byron Bay, over a thousand miles north of here. We need to get them there within a day, and the only realistic way of doing that is for someone to check them in as luggage on a domestic flight. That someone is me.

Our hops are picked and packed in a large foil bag and refrigerated to prolong their cursory shelf life. The foil bag is sealed inside a plain, corrugated cardboard box with no markings. It's about five feet high and two feet square, and weighs about twenty-five kilograms. I find that with a quick hoist and swing I can balance it on my shoulder just fine.

By the time I'm on my way to the airport there's a definite resiny, fruity smell coming through the cardboard, and it occurs to me more forcefully than ever before that hops are related to the cannabis plant, and I'm about to attempt to take a large amount of them through airport security. I tweet a picture of myself with the box hoisted on my shoulder.

Pete Brown
@PeteBrownBeer

Just about to get on a plane with 25kg of fresh hops. This should be interesting!

Replies aren't long in coming.

Stephen Beaumont
@BeaumontDrinks

@PeteBrownBeer I see a strip search in your future.

Brookston
@Brookston

@PeteBrownBeer Ask Sam Calagione from @dogfishbeer about his experience getting stopped by security carrying a brick of hops through O'Hare.

This second one stops me short. Joking about cavity searches because of a cannabis-related plant is banter. But the real danger of it happening isn't quite as funny. I start to worry that maybe the real reason Stone & Wood have been so generous in inviting me down here is that they need a mule.

I Google 'Sam Calagione airport hops' and find a passage from the Dogfish Head founder's first book, *Brewing up a Business*, in which he was stopped while trying to board a plane in Chicago after a sniffer dog took a dislike to his stash of whole-leaf Palisade hops. 'Of the five people in the room I definitely held the minority opinion on whether a full-scale cavity search was necessary,' he writes. 'But I was the only one in the room without a gun so I did a lot of listening.'

Calagione's plight was worsened by the discovery of Randall the Enamel Animal in his luggage. In the eyes of airport security, the only thing this strange contraption resembled was an elaborate bong.

In fact, the Enamel Animal was an invention of Calagione's to make beer even hoppier, yet another attempt at preserving some of the freshness and diversity of the harvest. It was a long cylinder, a modified filter that he filled with hops before passing freshly brewed beer through it, to steep it with the fresh hop flavours lost in the brewing process, like dry-hopping on steroids. It's an idea that's now become common across the craft brewing world, as brewers yearn to capture those short-lived essences.

Calagione was lucky: one of the security men lived in Delaware, where he was based, and had heard of Dogfish Head, while another was a fan of Sierra Nevada's ales, and Calagione's impassioned speech on the need for hoppier beer in America convinced them. His beery bong and weed were repacked and covered with special 'Inspected by the Department of Homeland Security' tape, and he was on the next plane out of Chicago.

Hobart Airport is tiny, and there are no sniffer dogs. The hops have already started to decompose in the day since they were packed, and what was 25 kilograms now weighs in at 23.8 kilograms, meaning I don't have to pay any excess luggage charges. If the check-in assistant notices the fruity, resiny aroma coming from the large cardboard box, she doesn't comment on it.

Half a day later I'm reunited with my hops in Byron Bay. As soon as I step out of the airport, I realise why the brewery team found Tasmania a little chilly. Byron is a tropical paradise, a small town on a rocky promontory between two shining white beaches. This is where busy Australians dream of coming to retire, and the decision to open the brewery here was a personal one for its three founders. The brewers go surfing every morning on their way into work, and you have to believe some of this attitude comes over in the beer itself.

Stone & Wood's flagship is Pacific Ale, a beer that was designed specifically to be perfect for the climate in Byron and to be evocative of the place when drunk elsewhere. It's a pale golden ale, slightly hazy because it's unfiltered and unpasteurised, and is brewed exclusively with Galaxy hops. The passion fruit aroma is vivid on the nose, and what's pleasing about it is that despite all that aroma the level of bitterness is very low. There's long been an assumption in craft brewing that a hoppy beer has to be hoppy all the way through: if it's high in aroma hops, it should also have a lot of hop bitterness. But there's no technical reason why that should be so. Bittering hops are added early in the boil, which isomerises their alpha acids, while aroma hops are added at the end of or even after the boil, to preserve their volatile aroma compounds. Instinctively it might feel like adding a lot of one without the other could make a beer unbalanced, but Pacific Ale is one of a new breed of hoppy beers that combine strong perfume with great delicacy.

Because of our long-distance travel and the time delay and other risks involved with it, Stone & Wood aren't using the fresh hops to brew the beer, but to 'dry hop' a freshly brewed beer while it's still in the fermentation vessel. Of course, the whole point of these hops is that they haven't been dried, so no one is really sure how to refer to the dry-hopping with wet hops that we're doing.

The brewers are waiting for us when we arrive at a place that looks like you'd imagine a brewery on a desert island to be. It's impossibly lush, coated in palm leaves and glistening with moisture, and I can't believe anyone working here actually feels like it's work at all. With only the briefest of introductions, we set to work loading the wet hops – now quite sweaty and soggy – into a bunch of muslin sacks. We tie these and then drop them into the fermenters, essentially using hop teabags to add more flavour to the fresh beer.

I then get a few days to relax in Byron while the hops steep. Finally, the beer is kegged and we're off up the road to Brisbane, where I'm presenting it at a special event as part of the city's Brewsvegas beer festival.

When I first heard of green hop beers, I imagined they would offer greater peaks of hoppiness. But I was wrong. Imagine a simple graph where one axis is the *range* of different hop flavours and the other is the *intensity* of those flavours. I thought that if you had a hop that was resinous and piney, making a beer with that hop when it was still wet would massively amplify the pine and resin, giving it a taller spike on the graph. But that's not true. What happens is that the range of flavours is broader, so as well as the pine and resin you might get greener, grassier, sappy flavours. There's an extra sweetness, too, sometimes reminding me of boiled sweets.

Archive is a big warehouse of a bar in a stylish Brisbane suburb, and the room we're in is busy. There's no ceremony when the New Pacific Ale is tapped – Australia is refreshingly straightforward and practical – and soon everyone is drinking deep. The difference between the dry/wet-hopped version and the standard version is not as dramatic as in other green hop beers I've tried because we didn't brew with the green hops, and also because Galaxy has that rare consistency from field to glass anyway. But the hop is definitely fuller and rounder, not different, but more present. We've captured something ephemeral. But even now, as it sits in the keg, those compounds will be starting to think about disappearing. Best we drink more of the beer while they're still there.

And as I do, I think about the blissed-out Stone & Wood family in the Tasmanian hop paddocks, about Orwell's pickers in Kent and the tattooed craft beer hop fanatics. Exploring each of beer's ingredients has taken me deep into science and nature, and revealed wonders. But my exploration of hops has been more emotional, hedonistic rather than studious. This is why hops are beer's superstar ingredient, and, finally, I think I understand where it comes from. It all comes together, the science and the sensory, the real and the romantic.

Those 400 different aroma compounds make the hop unique among plants. Nothing else offers such a variety and such a concentration. And a huge part of this character is momentary. The perfumes of the hop emerge in midsummer, when the flowers are on the bine, growing in volume and intensity as we all bask in the sun. If they weren't harvested they'd soon petal and disperse, eventually vanishing back into the ecosystem. When we harvest them instead, we're on a doomed mission to salvage and preserve what we can. We dry them so they don't rot, and in doing so we preserve a core of their magic but sacrifice the more volatile essential oils. When we brew we sacrifice another layer of aroma and flavour – there's no choice – and then we dry-hop beers or brew with more and more hops to saturate the finished beer with as much hop essence as we can. But it's like holding a handful of sand. Whatever you do, some of it is always running through your fingers, disappearing even as the finished beer sits inside its container. And this is what makes the hop field a magical place. We know that here, on the day the fresh hops are being harvested, we have our only chance to savour the full character of the hop. The moment of perfect ripeness, the fullness of those oils, is the same moment the hops must be picked, and that's the instant their character begins to fade. If you love hops, the harvest itself, in the middle of the garden, is heaven, and everything else an echo of it that is always fading, but always evoking that heaven.

11. EKG, PGI

Back in Kent, back at the time of the UK hop harvest six months before I board the plane for Australia, John Humphreys from Shepherd Neame takes me to see Britain's most important hop grower. This year – 2015 – is the sixty-fifth consecutive hop harvest Tony Redsell has worked on. Now well into his eighties, he remembers when families used to come down from east London and remembers the introduction of the first picking machines that replaced them. He still walks though his fields every day, inspecting the crop. Tony has the UK's largest hop gardens, with 220 acres of English aroma hops on three sites near Faversham. He mainly grows East Kent Goldings, and was the driving force behind that variety gaining protected geographical indication (PGI) status from the European Union.

When John introduces us, Tony gives me a weary smile. I'm the latest in a long line of journalists who have come to talk to him, as they do at harvest time every year, and right now, at 7.30 on a sunny Saturday morning in mid-September, he's a busy man.

'I'm not going to show you around,' he says. 'John, you can show him what he needs to see. Try not to get in the way. When you've had a look around I can give you five minutes. I'll be over here in the office.' And he walks away.

East Kent Goldings are, as the name suggests, only grown here. The hop has a low yield and a low alpha acid content, and is susceptible to downy and powdery mildews, and wilt. But when it's in a British cask ale that just hits the right condition, it's a warm glow of floral, honey and fruit flavours with a hint of spice. Drinking an East Kent Goldings–hopped beer in Faversham, it strikes me that while the Americans talk at such length about preserving the powerful character of their hops, the same applies to gentle English hops, too. The way we treat our beers from the point they're packaged to the point of purchase leaves a great deal to be desired, and I realise that part of the reason many people think of British real ale as boring, and British hops as 'twiggy', is that most of the time we're not drinking them fresh. While America obsesses about cold chain distribution, Britain often leaves casks of ale sitting in brewery yards and on unrefrigerated lorries and in distribution centres with no thought for the impact of temperature. We might accept that serving temperature is important, but still give little thought to storage temperature, and whether this might have any impact on the quality of a beer. Every supermarket chain in the country stores and displays bottled and canned ales at ambient temperatures, while their American counterparts keep them in refrigerated storage. The flavours of British and American hops may be different; the effect of warm temperature on them is the same. Many people still think real ale should be served at room temperature, unaware that such a stipulation dates back to when our rooms were much cooler than they are now.

British hops are increasingly seen as the poor relation on the global scene. It's uneconomic to grow them, they're not that interesting to many drinkers and brewers, and the UK hop research programme gets no government funding. The enthusiasm for hops that I find around the world is tinged here by sadness and pessimism about the future. And at the risk of sounding like a thirteen-year-old, that's just not fair.

Tony Redsell is dry and laconic. It may be his manner, but when we meet after the tour of his farm and hop-processing sheds, I get the clear impression he's really not interested in speaking to me. So I decide to go for broke and ask him, a little more bluntly than I'd been intending, a question that's been building in my mind over the past few weeks of hop picking, fuelled by each harvest I've witnessed.

'Why are you doing this?' I ask. 'Look, it costs ten grand per acre to put in the wires and poles. It's a difficult crop to grow well. And even if you do, people want foreign imports instead. You could plant these fields with almost any other crop and it would be easier to grow, cheaper to harvest, more consistent, with a better yield, and you'd be able to sell it for more money. There's no economic case for growing hops in Kent, is there? So why do you?'

His face and voice change instantly, filling with passion.

'Because hops are my lifeblood!' he roars. 'I've grown hops for over sixty years and my dad grew hops before me, and before him hops have been grown here for hundreds of years. Because British hops give British beer its special character! East Kent Goldings create a wonderful aroma in beer. There's a romance about East Kent Goldings, the romance of a variety that was selected in 1790 and is still here, renowned the world over. It epitomises the romance with the entire hop industry, and at the moment it is being abused. If you collate the statistics for the whole industry, EKG has a better yield than so-called "Goldings", many of which aren't Goldings at all!'

'Thank you,' I smile, 'That's exactly what I needed.'

– FIVE –

Yeast

'In the great richness of nature I have found a source of peace of mind and a happiness which no one can take away from me.'

EMIL HANSEN, zymologist (1842–1909)

1. Space Booze

When I'm writing a book, as I reach the point where I need to force myself to stop reading and making notes and start writing the thing up, I take down a large picture from my study wall and begin to plot out the book in the empty space, using multicoloured Post-it notes. Every story, anecdote or theme gets its own sticky note, and I cluster them together and move them around until the shape and structure of the book reveals itself.

In some senses this book was easier to plot than most: I have four distinct main sections, each getting a different coloured Post-it. During my initial burst, when I was just scribbling notes as fast as I could from the top of my head and throwing them at the wall, I managed to get probably 70 per cent of the book up there in one session. It was shaping up nicely, but there was something bothering me about the yeast section. I had lots of great stories, all the different encounters you'll shortly be reading about, and quite a lot of amazing facts I'd discovered about yeast, about what a mysterious and still patchily understood organism it is, and about how different styles of yeast make dramatic contributions to the flavour of beer, to the extent that yeast is often the key determinant that distinguishes different styles of beer from each other.

But there was something missing. I stared at the wall for five minutes, with growing frustration. *Brettanomyces.* Check. Wild yeasts. Check. The origins of modern lager brewing. Check. Dammit, what was I missing?

And then I realised – it was fermentation.

I was furious with myself. How can you possibly write about yeast and not think of fermentation? That's the whole point of yeast in beer! Yeast is what *makes* beer!

But the exercise had revealed that fermentation wasn't the *whole* point of yeast. The stuff I'd been writing down off the top of my head was the stuff that had made the greatest impression on me over the previous months of research. I already knew about fermentation. I'd been delving into the flavour-giving properties of yeast because much of the time among beer enthusiasts, if not brewers, this aspect of yeast's contribution is under-appreciated. But in shining a light on that, I'd almost forgotten about the biggest miracle in the whole of brewing and, in some ways, the whole of existence

Hold on tight: this next part is a bit of a ride.

The constellation of Sagittarius, one of the twelve signs of the Zodiac, is known affectionately as 'the teapot'.* Unlike many of the shapes we can supposedly see in the stars, this one is quite easy to get: viewed in the northern hemisphere, if you look at it the right way here's its handle and here's its spout. And if you're ever lucky enough to see the night sky in an area free from light pollution, you can see 'steam' coming from the spout. That steam is the centre of the Milky Way. The first time I saw it properly, from the helm of a sailing ship halfway across the Atlantic, the centre of our galaxy was a dense, creamy wash, as if someone had taken a thick paintbrush and made a sweeping stroke down the middle of the sky.

The constellation of Sagittarius is close to the centre of our galaxy, right in among the action. As a result, it lends its name to a giant molecular cloud near the heart of the Milky Way. This cloud is one of the largest in the galaxy, about 150 light years across, and has a total mass equivalent to 300 times that of our sun. As that's a tad large, astronomers divide it into regions to study it, designated north (N), middle or main (M), and south (S). Sagittarius B2N is composed of various types of complex molecules. In particular, it contains vast amounts of alcohol – about a billion billion billion litres, give or take. This includes vinyl alcohol, ethanol and methanol.

So there's a cloud of booze at the centre of the galaxy, just hanging in space, OK?

This is incredibly exciting, and not just because of the simple fact that it's true, and not because it means God, if you believe in that sort of thing, is a massive boozer. To scientists, the presence of vinyl alcohol in particular at the centre of the universe is exciting because it is a complex organic molecule, and plays a role in the formation of more complex organic molecules, in particular amino acids, an essential precursor to life. Some of the molecules of these substances may contain up to six or more atoms, meaning complex chemical reactions have to take place for them to form. 'The discovery of

---

* Of course when the constellation was first named by Ptolemy in the second century BCE they didn't have teapots. For him, Sagittarius was an archer. I find this much more difficult to see, but he's meant to be firing a bow into the heart of Scorpius, as the two constellations race around the sky.

vinyl alcohol is significant,' said Barry Turner, a scientist at the National Radio Astronomy Observatory in Charlottesville, Virginia, who discovered the cloud's contents in 2001. 'It gives us an important tool for understanding the formation of complex organic compounds in interstellar space. It may also help us better understand how life might arise elsewhere in the Cosmos.'

The best hypothesis for the existence of the cloud is that vinyl ethanol particles attach themselves to silicon dust motes that are covered in a layer of water, ice and carbon-based compounds. The region is dense with stars. If the dust particles move towards a star, the alcohol evaporates to form a gas cloud, and in this state emits signals our radio telescopes can pick up. But what if these dust particles move in the other direction? As archaeo-botanist Patrick McGovern surmises:

> *Scientists hypothesize that the vinyl ethanol molecules in particular . . .*
> *might have been held in place on interstellar dust particles [which] . . .*
> *might have been transported through the universe in the icy heads of*
> *comets. At high velocities, the ice would melt, releasing the dust to seed*
> *a planet like Earth with a kind of organic soup, out of which primitive*
> *life forms emerged.*

That's right: booze from outer space may well have kick-started life on Earth. And if it did so here, it could have done so elsewhere in the galaxy. Of all the sentences I ever thought I might put down on paper when I started writing about beer, I never saw those last two coming.

The question that then formed in my mind was this. On Earth, alcohol is created by the action of yeast digesting and converting sugar. Does this mean there are giant swarms of intergalactic yeast out there? Probably not: the best hypothesis scientists currently have is that the birth of a new star throws out all kinds of chemical compounds, including various alcohols. Stars are born at the centre of the Milky Way – the core of the cloud is a star nursery sixteen light years across and ten million times brighter than the sun.

So alcohol is created by two things: a microscopic fungus, and the birth of a new star. Given the current state of scientific funding, it might be a while before we figure out how to give birth to stars. But we do have microscopes. So for the time being, the brewing industry must make do with studying microorganisms that ferment sugar.

2. 'Sugar Mould'

At the start of this book I introduced the equation that describes how plants turn light, water and air into sugar, and said that this is not the main equation that brewers revere. Once you have your sugar, this second equation is the one that describes the process of turning it into alcohol:

$$\text{Sugar} \xrightarrow{\text{Yeast}} \text{Ethanol} + \text{Carbon dioxide}$$

Once again, it looks like a miracle, and never ceases to make me pause in wonder no matter how many times I write or speak about it. Once more, it makes a bit more sense if you substitute chemical symbols for words:

$$C_6H_{12}O_6 \xrightarrow{\text{Yeast}} 2CH_3CH_2OH + 2CO_2$$

Now, you can at least see the logical sense of it, even if the process still seems magical.

Equations like this, and this one in particular, were made possible by the work of Antoine Lavoisier, the French nobleman and chemist who discovered oxygen and hydrogen. He published the first quantitative work on the conversion of sugar into ethanol and carbon dioxide, and in doing so established the law of conversion of mass: in the equation above, if you add them up, there are the same number of carbon, hydrogen and oxygen atoms after the arrow as before. While Lavoisier wasn't the first to suggest this, his experiments with turning grape juice into wine gave it its definitive expression:

> *The whole art of experimenting in chemistry rests on this principle; in all experiments one is obliged to assume an actual equality between the principles [that is, elements] of the substances examined and those obtained by the analysis of these substances. Thus, inasmuch as grape-juice yields carbonic acid gas and alcohol, I can affirm that grape juice = carbonic acid gas + alcohol.*

The general acceptance of this law was the final death knell for belief in magic, the spontaneous appearance of matter and the idea of alcohol as a gift from the gods. But it would be another century before the process of fermentation was definitely linked to the actions of microorganisms

Yeasts are not the only microorganisms that ferment, and alcohol is not the only by-product of fermentation. In its broadest sense, fermentation is the action whereby microflora release energy from organic material by transforming it. It's a process that often happens without oxygen (although alcoholic fermentation does normally require oxygen) and is often 'switched on' when a microorganism is starved of oxygen. Yeasts ferment sugar into alcohol. But the broader family of microflora in which they sit ferment all kinds of substances. They ferment milk into cheese. They ferment vegetables into sauerkraut and kim-chi. Coffee, chocolate, bread, salami, soy sauce and yoghurt are all products of fermentation. And as Michael Pollan points out, fermented foods invariably taste more intense and are valued more highly by the cultures that produce them.

But that last sentence is tricky and has the potential to confuse: when I wrote 'the cultures that produce them' I meant 'as in, the French create wine, the Japanese create soy sauce', and so on. But it would be more correct to say 'the cultures that produce them' are the vast armies of microflora that are all around us. Sandor Katz is one of the world's most passionate advocates of fermentation in all its guises, and certainly its most eloquent. 'Fermentation is everywhere, always,' he writes in his book *Wild Fermentation*:

> *It's an everyday miracle ... Microscopic bacteria and fungi are in every breath we take and every bite we eat ...*
>
> *Microbial cultures are essential to life's processes ... [and] we humans are in a symbiotic relationship with these single-cell life-forms ... Not only are we dependent on microorganisms, we are their descendants: According to the fossil record, all forms of life on Earth spring from bacterial origins.*

In modern times we've been taught (mainly by people trying to sell us things) that bacteria are bad, and that sterility is good. But if we did somehow manage to eradicate bacteria from our lives, we'd die pretty much instantly.* It's

---

* Sandor Katz developed his interest in fermentation when he was diagnosed HIV positive and developed AIDS in 1999. He remains in robust good health – a condition he ascribes largely to a diet of wild-fermented food and drink.

recently been established that you – your body, your corporeal presence – is only 10 per cent you. Nine in every ten cells you carry around – on your skin, in your hair, in your muscles and especially in your gut – belong to bacteria that we depend on to break down food for us and move essential nutrients around. They account for about three pounds of the average adult's weight – roughly the same as your brain.*

Up to a third of the world's food is produced by fermentation. Before refrigeration, it was the main way we preserved food. It's essentially the process of partially controlled rotting, and we humans are not the only creatures that take advantage of it. When squirrels bury acorns, they aren't just 'storing' them like we learned to love as kids; they're pit-fermenting them. Some species of birds sour seeds in their craw. And a variety of animals from fruit flies through wild pigs and deer to elephants will actively seek out and fight over rotting, fermenting fruit before settling for fresh fruit if they can't get it. In 2004, biologist Robert Dudley expounded the 'Drunken Monkey' theory of evolution. He points out that when ripe fruit is bruised, this allows yeast to ferment the sugars in the fruit to produce alcohol. The aromatic compounds produced are light and volatile and float through the air. Animals that are sensitive to these compounds and find them appealing are thereby drawn to sugar-filled, energy-giving fruit before animals that are not, meaning that if you're attracted to the smell and taste of booze, you're more likely to survive in a hostile, competitive environment.† Dudley suggests that while this might help explain our success in evolving as a species, it might also explain modern addiction: we're genetically programmed to seek out alcohol, which, like our predisposition to sugar, is based on the assumption that these are scarce resources. When we have them in abundance, sometimes we can't stop consuming them.

So there are some interesting theories and some obvious facts about the benefits and attractions of fermentation, particularly alcoholic fermentation, to humans. But why do yeasts do it? What is the evolutionary advantage for them?

---

* I got over the initial gross-out of this astonishing fact by thinking about how my body is home to billions of creatures for whom I am the universe. If you think about it, each of us is a god in the eyes of our bacteria. Or would be, if they had eyes.

† It's also worth mentioning here that fermentation creates new nutrients: several B vitamins are synthesised in the fermentation of beer, for example.

In its strictest, tightest sense, the reason yeasts eat sugar is the same reason we do: the production of adenosine triphosphate, or ATP to its friends. ATP is the molecule that gets energy to where it needs to go in our cells. It's the basis of life. And yeast makes it by metabolising sugar. Alcohol and carbon dioxide are the by-products of that metabolism.

The creation of alcohol may have initially been a random genetic mutation, but it was one that proved very beneficial for yeast. Alcohol is, ultimately, a poison. If we drink too much of it, we'll die. We use alcohol to sterilise items such as surgical equipment because it kills any bacteria on that equipment. But yeast can tolerate alcohol up to a certain strength. When it finds a source of sugar and begins to feed, by excreting alcohol all over the place, the yeast is creating an environment that is hostile to other microorganisms that might otherwise compete with it – a process Michael Pollan likens to a child licking all the cookies on a plate so he doesn't have to share them with the other kids.

Saccharomyces cerevisiae, which translates roughly as 'sugar mould' or 'sugar fungus', is the main family of yeast responsible for brewing, wine-making and bread baking, and is commonly written as *S. cerevisiae* because even scientists get tired of typing *Saccharomyces* after a while. *S. cerevisiae* is the main star in the story of beer fermentation, but not the only one, and we'll be meeting some of its relatives later.

Despite what many of us have written in the past, *S. cerevisiae* is not airborne. It lives on the skins of fruit, or even in their flesh. It hibernates in the stomachs of wasps. It travels around on dust motes or on the hairs on the legs of fruit flies. The more you learn about it, the more unlikely sounding and incredible it becomes, and when I share stories of my yeast education in the pub, my friends usually think I'm taking the piss, or drunk, or have gone insane with the pressure of the deadline for this book. But it's all true. And here's my favourite story of *S. cerevisiae*'s superpowers.

Sometimes *S. cerevisiae* finds itself in an environment where it has consumed all the available sugar. Under these conditions, the yeast can reverse the process by switching on an enzyme which allows it to consume the alcohol it has created and use it as an energy source.

There's no way of sugar-coating this, so let's just get through it without sniggering. Or retching. A good analogy of the evolutionary benefits to yeast of producing alcohol is to imagine that your poo was so noxious that you could use it as a defensive barrier that killed any thief or predator who came into contact with it, so you could smear your poo all over your refrigerator or food cupboard to protect its contents, so no one else could come near it. But then, if you found that the food cupboard was empty, you could lick your own poo from the outsde of the refrigerator and find it highly nutritious. I'm afraid that's an entirely accurate analogy for the relationship between yeast and alcohol. It takes the curious phenomenon whereby you find the smell of your own farts quite tolerable but those of other people to be disgusting to an entirely new level.

As Michael Pollan writes in *Cooked*, 'Of all humankind's fermentations, alcohol is the oldest and by far the most popular, consumed in all but a small handful of cultures for all of recorded history and no doubt for a long time before that.' In every part of the world, humans figured out how to encourage and eventually exert a degree of control over the fermentation of whatever naturally occurring sugars were growing around them at the birth of civilisation or even before. Fermenting fruit is relatively easy, because fruit went down an evolutionary path on which there are benefits to it being eaten and having its seeds deposited out the other end by the happy, sated animal, or even in rewarding insects or birds with sugar or alcohol in return for pollination. Grain is trickier, because it evolved to keep its sugar for its babies and it doesn't want to be eaten or fermented, either by animals or microflora. Our culture is founded on our relationship with yeast cultures. We've worked in partnership with yeast for thousands of years, jimmying open the locks on nature's defences to give it access to rich sources of sugar, and it's given us booze in return. The history of the development of brewing is in large part the history of us learning more about yeast, how it behaves, what it doesn't like and what keeps it happy. As Pollan writes:

> Like a gardener, [brewers] find themselves in a lively conversation with nature. All work with living creatures that come to the table with their own interests, interests that must be understood and respected if we are to succeed. And we succeed precisely to the extent we manage to align our interests with theirs.

That lively conversation continues today. And while we've made recent leaps and bounds in our understanding of our microscopic partner, no one involved in the study of yeast would argue that we're anywhere close to completing the picture.

Different yeasts have different behaviours, different preferences and different tolerances to the alcohols they produce. This plays a huge part in determining the character of different drinks. Yeast will ferment sugar to a certain level, and when the environment gets too boozy they can't work any more. Wild yeasts tend to be able to get to about 5 per cent ABV and then give up. But just like people, in certain environments some species develop different attributes. Champagne yeasts are generally recognised as being the strongest, but yeast working on its own can only rarely produce a liquid that's more than 18 per cent ABV. In an environment such as a brewery, yeasts self-select for conditions they prefer, and evolve quickly to suit their environment. Without understanding how and why, we've been unwittingly breeding and domesticating yeasts for hundreds of years.

3. 'We're Just Here to Keep the Yeast Happy'

It's very early on a Wednesday morning. The sky is full of daylight and the clouds look freshly scrubbed, but the light seems fragile and uncertain, as if the day might still change its mind and night could steal back at any moment. This is the kind of early that, if you're not used to it, can make you slightly hysterical. But I'm also late: when I get to the Marston's Brewery in Burton upon Trent just before 6 a.m., the team I'm here to meet have already been hard at work for two hours.

Getting yeast to ferment readily available sugar is easy. Given the right temperature and conditions, it's much harder to *stop* yeast from fermenting everything.* But getting yeast to ferment in the way you want it to, and getting it to ferment the same way every time so you can sell a brand of beer that has a consistent flavour, is much trickier. Talk to a brewer for more than five minutes and you soon realise it's a process over which we only

---

* As you'll know if you've ever had to throw away a carton of fruit juice that's gone sharp and fizzy, the carton bloating with gas. That's natural yeast, fermenting the sugars into alcohol and carbon dioxide. Even fresh orange juice has an alcohol content of around 0.5 per cent ABV.

have tentative guidance rather than any kind of authoritative control. An old adage among brewers is, 'We don't make beer; we simply gather the ingredients in the right place. The *yeast* makes the beer.'

If you want the yeast to brew beer the way you like it, you need to keep it happy. A lot of brewing practice is essentially little more than playing babysitter-cum-concierge to a microscopic organism, and long before the behaviour or even the existence of yeast was understood brewers were using observation, trial and error to build brewing systems that seemed to work, even though they had no idea what was happening, or why.

One of the earliest of these was the beer stick, almost a magic wand in ancient brewing, that survives today in the production of African sorghum beer and kvass in parts of Scandinavia. Once the ingredients are assembled, they're stirred with a stick especially reserved for that use, because it has special properties that start the fermentation. We now know these special properties are yeasts from previous brews, lying dormant on the stick until they're given a new source of sugar.

When it comes to understanding the world around us, before we had accurate measurement and scientific proof, science, superstition and religion were all different sides of the same thing: observing the world and what happened within it, and drawing conclusions from those observations. We're programmed to see patterns, and sometimes we see them where they don't exist. Once, we observed that the sun came back in the spring if we made sacrifices to the gods. The ancients making sacrifices had the same sized brains as us and were just as thoughtful and intelligent; they simply lacked the sum of stored knowledge we eventually accumulated.

Similarly, we once thought of fermentation as a gift from the gods. The difference between a good and a bad brew was sometimes attributed to spirits. The five-pointed star you see on label designs for beers such as Heineken, Stella Artois, Newcastle Brown and Sapporo, to name a few, can trace their roots back to the star that was hung above medieval brewing vessels to keep evil spirits from spoiling the brew. It took us far, far longer to work out that those evil spirits were wild yeasts and other bacteria than it did for us to work out the relationship between planets, stars and moons.

That process of discovery was a gradual one. Medieval brewers began repitching yeast from one brew into the next, realising there was something in the rocky-headed foam that kept fermentation going. 'Godisgoode' went from being an observation on the miracle of fermentation to being another name for this physical substance that we could see in the brewing vessel We had no idea that it was eating sugar and pissing alcohol, but we knew we needed yeast to brew – many possible etymologies for the word 'yeast' go back to Old English or German words meaning 'foam' or 'froth'.

Centuries of trial and error led to a variety of different fermentation systems. As yeast was repitched, brewers unwittingly domesticated and evolved it. Yeast is highly prone to mutation. Like any other living creatures, random mutations that like the immediate environment lead to adaptation, and yeast, a single-cell organism, goes through different generations very quickly. Although all brewing yeast belongs to the same family within the same species, just as humans who settled thousands of years ago in Africa look very different from those who made their way to Sweden, so a yeast in a Victorian brewery in Birmingham can have developed very different characteristics, strengths and weaknesses from one in a Trappist monastery brewery in Belgium – or even a Victorian brewery up the road in Burton upon Trent.

As superstition slowly evolved into science, brewers discovered that different yeasts preferred different fermentation conditions. A fermentation vessel is essentially any container that can allow yeast to ferment a volume of sugary liquid. The earliest fermenters were clay pots or perhaps even holes in the ground. They can be wooden barrels or stainless steel vats, open to the air or closed, tall and conical or horizontal. Different methods and structures have co-evolved in different places with the yeasts they serve. Sometimes, they become ornate to the point of eccentricity.

I'd always been aware of 'Yorkshire Square fermentation', but never quite sure of what it entailed. I assumed it consisted of square, slate-built open fermenters, and this was enough to create distinctive beers that, being from Yorkshire, would have been the best in the world. So I was shocked when, on a visit to the Black Sheep Brewery in Masham, North Yorkshire, I was shown one in action. A Yorkshire Square is a covered chamber with a round hole, about eighteen inches across, in the middle. As the beer ferments, it punches up through this hole and sits in a shallower trough on top of the main vessel. The beer itself runs back into the main vessel through 'organ pipes' around the sides, but the yeast stays in the trough on top.

But here's the good bit: for six minutes every three hours, the beer is 'roused' – a pipe that ends in something resembling a Martian death ray sucks beer up from the bottom of the fermenter and sprays it all around the top of the yeast tray. The rousing introduces great quantities of oxygen to the beer, and that makes the yeast go wild. Within minutes it's pouring up through the hole, foaming everywhere in a vigorous, hyperactive fermentation. According to Rob Theakston, Managing Director of Black Sheep, 'The yeast loves it.' I'm not surprised – I suspect I would, too, lying on a warm plate, being sprayed with beer every few hours.

The Yorkshire Squares are a very impressive and very elaborate system to keep beer as happy as possible while it's fermenting. But my favourite variation on this theme, here in Burton upon Trent, is one of the wonders of the brewing world.

✿ ✿ ✿

The Burton Union room at Marston's is unique, astonishing and confusing. At first glance it reminds me of a big Pinewood Studios sound stage on which the climactic battle of a James Bond movie is being orchestrated. Fermentation vessels three storeys high run down each side of a massive space full of gantries and ladders and walkways, all surrounding and serving a series of elaborate constructions in the centre of the room.

A union set is a row of wooden barrels with a large metal trough sitting on top of them. The barrels are massive, and are held in a frame around head height. A big metal X with a bolt in the middle holds each barrel in place, lying suspended on its side. From the apex of each barrel rises a swan-necked stainless steel spout that curves over into the trough that sits above the barrels and runs the entire length of the set.

As we watch, one of the Marston's brewers is hauling long, thick rubber piping across the floor, connecting the union set in the middle to one of the tall, steel fermentation vessels around the sides of the room. A batch of Marston's Pedigree was brewed on Monday and put into the tanks for the fermentation to start, to get it going and overcome any problems. Now it's well under way, the fermenting beer is being transferred to the union sets.

The barrels are linked by a series of pipes so the beer from the tank is dispersed evenly between them. Over the next few days, the beer will complete its fermentation in these wooden barrels.

The beer started flowing at 4.45 this morning, so two sets are almost full (they're filled two sets at a time, blended for consistency). As we watch, some of the swan necks coming up from the barrels on the right-hand side of the trough start to fob with creamy froth. 'They always start fobbing on one side before the other. No one knows why,' says Genevieve Upton, the Marston's brewer showing me around. 'You'd think they'd go in a particular order, but it's pretty random, except it's always one side before the other.'

Soon all twenty-four taps are gushing with foam. It's fast at the start, flowing from the swan necks in big gouts, running down the long, stainless steel trough, thick and creamy like shaving foam. Soon the whole trough is covered. I've seen the unions in action before and remember them being much more sedate than this. Genevieve tells me it'll slow down by this afternoon.

The Burton Union system is commonly credited to a brewer called Peter Walker, who patented a version of it in 1838. But Walker wasn't the first to brew with a system similar to this, and there's no record of his particular design actually being used in brewing anywhere. There is no other record of anyone else before or after claiming the credit for what we recognise as the Burton Union system today, so Walker is cited as its inventor even though the truth is the system evolved over a number of years, in relationship to the yeast it served.

When you look at the bizarre complexity and surreal beauty of the union system, you wonder why and how any brewer could possibly have devised it. And the reason for its existence is that it keeps the yeast happy. Fermenting beer in a system like this rather than in conventional fermentation tanks has two main benefits. Firstly, the steady pumping of beery foam up the swan neck pipes is created not by any external force, but by the action of yeast creating carbon dioxide. Most of what that CO_2 pumps into the trough is yeast, with a little bit of beer mixed in. The beer runs into a collection trough and from there back into the barrels, but the yeast stays in place in the trough. By the time fermentation is complete, all the yeast is in the trough and all the beer is in the barrels, remarkably bright and clear.

The second benefit is that the yeast in the trough is remarkably healthy. When yeast ferments it propagates at a rapid rate, growing exponentially in volume. Marston's take the yeast from the trough and keep it in yeast storage tanks, known as 'sputniks,' which sit at each end of the union room. What they don't need goes to a factory on the other side of Burton to become the core ingredient of Marmite – Marston's sends a couple of tankersful every week.

The yeast they keep is repitched into the next brew and is remarkably healthy. Yeast reproduces by splitting in two to form new cells, and in theory it should remain identical for generation after generation. But yeast is prone to mutation, as well as infection. The Marston's Brewery is part of a much bigger group that brews a wide variety of beers here (Pedigree is the only beer that goes through the unions) and keeps up to eight different yeast strains on site. All behave differently, and need to be treated differently. One of these is the yeast for Bass, once the biggest beer brand in the world, now owned and neglected by Anheuser-Busch Inbev, for whom Marston's brew the beer under licence.

'The Bass strain would have gone through the system back in the day, but it doesn't any more,' says Genevieve. 'Now we have to repropagate the Bass yeast from the lab culture much more often. It changes over the course of eight weeks, declining in how it ferments. We only have to repropagate the Marston's yeast once every two years.'

A Burton Union set is essentially an adventure playground for yeast that keeps it in perfect condition. But it's also the world's biggest lava lamp, a spectacle that brings you to a joyous, meditative state. 'You fix your eye on one and lose yourself in it, and then you turn around and the other one is belting out. You've got to keep your eye on it the whole time,' says Genevieve.

We've been standing staring at the Union set for half an hour, lost in it. Where there was once a creamy white foam there's now a brown scum forming where the yeast is oxidising. But under each spout there's a white eruption, like a fishing pool cut into ice, where more yeast continues to pour into the trough. The yeast is much fluffier than it would be in a traditional fermentation tank. You can almost see that it's happier.

Cleaning and maintaining the Unions is a laborious and expensive task that until recently required brewers to fill each barrel with water and spin it around. When the brewing industry underwent massive consolidation in the second half of the twentieth century, the Unions were phased out almost everywhere. Marston's is the last brewer in the world that has traditional sets still in use. Brewers from around the world come to see them in action. 'Some brewers from big industrial set-ups have never even seen yeast before because everything they do is automated,' says Genevieve. 'They stand here on the gallery and stare, mesmerised.'

One brewery that visits every year is California's Firestone Walker. They were so enraptured by the unions that they've built their own modified system based on what they've seen at Marston's, evolving it again. Marston's and Firestone Walker remain the only two commercial brewers anywhere using a Union system.

Several things strike me as I stay there on the gantry gazing down, unable to tear myself away. One is the force with which I'm reminded that beer is a living product. Another is sheer peace and happiness, the lava lamp doing its job, and I feel lucky to be able to see beer here in this state. This is what it's all about. Shorn of the context of any debate going on outside the walls of the Union room, being inside watching the visual poetry of the Unions in action and the intense physical labour of the brewers manhandling hoses and running up and down to check everything is working, I'm watching the perfect example of craft brewing in action.

'There are so many parameters to doing a good job and getting it exactly right,' says Genevieve. 'Sometimes, you do feel like an artist when you're working here.'

4. *Saccharomyces carlsbergensis*

We owe the birth of modern brewing to an epic family feud.

Up to a very recent point, advances in the scientific understanding of the ingredients of beer were all about improving its quality.* But there was only so much that could be done with the other ingredients while yeast remained a mystery. You could have the best quality hops and barley and figure out your water chemistry, but if you were not on intimate terms with the other living organism involved in making beer, it could easily dictate the overall character of the beer based on factors humans had no control over, and even the most talented brewer in the world was powerless to resist such whims.

J. C. Jacobsen was a brilliant and driven man. Although he was by trade a brewer and a businessman with no formal scientific training, he had an amateur fascination with science that suggested at times he'd ended up in the wrong career. He was convinced that science was the route to better beer at a time when many saw brewing as a natural art that should remain free from tampering.

---

* Arguably, over the last few decades many of the scientific leaps in understanding beer have not been about improving quality, but about cutting costs without the drinker noticing: speeding up the process, and using fewer or cheaper ingredients.

Jacobsen set up the Carlsberg Brewery in 1847, naming it after his son, Carl. In 1845, he had travelled to Munich to visit his friend and mentor Gabriel Sedelmayr at the Spaten Brewery. He returned to Copenhagen with a sample of precious Bavarian lager yeast stored in a hatbox, pausing at streams to keep it cool so it wouldn't spoil. His passion and rigour for brewing and science, and the popularity of the Bavarian-style lager he introduced to Denmark, meant that by the 1870s Carlsberg was already the biggest brewery Denmark had ever seen, and J. C. Jacobsen was a rich and powerful man.

Jacobsen had a very specific vision for the brewery and how it would develop in his lifetime and beyond, and groomed Carl to be his successor, insisting the boy received the scientific education the father never had. But Carl had different ideas from his father about how the brewery – and his own life – should be run. The two feuded constantly from when Carl was a young man until just a few months before J. C., known to his employees as the Captain, died in 1887.

J. C. had decided that as he was brewing lager, Carl should brew ale instead, and he set his son up with a separate brewing annexe when he finally allowed him to return home from a year-long study tour in 1871. Carl ignored his father and brewed lager instead. Incensed, J. C. drew up a new will in which, instead of making Carl his heir, he left everything to a newly created Carlsberg Foundation, a charitable body run by scientists. The Foundation was created in 1876, with its main focus being the management of the Carlsberg Laboratory, created the year before. Anything discovered or created by the laboratory was to be for the benefit of everyone, not just for the profit of Carlsberg.

When Emil Hansen joined the Carlsberg Laboratory in 1879, everyone felt the daily tension between father and son. In 1881, Carl left his father's business entirely and built a new brewery, which he called *Ny* (new) Carlsberg, right next door, forcing J. C. to rename his *Gamle* (old) Carlsberg. Hansen wrote in his diary:

> These two crazy people are putting up signboards bigger than the other's down there, because each of them is trying to cover the other's street name. They are making themselves objects of derision even to the workers, and the scandal has found its way into several newspapers, even in the provinces.

Emil Christian Hansen was no stranger to such conflicts. Born in 1842 to a poor family in Ribe, a tiny town in south-west Jutland, he struggled and fought throughout his entire life. In many ways, J. C. Jacobsen was the father Emil Hansen might have wished for. His own father was an itinerant painter and probably an alcoholic, keeping his family and livelihood together by his wits alone. Emil, by contrast, was quiet and serious, brooding and intense, and he grew up to be a paranoid loner, driven by anger and a sense that he was eternally being overlooked and snubbed. He was fiercely bright and excelled at school, but his poor background prevented him from pursuing a classical education. He never felt he got the recognition he deserved, even after he won a gold medal for a ground-breaking paper on the behaviour of fungi in 1876. But his interest in microorganisms eventually led him to the Carlsberg Laboratory, where he would change the world.

As in all avenues of science, Hansen was building on the work of others. In the middle of the seventeenth century, a Dutch draper called Antonie van Leeuwenhoek developed an interest in lens making because he wanted to better analyse the quality of thread. He ended up revolutionising the microscope and ultimately became known as the 'father of microbiology'. During his microscopic studies of everything from thread to mould, bees to lice, he put a drop of fermenting beer under his lens and saw what we now know to be yeast cells. He drew these and sent them to the Royal Society, but no one could figure out what they were and the discovery was forgotten for 150 years.

The main reason it took so long to figure out what yeast was and what it did is that biology and chemistry were being studied separately and each had their own idea of how things worked. Antoine Lavoisier worked out the conservation of matter and that sugar was equal to alcohol and carbon dioxide, but he didn't work out how that conversion actually happened – was it a simple chemical reaction, or was it the action of some kind of agent?

Finally, in 1837, German biologist Theodor Schwann brought together the discoveries of van Leeuwenhoek and Lavoisier. He proposed that the blobs seen under the former's microscope were cells, and was the first person to state that 'All living things are composed of cells and cell products.' From this revolutionary perspective, he argued that the cells in fermenting booze were the agents of transforming sugar into carbon dioxide and alcohol. He called them *Zuckerpilz* – German for 'sugar fungus'. His colleague Franz

Meyen thought this might sound better in Latin. When he translated it, he got *Saccharomyces*. But not everyone was convinced.

If Theodor Schwann was the founder of cell theory, Justus von Liebig was the father of organic chemistry, and chemists preferred the neat equations established by Lavoisier. A great many processes and transformations in nature are simple chemical reactions that can be achieved by the application of heat, the introduction of water or other changes to environmental factors, with no other agent weighing in. Why couldn't fermentation be one of those?

If I had lived at a time when it hadn't been proven, I don't think I would have accepted how the action of yeast really works either. But Liebig found the whole idea so ridiculous he went beyond the robust and sometimes personal criticism that was common at the time and published a paper that took the piss out of the cell theory of fermentation, writing that when yeast was placed in a sugar solution it 'becomes obvious that they are the eggs of small animals', which hatch out into creatures that have heads with tubes on them, stomachs, intestines and little pink anuses, from which they excrete alcohol as the sugar is digested 'in the blink of an eye'. Liebig was trying here to make the process sound as ridiculous as he possibly could. He never accepted the truth of yeast-based fermentation in his lifetime. To have done so, he would have had to accept that what he wrote as an attempt at cruel humour was, shorn of its wilder embellishments, pretty close to the truth.

Louis Pasteur's strength was that he was both a chemist and a microbiologist. He was the first to understand and show the broad spectrum of fermentation, finally establishing beyond doubt (save among a few people like Liebig) that not only did yeast ferment wine and beer, but microorganisms also soured milk, wine and beer, and were responsible for various diseases.* He published *Études sur le vin* (Studies on Wine) in 1866, and followed this up with *Études sur la bière* (Studies on Beer) in 1876, the year after the foundation of the Carlsberg Laboratory.†

---

* Over a busy career, Pasteur finally disproved the idea of spontaneous generation, that life could just spring into existence, and provided the basis for modern antiseptic sterilisation and vaccination. He established that bacteria could be killed by heating liquids to temperatures between 60 and 100 degrees Celsius (140 and 212 degrees Fahrenheit), and gave his name to the process of pasteurisation.

† It's worth pausing for a second to note here that, in French, wine is masculine and beer is feminine.

As well as establishing that yeast was the agent of fermentation and that other microorganisms could spoil beer, Pasteur demonstrated the behaviours of different kinds of yeast. He showed that Bavarian-style lager yeast tended to gather together and sink to the bottom of the brewing vessel after fermentation, while ale yeast floated to the top. Top- and bottom-fermenting yeasts behave differently in other ways, preferring different temperatures, fermenting at different speeds and giving the finished beer differing characteristics. The type of yeast remains the key differentiator between ale and lager, despite many drinkers believing it has something to do with colour or serving temperature.

Pasteur was a rock star scientist. Everywhere he went he was garlanded with medals and prizes. J. C. Jacobsen adored him, the personification of the application of science to brewing he had always yearned to do himself. In the portrait Jacobsen had commissioned of himself not long before his death, he stands at a table covered in scientific equipment and papers. His copy of *Études sur la bière* is prominently displayed.

Emil Hansen also owned a personal copy of *Études sur la bière*, which still survives. On a page where Pasteur discusses procedures for cleaning yeast cultures Hansen has written, 'How do you get that absolute pure culture', and 'This question is much more complicated, since not one but several yeast species survive the mentioned treatment.' You can almost feel the professional jealousy coming off the page, the sense from Hansen that he could do better.

In 1882, Hansen visited the laboratory of German microbiologist Robert Koch. This could have been perceived as a direct dig at Pasteur, whose motivation in his research on beer included the desire to pay Germany back for France's humiliating defeat in the Franco-Prussian War. (Pasteur requested that any beers made using his methods should be referred to as *bières de la revanche nationale*, or 'beers of the national revenge'.) But there was a directly useful reason for doing so. Koch had pioneered the technology of using nutrient gelatine plates to culture colonies of bacteria. Hansen had already managed to isolate single yeast cells by suspending yeast cells in water, counting them and then diluting the water again and again until he only had half a yeast cell per millilitre. In this way he was able to isolate a single yeast cell. With Koch's gelatine plates, he was then able to culture up a yeast from a single cell, keeping it pure.

Carlsberg and rival Danish brewery Tuborg had at this point been struggling with spoiled beer and were desperate to know why. Carlsberg was suf
fering from a 'beer disease' that was turning the beer sour. In 1883, Hansen
isolated four separate strains from the yeast being used at the Carlsberg
Brewery. Using his new cultivation techniques, he cultured up enough of
each separate yeast to brew different samples of beer. One strain, which
he named Carlsberg *Unterhefe* 1 (bottom yeast 1) gave consistent, bright
beer with good flavour and stability. *Unterhefe* 2 also created good, clear
beer, with a slightly fuller taste than *Unterhefe* 1, but the beer it produced
didn't keep for long. The third line was a variant of *S. pastorianus,* a bottom-
fermenting yeast named after Pasteur. Its beers were excessively bitter and
smoky, and this strain was identified as the culprit of the beer disease. After
some doubts about Hansen's earlier work, the Captain was now convinced.
In 1884, the entire production of the Old Carlsberg Brewery was switched
to *Unterhefe* 1, which was renamed *S. carlsbergensis.*

Because the Carlsberg Foundation was and remains a charitable organisation, the trustees felt anything discovered on their watch should not be
patented and kept for profit, but shared with the scientific community, to be
used by all. Hansen's single strain yeast technology spread rapidly around
the world. To this day, anything developed in basic or applied research at
the Carlsberg Foundation cannot be patented.

The impact of Hansen's work was immediately apparent on the global
brewing industry, and *S. carlsbergensis* joined *S. cerevisiae* as one of the two
dominant brewing strains across the world.* Using a single strain yeast meant
that for the first time a consistent flavour could be almost guaranteed rather
than simply hoped for. A guarantee of consistency is the basis of any brand:
the people who buy them do so because they expect every can of Coca-Cola,
every Big Mac, every bottle of Heinz Tomato Ketchup, to taste the same as
the last. Now, this guarantee could be extended to beer, which meant that

---

* Hansen was the first to establish that different species of yeast existed as well as different strains. In his
experiments, he was insistent that the *S. pastorianus* strains he had used in his experiments were quite
different from the yeast he named *S. carlsbergensis.* But genetic research in the late twentieth century
established that *S. pastorianus* and *S. carlsbergensis* were synonyms for the same yeast. While some
people – particularly at Carlsberg – still preserve the old distinction, the global scientific community
has renamed *S. carlsbergensis* as *S. pastorianus.* More than a century after Hansen's and Pasteur's deaths,
the rivalry continues.

breweries big enough to take advantage of refrigerated transport and new brewing technologies could offer a consistent product on a bigger scale than ever before. Pasteur published *Études sur la bière* in 1876. Hansen started work at the Carlsberg Laboratory in 1879, and published the first of his thirteen papers titled 'Studies of alcohol yeast fungi's physiology and morphology' in 1881. The foundation dates of many of the biggest beer brands in the world today point to what marketers love to call 'first mover advantage': Heineken, Tuborg and Beck's were first brewed in 1873, Budweiser in 1876, Foster's in 1888, Asahi in 1889, San Miguel in 1890 and Castle Lager in 1895. Single strain yeast is by no means the only factor that helped these brands become long-lived giants, but they wouldn't have grown so big without it.

5. Of Flavour and Fruit Flies

If you feel sorry for anyone at Carlsberg that they didn't get to enjoy the full profits of such an important discovery, your worries would be put to rest by a visit to the Carlsberg Laboratory, now renamed the Carlsberg Research Foundation. The brewer's astonishing success is here in the bricks and mortar – and, more to the point, in the marble and the gilt and the statues and the mosaics and the ornamental gardens.

I'm being given a tour of the Foundation by Professor Claes Gjermansen, who has worked here since the early 1980s, studying yeast. I had expected to find a laboratory, but it's more like an entire university campus. Carl Jacobsen was an artist in the same way his father was a scientist, a passionate advocate rather than an expert practitioner himself. He amassed a huge collection, and in 1903 Carl donated New Carlsberg and many of its collections to the Foundation, calling the move 'a reconciliation offering to eradicate every trace of an ancient disharmony between a father and his son'. Now, sculptures sit and stand and paintings hang wherever you look, art and science combined and celebrated together, running through the whole place like the Jacobsens' DNA.

About a hundred people work here today, which is not as many as it once was, and the place feels half empty. Claes takes me on a tour of the whole building, which includes a dusty old library on the top floor, lined with rows of old brewing research journals from around the world. Portraits of dead scientists line the walls. A set of bongos sits in front of a neatly leather-bound set of periodicals from the nineteenth century. All the content of these volumes has been digitised, so the space is seldom used for its original purpose and there's a full band set up for practice in the centre of the room. 'I used to enjoy going through the journals and getting inspired by the titles,' says Claes. 'Now I just sit at my own computer.'

We find a row of Carlsberg Research Foundation journals. 'I wonder if my first piece is in here?' says Claes, picking up a volume from 1981. He gets excited when he finds it, but even more animated when he discovers a beautiful plate on guppy genetics from 1922. There's a fascinating story about how the eel got to Europe from the Sargasso Sea. No one has yet figured out how it returns from Europe to the Sargasso.

By the time Emil Hansen died in 1909, he had at last received the recognition he always craved, and was a rich man in his own right. He's commemorated here by a lavish marble monument – not quite as lavish as that to the Captain, obviously – and his lab is pretty much as he left it. The machine he invented to continuously propagate pure yeast strains sits in the museum, and other machines like it were still being used late into the twentieth century.

Not wanting to look like a heel, Hansen also donated his fortune to the Carlsberg Foundation, but, not being a Jacobsen himself, he helped ensure his own immortality by insisting that the money be used as a prize fund to reward scientific research on yeast.

In 1993, Claes Gjermansen won that prize. Up to that point it was believed that brewers' yeast couldn't 'spoilate' – it couldn't reproduce sexually. Claes proved that it could – if you reduced the temperature it was in.

This is typical of the work being done on the campus today. Other breweries have laboratories to ensure their yeast remains healthy and to spot any problems. At Carlsberg, they're still trying to unlock the many mysteries that remain under the microscope.

I can comprehend about half of what Claes shows and tells me, but it's all pushing forward our understanding of yeast. He shows me the Multiform Carlsberg System, a carousel containing sixty identical two-litre tubes. Using this, cells can be removed and analysed at any point during fermentation. Yeast behaves differently in a lab on a Petri dish than it does in a big fermentation vessel, and this machine solves the Schrödinger's Cat dilemma of whether the act of analysing the yeast changes its behaviour. It's now been copied around the world. The Carlsberg Foundation's contribution to science didn't end with Hansen, nor with Sørensen's establishment of the pH scale in 1909.

We finish our tour in the museum bar, where the latest beers in the *Semper Ardens* Research Project, whereby Carlsberg brews a range of interesting beer styles from around the world, are on offer. The first beer in the range was Carlsberg Trappiste, a 9 per cent Belgian-style ale that Claes was clearly proud to work on. Today I settle for the Jacobsen Extra Pilsner. It's full-bodied and juicy, with a big hit of peppery Žatec hops at the end.

'It's not stale and there are no off-flavours,' offers Claes, the scientist.

I ask him what he's currently working on.

'Diacetyl,' he replies.

The holy grail of lager brewing is to be able to reduce fermentation time with no adverse effects. Lager yeasts enjoy a long period at cool temperatures. If they don't get that, you can get undesirable flavours in the beer.

One of these flavours is diacetyl, a compound produced by yeast early in the fermentation that tastes heavily of butterscotch. It can be a positive attribute in British ales if it's not too heavy, but to most palates it ruins lager, and is technically regarded as a fault. During the long, cool, storage period traditional for lager, the yeast will eventually reabsorb diacetyl and clean the flavour up. But what's been frustrating Claes is why the yeast produces it in the first place.

'What is the evolutionary advantage to yeast of producing these compounds?' he asks, as if I might have the faintest idea. 'They are not produced for the benefit of the yeast. Is it an antibiotic?'

Now, he thinks his peers have figured it out.

'The fruit flies like them. It means that when the yeast produces them, it is more likely to be spread by fruit flies, and this helps ensure their survival.'

I later learn that the relationship between fruit flies and beer is of mutual benefit. As you'll know if you've ever drunk in a pub beer garden on a hot day and had to swat them away or fish them out of your glass, fruit flies enjoy a drink. But alcohol does more than refresh them and make them happy: it actually helps keep them alive. The common fruit fly or vinegar fly, otherwise known as *Drosophila melanogaster*, is vulnerable to an even smaller pest, a tiny parasitic wasp that lays its eggs in the fruit fly's stomach. When the larvae hatch, they eventually burrow their way out, like Ridley Scott's alien xenomorph, and kill their host. But there's an antidote: while the fruit fly enjoys a drink, the tiny wasp larvae do not. If they're in a fruit fly's stomach when alcohol comes down its tiny little neck, the larvae shit themselves inside out and die.

And people say drinking is bad for your health.

6. Re-Brew

It sounds like a tall story, especially coming from the PR department of one of the world's biggest breweries.

Recently, someone at Carlsberg just happened to be moving some stuff around in the cellars, and they just happened to find three bottles of beer brewed in 1883, which just happened to be the year that Emil Hansen successfully isolated and cultivated single strain yeast cells. And one of these bottles just happened to contain some yeast cells that were still living, which they were able to successfully repropagate and therefore recreate the first modern beer.

And would I like to come back to Carlsberg to taste the recreated beer?

I don't really believe the premise. But I do want to go back to Copenhagen. I might learn something I've missed before.

Carlsberg have certainly pushed the boat out. I'm one of forty writers from around the world who have been brought to Copenhagen, given two nights in a hotel and offered a celebratory dinner cooked by a Michelin-starred chef with the Crown Prince of Denmark in attendance. There's clearly a lot riding on this.

We're invited to take a seat in what used to be the dining room in J. C. Jacobsen's house. A domed glass ceiling sits above a marble floor. The walls are marble, too, covered with bas-reliefs of scenes from Greek mythology. Twenty fluted marble columns create a central space that's now lined with rows of chairs, with a PowerPoint presentation at the front. A Venus de Milo stands in the centre of the ornamental garden outside, staring in through the glass doors. The Jacobsens moved here in 1854, just seven years after the brewery opened. For all the talk about what happened here in the 1870s and 1880s, Carlsberg was clearly very successful even before then with its Bavarian-style beer.

First, we get a series of speeches from everyone who is anyone within Carlsberg and the Carlsberg Foundation. We're told that the brewery has always been about science and innovation, about scientific social responsibility as well as corporate social responsibility. We're told the Carlsberg Foundation is unique, that it supports not just research in brewing science, but within the national sciences, humanities and social sciences. Carlsberg aims to maintain brewing 'at a high and honourable level', balancing short- and long-term benefits.

Over the course of the morning, my scepticism is carefully and meticulously worn away. When we're shown the cellars – which extend some thirteen kilometres in total – and the amount of junk in them, I accept that you could stumble across old beers that have lain undisturbed for 130 years. We're invited to rifle through a few crates ourselves, and find some intact, dusty bottles from 1913, but apparently Carlsberg was pasteurising by then so we have no chance of repeating the original discovery.

When we're shown the lab, and the detailed genome of the 1883 yeast and how it compares with its cultivated modern-day descendants, showing some minor but definite mutations even though the yeast has been repropagated from the lab regularly over the years, there's no doubt the discovery of the yeast is genuine.

We're shown six test tubes of beer that's identical in every way except it's been fermented by six different yeasts: lager, ale, Belgian Trappist, *Brettanomyces*, wheat beer yeast, and a new, experimental, super-fruity strain. They taste quite different from each other. It's astonishing how much difference yeast makes to the flavour of beer.

Then we're in the pilot brewery where the recreated beer, dubbed Re-Brew, was born. They've tried to get it as close as possible to how it would have been in 1883, which is not easy given the changes to hop and barley cultivation in the last 130 years. They've specially recultivated an old landrace barley variety known simply as *Gamledansk*, or 'Old Danish', and used it to make Munich, Caramel and dark malts. The water was purified and then had salts added back in that accord with water analysis from the 1880s. All they know about the hops is that they were whole leaf hops from the Hallertau region, so they've plumped for Hallertau Mittelfrüh, a Noble Hop that was the most popular variety back then.

By the time we're back in the Captain's old dining room, there's a nervous curiosity building among the writers. Surely if the pure yeast story is genuine then it'll just taste like a modern beer? We want it to taste different and interesting, but if it does, wouldn't that throw the whole claim about replicable yeast strains into disarray? But if it doesn't, if it just tastes like modern beer, which in theory it should, why all the fuss?

'Flemming will initiate the tasting ceremony.'

Flemming Besenbacher, the chairman of the Carlsberg board, steps forward through the tightening crowd. This is the closest I've ever come to beer drinking being performed as a religious rite, as it was 10,000 years ago. The anticipation has been built up to an absurd degree. When you're in a group situation like this, a collective neurosis takes hold. Everyone in the room is focused on the wooden cask. For a few moments, nothing else happening anywhere in the world is as important as what's going on here right now. This is the most miraculous thing the world has ever seen. Nothing is as valuable as a glass of this stuff.

It pours slowly from the cask into a glass shaped like a brandy balloon. The glass has been specially designed and hand-blown for the occasion. Slowly, the number of glasses multiplies. Everyone forces themselves into polite restraint, while suppressing the urge to kill everyone else in the room to get the first glass. About a thousand years later, I finally have a glass in my hand. The beer is a deep, reddish brown. There's a faint but intriguing aroma that bears hints of honey, marzipan and caramel. I take my glass into a corner and contemplate it for a while without drinking it. I want everyone else to disappear, so it can just be the two of us. I photograph it. I stroke it. And, finally, I raise to my lips.

And it's . . . clean. It's rounded, well-balanced, with a slight rough edge around smooth caramel notes. It's more interesting than I thought it might be. But it's not special. It's OK. Better than OK, it's quite good. It could have done with a little longer fermenting and conditioning, and I suspect the slowness of the yeast came as an unpleasant surprise to the brewers. I'd love to taste it again after they've been given another week with it.

And then I realise that this cleanness, this lack of drama, is the whole point of the beer. I try to imagine what it must have been like to taste a beer like this for the first time in 1882 or 1883, when the first ever beers from laboratory-cultivated, single-strain yeasts were brewed here. How did it feel to taste a beer with no off-notes, no sour or wild notes, and know that, as a brewer, you could reproduce that beer exactly next time, and the time after that, that you could produce a beer that only tasted of the ingredients you had deliberately included, distinct and uncluttered by elements you didn't want but couldn't control?

I succeed in my thought experiment. The room – emptied of chairs and now resembling some kind of Roman bathhouse – helps me realise what a revolution this beer was when it was first brewed. It swept through brewing so quickly that for over a century we've known little else than laboratory cultivated yeast. We've grown accustomed to it. Some of us have got bored of it. Which is why, just as with floor malting and heritage barley and original water sources, we want to go back and experience what beer was like before Hansen and Pasteur changed it forever.

7. The Call of the Wild

You wouldn't be reading this book, and I wouldn't have written it, if a man called Michael Jackson* hadn't got off a train and bumped into a mysterious man wearing a John Lennon mask.

In the late 1960s, Jackson was a journalist stationed in Amsterdam. Bored of lager – which he saw as the 'dry white' of the beer world – and missing the 'burgundy' that was British ale, he followed a colleague's recommendation and travelled to the Catholic south of the country where old festivals still retained an anarchistic air. On the train, he made the mistake of engaging in conversation with a Protestant from the north who warned him that everyone on the streets in the southern towns would be drunk. The history of modern beer changed when Jackson became so frustrated with this man that he got off the train at the next stop, with no idea where he was, just to get away from him. 'I was sucked into a crowd, beers in hand, who seemed to be in endless circulation through the station café. The station square was full of drinking, dancing and Beatle [sic] music. The whole town was drunk, and soon I was too,' he wrote later. 'Amid the endless golden glasses of Dutch lager, someone wearing a John Lennon mask handed me a chalice containing a darker beer. Caution long to the winds, I took a gulp. I was quite unprepared for the richness of the brew and, a moment later, the hit of alcohol, somewhere around the top of the head.'

---

* He always used to make it clear that he was 'not the gloved one'.

The man in the mask asked Jackson if he liked the beer. When he replied that he did, the man said, 'That is a Trappist beer. If you like that sort of thing, you are in the wrong country. You really ought to go across the border.' And then the crowd separated them. Jackson never found out who the man was, but the following morning, hungover, he did as the man suggested and popped over to Belgium for the first time in his life, 'a refugee from The Netherlanders' annual moment of uninhibition'.

In a sense, he never left. Jackson would go on to invent modern beer writing, publishing the first definitive review of beer around the world, defining the notion of beer styles, fanning the spark of American craft brewing into the flame it is today, and championing great beer wherever it is brewed on the planet. But Belgium was his passion, the centre to which he always returned.

Traditional Belgian brewing was dying out when Jackson crossed the border. The brewers and drinkers of traditional styles were ageing, and their children were only interested in pilsner-style lagers. But when Jackson began to chronicle his discoveries, particularly in America, these dusty, half-forgotten breweries suddenly began receiving enquiries for large transatlantic export orders. The Belgian tradition was saved, and went on to inspire brewers around the world. When a young craft brewer finally grows weary of hops, she turns to Belgian styles for inspiration.

Usually, if a brewer tells you their beer is 'Belgian style', what they mean is that they're using the kind of yeasts that Emil Hansen tried so hard to eradicate from beer. That's a massive oversimplification of what 'Belgian' is: the range of Belgian beers is so diverse no one characteristic can sum them up in their entirety. But the way some Belgian beer styles use yeast is the main thing that had made them famous – some might say notorious – in the world of beer.

Michael Jackson referred to Belgian lambic as 'the champagne of beers', and he knew best. But lambic and I have history. Like Bamberg's smoked beer, I've never really got on with it and always suspected that its biggest fans were trying a little too hard. The most famous lambic brewer in the world is Cantillon, in the Brussels suburb of Anderlecht. Last time I was here was in 2005 with a minibus full of beer writers. As the whole group swooned while brewer Jean-Pierre Van Roy presented his beers for tasting, beer writer Ben McFarland and I caught each other's eye and pointed to our glasses, mouthing 'Really?' and rolling our eyes at each other, before turning back and nodding vigorously with the rest of the group. One man was actually moaning with pleasure.

Cantillon don't add any yeast to their beer: they allow it to be inoculated with whatever is in the air in the Senne Valley. The local population of microflora help produce a beer that's sharp, sour, tart, and, to many, not like beer at all. Before now, the best use I've ever found for a Cantillon beer was at a beer and oyster matching dinner. Cantillon's Rose de Gambrinus, dubbed 'the Laphroaig of beers' thanks to its ability to divide opinion into adoration and horror with very little in between, was put into service as the base of a shallot vinaigrette. It worked perfectly.

Apart from that, I've always given Cantillon beers a wide berth, but they stake out the opposite end of a scale of yeasty character and philosophy pinned at the commercial end by Emil Hansen. I can't write about yeast without exploring them again, so here I am, on a Saturday morning in late spring, in a seedy Brussels suburb, preparing myself to drink sour beer. I hope you're grateful.

The first thing I notice is that the Cantillon brewery is much busier than it used to be. There's a bar and seating area that weren't here on my last visit, and about fifty people are milling around, some waiting for a brewery tour, others settling into a mid-morning drinking session. Most of them wouldn't have been old enough to drink when I was last here a decade ago.

The whole place is suffused with a sweaty, cheesy aroma, and I don't think it's coming from the mostly male, very earnest beer fans. The beer is a product of this entire building, not just the brewing vessels within it, and in turn the building itself has been impregnated with the beer. They've fused into two aspects of the same creation.

Jean-Pierre Van Roy – the third generation of Cantillon brewers – is still here. There's a framed photograph of him above the merchandise stand, next to his predecessors, wearing an ill-fitting suit. Today this master brewer, the most famous creator of lambic beer in the world, is sitting by the door in his flat cap and scarf, collecting admission fees as we enter.

I approach the new bar and decide to head straight in and get this over with. Cantillon Lambic, young and fresh, is served from the cask, and there's a creamy surge before it settles down. It looks pale and innocent, indistinguishable from a lager from a short distance away. Closer to my mouth and nose, it's doughy and sweaty, like an adolescent's bedroom. As I raise it to my lips, my tongue involuntarily curls away, attempting to hide at the back of my mouth. I have to force it flat to accept the beer

It's raw and brash, like the teenager who inhabits the bedroom conjured up by the nose. Initially I find it difficult to pick out specific flavour notes, because my tongue is still trying to get away from it of its own accord, a physical reflex that I'm still struggling to control. I give it my full attention, sipping again, trying to settle my palate as I've done many times before. And the beer begins to unfold. There's the sharp citrus of grapefruit with a kind of sweaty fruitiness, and, underneath, a grainy malt character.

'Prochaine tour en français?' asks one of the people working here. It really is much busier than it used to be, and there were no guided tours when I visited for the first time on my first trip to Belgium in 2004. Back then it was just Jean-Pierre and his family. We didn't hit it off that time either.

I decide to move on to the geuze. You may not be astonished to hear that young buck lambics aren't to everyone's taste, so the practice here is to age them in wooden barrels and then blend them to achieve a pleasing whole. As you age the beers they get richer and mellower, calmer, and yet more complex, just like people. But a geuze has an advantage over us in that it's a mix of the best bits of young and old, a blend of beers aged usually between one and three years.

Cantillon geuze has a richer, mustier aroma than the lambic. It's much drier on the palate. The tartness is subtler, like good home-made lemonade rather than sharp grapefruit juice. But the dryness is really something – it's the most interesting characteristic of a beer that's often described as 'sour'. It has a real depth to it. When I was writing about cider (to which many lambic beers bear a close resemblance) it struck me that 'dry' is often used to describe an *absence* of flavour, the opposite of sweetness in a drink where all the sugar has been fermented out. Whereas this is dryness as a solid presence of something. There's bread and dried fruit. It's a complete beer, moreish and yet satisfying, too, so you want to keep returning to it and drinking more, but slowly and steadily. It gets finished much more quickly than the lambic and I'd quite like another but –

'Next tour in English?'

About a dozen of us step forward.

Cantillon has been a family brewer since 1900. It's still brewing the same beer, using the same recipe, even most of the same equipment, and the same wild yeasts from the local environment. These are collected when the wort sits in a big copper tray called a 'coolship,' under the eaves on the top floor of the brewery. While there's a roof over it, the sides of the room are open to the elements. Our guide tells us that Cantillon is 'the last one representing this tradition' and describes the beer as 'a wine of cereals, a contact between the air, full of yeast, and the wort. The wort cools in the open air over one night. No control. Nature decides.'

Yeast can't actually fly through the air of its own accord. It relies on various different ways of getting around from one sugary stash to the next, from dust motes to fruit flies. When you've been brewing for as long as Cantillon, there's also a culture that's evolved here in the room, on the roof beams above the vat. Wild yeast isn't just wild yeast: there are microorganisms in the room that prosper because they like it here, adapting over time to the man-made environment, probably living in the wood and falling into the cooling beer.

Because they're reliant on having only the right cultures being present in the air, brewing at Cantillon traditionally takes place only from November to March. The perfect temperature for the night-time rest is between minus 3 and plus 8 degrees Celsius (27 and 46 degrees Fahrenheit). Warm summer temperatures mean other cultures thrive, which even by Cantillon's standards are not right for the beer. Jean-Pierre Van Roy's grandfather enjoyed perfect temperatures pretty consistently between mid-October and May, but global warming means Jean-Pierre himself has never experienced such a long brewing period. Now, even November to March is starting to look threatened. In November 2015, Cantillon had to pour away three brews because the temperature was between 10 and 15 degrees Celsius (50 and 59 degrees Fahrenheit). As the brewing period shortens, so does the amount of beer the brewery can create. 'We only have five months to brew and our production is very limited,' Jean-Pierre told the press after pouring away his beer. 'If we lose a week we can survive, but three weeks or more would be more complicated.'

Once the beer is inoculated with the yeasts in the environment, it's put into wooden barrels to ferment. The smell as I walk into the barrel room is incredible. It's incense and sherry and a hint of vinegar, and something I identify as cedar wood, but probably isn't. There's a heavy silence in the room, almost as if it's the presence of something rather than an absence of noise. The voices of other tours in adjacent rooms fall away. People in this room automatically lower theirs. I could very easily over-romanticise this place, but it's very peaceful and I don't want to leave. I want to settle in and read a book here – or write one.

My final Cantillon beer of the visit is a sixteen-month-old lambic, straight from the barrel, unblended, but softened by age. It takes three years to make a complete geuze, so this one is almost halfway there. It's completely still, with a bit of haze. It has a brash, funky aroma, and to drink it's tart and dry, much more restrained than the young lambic from earlier. It really is very wine-like, even to the point of having a bit of tannin. It makes me realise that 'sour' beers and the yeasts that create them are often misunderstood and misrepresented.

Brettanomyces is the wild, uncouth relative of *S. cerevisiae* and *S. pastorianus*. It was first classified at the Carlsberg Brewery in 1904 by Niels Hjelte Claussen, a younger colleague of Emil Hansen, who was investigating the marked differences between continental beers produced with new single strain yeasts and the more complex character of British ales, the finest, strongest examples of which were aged in wooden barrels for up to a year. Experiments attempting to brew these ales with new single strain yeasts had resulted in beers lacking in character, and Claussen wanted to know why. He discovered a different strain of yeast, identifiable by its long, torpedo-shaped body compared to the lemon shape of *Saccharomyces*, and said it probably existed 'as a general infection' in most British breweries, 'and it may probably be found in all such places in the pipes, utensils and vessels of the breweries where such infections may creep in and get fixed'. In honour of where it was found, Claussen named his discovery 'British fungus'. Under the custom of translating scientific names into Latin, this became *Brettanomyces*, and was applied to a family of different yeasts identified by Claussen.

Claussen's use of the word 'infection' here is the root of continuing debate over the nature of *Brettanomyces*. Many accounts of Claussen's discovery claim that he was trying to explain the spoilage of British beer. In fact, he was trying to explain its appeal, and why its character didn't translate to beers brewed with pure cultivated yeast strains. As he told a meeting of English brewers in 1904, *Brettanomyces* was 'absolutely necessary to bring English stock beers into proper cask and bottle condition, and to impart to them that peculiar and remarkably fine flavour which, in a great measure, determines their value'.

But the word 'infection' is invariably used in a negative sense. In the age of scientific brewing, it seemed *Brettanomyces* (I'm going to switch to

'Brett' now, because, understandably, that's how most brewers refer to it) was a variable still outside brewers' control. And while it may have been a desirable characteristic in strong, aged, stock ales, it was more intrusive in cleaner, lighter beers such as continental lagers or the new weaker British 'running ales' that would eventually become known as real ale. Brett produces acetic acid – the base of vinegar – as well as flavour compounds that are musty, earthy and spicy, evoking the positive aspects of the farmyard barn, and sometimes sourness. In the right place, balanced with the right flavour elements from beer's other ingredients, these attributes can be seen as beneficial, adding extra depth. In 1908, one brewer sent a letter to the editor of a Chicago publication called *The Western Brewer: and Journal of the Barley, Malt and Hop Trades* saying he had been 'advised' to use Brett to 'improve the flavour and taste' of his ale. But in most brewing traditions Brett was seen as a fault, an infection in the common sense of the word, and was stamped out.

Although not quite everyone agreed.

The discoveries of Pasteur and Hansen didn't hit everywhere at the same time. The isolation of single strain yeasts presented brewers – or at least, those possessing deep enough pockets – with a choice. Pasteur first shared his methods with British brewers, who created beer on an industrial scale for industrial workers in towns and cities. That Hansen's best yeast happened to be a bottom-fermenting strain was the final boon needed for golden, pilsner-style lager to conquer the rest of the world. But lagering capabilities, refrigeration and lab facilities adequate to keep single strain yeasts were all expensive. The big brewers of Copenhagen, Munich and Amsterdam made heavy investments and grew huge, setting pale lager on a path that would eventually lead to it accounting for more than nine in every ten beers in the world.

Belgium was different. Brewing was an activity for the farmhouse, the small town and the monastery. Pasteur's influence took longer to get here. And when it did, it wasn't adopted in quite the same way as elsewhere.

By the beginning of the twentieth century, Belgian brewing was under threat from the popularity of British ales. Competitions were held to create beers that were distinctly Belgian in style. The Trappist monasteries – many of which were only just returning to brewing after having their ancient tradition smashed by Napoleon Bonaparte – built modern new breweries, embracing technology but maintaining the rural tradition. The beers got stronger, especially after a new law in 1919 prohibited the sale of spirits in bars and other public places.

The Belgian brewing tradition became defined. It stood against the belief that science was the only master. It didn't reject Pasteur's work, but the Trappist monks in particular believed it was being taken too far, creating beers that were purer and cleaner, but lacking in some desirable characteristics. For the Trappists, science was always counterbalanced by a relationship with their god and with nature. The natural wonder of yeast was not to be confined and defined entirely by the laboratory.

While Brett isn't a defining feature of most Trappist beers,* it plays an important role in many of the other Belgian beer styles that defined themselves against conformity over the course of the twentieth century, such as saison, oud bruin, Flanders Red and lambic.

Brett is not the only source of the 'wild' character of these beers. Two genera of bacteria – *Lactobacillus* and *Pediococcus* – are also very popular in some exotic Belgian and German beer styles. These create lactic acid – the main source of the sour character of beer rather than the sharper acetic acid created by Brett – as well as other aroma compounds.

Together, the attributes of Brett, *Lactobacillus* and *Pediococcus* create a character that's best summed up as 'funky'. It's a mix of sour, earthy and spicy, cheesy perhaps, or sweaty, but sometimes quite sharp and unexpectedly refreshing, and never, ever boring. Brett has an intimate relationship with wood, and as the lambics at Cantillon age, it ferments slowly, changing and developing their character. It's a process that exists within certain parameters but is always variable within those parameters. While a young lambic is defined by whatever is floating around in and outside the brewery, geuze blends these wild elements to create something more agreeable and even more sophisticated. Some of the best geuze producers in Belgium, such as Tilquin, are not brewers at all, but blenders who buy fresh lambics from the best brewers to create their own unique beers from them.

Yeast has never really been as simple as 'wild' versus 'domesticated' – there are all sorts of shades between the two. Brett is a different yeast, but it's been

---

* Although if you want to experience the nature of *Brettanomyces* in a beer that's different from the norm, curious, complex and wonderful without being too scary, you can do no better than Orval, brewed by Trappist Cistercian monks at the abbey of the same name.

classified and documented just like any other cultured yeast. You can buy it as a pure strain from yeast labs – a strain with a different character, sure, but still *cultivated*, if you're not lucky enough to catch it from the air around you. Wildness and cultivation are not opposites, they're a dance, part of the interplay whereby we have domesticated yeast, and it has trained us to do its bidding. Different beers and different yeasts are points on a scale, positions within the dance. And now, some of us are sashaying back to the fringes.

8. The Brewery's Most Valuable Employee

'When I think about my yeast,' says Yvan de Baets, brewer at Brasserie de la Senne, 'I don't regard *it* as an ingredient, I regard *her* as one of the team. She's my best friend in the brewery.'

Yvan and a fellow home brewer founded Brasserie de la Senne in 2003. They started small and grew quickly, moving to a new brewery in 2005. They'd always dreamed of brewing in Brussels, and the Senne river is the same one that flows through the lambic region on the outskirts of Brussels known as Payottenland.

Brasserie de la Senne stands out from the ranks of Belgian brewing because of a greater focus on the potential of hops. But that doesn't mean they, like some, are simply trying to make hoppier versions of Belgian beers, or, if you prefer, Belgian versions of the global hoppy pale ale template defined by American craft brewing. 'It's a balance of traditional and modern,' says Yvan. 'We have a modern approach but are inspired by tradition. We use ancient European hops, and look for subtlety. We may be hop-driven, but we're also looking for malt and fermentation flavours.'

By fermentation flavours he means, of course, the flavour compounds given off by yeast. 'I have a very precise idea of what I want from the yeast. I know where to find it. I was given our yeast strain, and it's the greatest gift I've ever received. We use just the one house strain. It takes a lifetime to get to know your yeast – I only have one life, so I have one yeast. I prefer to adapt recipes to her rather than get a new yeast.'

The fermentation vessels here illustrate the point about mixing old ideas and new knowledge. 'I worked in a 1930s brewery which had circular, open fermenters, and I loved the ester profile they gave. So I studied tank geometry, and managed to build these to get the same profile. I wanted zero hydraulic pressure for the yeast – I wanted to put her under no stress at all. When a yeast is stressed she works faster, but she isn't happy, and she releases compounds that are signs of stress. These are vertical fermenters. There's some pressure in there, but we keep them half full, so there's lots of headspace. It's a swimming pool for the yeast.'

The fermenters are squat and round, and resemble something from the set of a 1960s *Doctor Who* episode. I've never seen anything like them before. The production capacity of a brewery is dictated not by the size of its brewhouse – the collection of big vessels in which malt is added to water, filtered, then seasoned with hops and boiled – but by the capacity of the fermentation vessels. It takes half a day to brew, but it takes around five days for a primary fermentation. There's no point brewing beer if you don't have the tank capacity to ferment it. Commercial brewers have got around this in several ways. They ferment beers faster, at higher temperatures. Whereas traditional lager fermenters, like those at Budvar, are horizontal, it makes better commercial sense to stand them on their ends and have vertical fermenters instead, maximising the amount of beer that can be fermented in a physical space, and collecting the spent yeast easily when it sinks to the bottom of the tank. And they look for ways to cut the conditioning time of lager. Budvar age their beers for 100 days. In some big commercial breweries, this process has been reduced to seventy-two hours.

And here's a man who only ever fills his precious fermentation capacity halfway, because he'd rather his yeast enjoyed a pleasant swim than getting stressed by making twice as much beer.

'We do two weeks for lagering a light beer, three weeks for something stronger. There's no extra technology in fermentation or lagering. There's technology in the brewhouse and bottling line. But here, in the fermentation tanks, this is where the beer is made. There's a secondary fermentation in the bottle or keg. All our beers are naturally conditioned. We keep them at 22 degrees for fifteen days, and test each batch.'

This secondary conditioning, which allows the yeast to mellow and finesse the beers, takes the total brewing process for a bottle of Brasserie de la Senne beer up to six weeks. That's an awfully long time for brewing an ale in the twenty-first century.

Regarding the yeast as one of the staff is a cute line. But if the yeast were a member of staff, and you were a responsible employer in a small company, you wouldn't deliberately keep that member of staff under constant stress in conditions she didn't enjoy. Yvan de Baets walks the talk, and accepts that he can only make half as much beer as his brewery allows him to as a result.

All of this would be a great folly if it didn't make a difference to the finished beers. The reputation and demand for Brasserie de la Senne's product strongly suggests that it does.

'We make naked beers. If there's any problem, the drinker will notice it,' says Yvan. 'We make beer that brewers like. People with mature palates, who aren't just looking for big and new all the time. Taras Boulba is the beer that best expresses this philosophy.'

Taras Boulba also happens to be one of my favourite Belgian beers. There's a delicate, fine haze, fruitiness with a slightly tart edge. It's dry without being bitter. 'There are some very mellow esters from the yeast,' says Yvan. 'This is very important for drinkability. That's what beer should be. There's no shame in it being a volume drink.'

I love that. I love the idea that within the rarefied circles of beer appreciation, someone might allow a Taras Boulba to slip down easily and declare it to be too mainstream, too easy to drink, and therefore too big and popular. It has a character that would fill the marketers of global beer brands with sheer terror on the grounds that someone, somewhere, might notice that it has flavour. It would never occur to those marketers that this character is precisely what many non-beer drinkers might need in order to make them reappraise this remarkable drink. And it would never occur to beer snobs that this wider acceptance just might be a good thing.

9. The Yeast Hunters

In November 2009, it rained.

The town of Cockermouth in Cumbria, Northern England, is accustomed to rain. It lies a few miles from the west coast, between the sea and the peaks of the Lake District, and collects a lot of rain dumped by the sea air as it attempts to get over the mountains. But Cockermouth had never known anything like this.

The ground was already saturated from weeks of rain, so there was nowhere for any more water to go when, on 18 and 19 November, just over twelve inches of rain fell in twenty-four hours. Cockermouth was built on the confluence of two rivers coming down through the mountains, the Derwent and the Cocker. When they burst their banks, the centre of town sank beneath eight feet of water.

The Jennings Brewery sits on a wedge-shaped promontory between the two rivers. The high-water mark in the brewery was recorded at six feet one inch. The brewing vessels were up one flight and weren't harmed, but many departments – including the yeast store – were flooded and ruined. The Jennings yeast – cultivated in the brewery since its foundation in 1828 – was lost. Without the house yeast, the same beers could never be brewed again.

But brewers take precautions against disasters like this. In the Second World War, many breweries across Britain were bombed and lost their yeasts forever. They could carry on as brewers, but with new yeasts the beers would be different from what they had been before. Some never reopened. So, in 1951, the Brewing Industry Research Foundation (now part of a bigger group called Campden BRI) set up the National Collection of Yeast Cultures (NCYC). Since 1980, this collection has been stored at the Institute of Food Research, on a campus just outside Norwich. And just in case anything terrible should happen here, a duplicate collection is also stored off-site.

Chris Bond has been working here 'since 1984 or 1985', and he's the Collection Manager and Quality Control Officer. Steve James is a Molecular Taxonomist and the Deputy Curator. Together they form a double act that's half comedy duo, half buddy-cop movie, feeding off each other, finishing one another's sentences, cracking in-jokes, arguing and rolling their eyes at old foibles, until they make yeast curation seem like not only the most interesting but also one of the most entertaining jobs in the world.

We meet in the canteen. The walls are decorated with beautiful silk-screen prints of different yeast strains, blown up and artificially coloured. They show yeasts in fission and in brewing, and Steve asks me if I recognise what any of them are. Fortunately I recognise *S. cerevisiae*, shaped like fat, slightly furry lemons with craters at the ends that will eventually bud into new yeast cells. Apparently, if you know enough about your microflora, some of these pictures are hilarious.

Yeast

The collection currently houses 4,100 different yeast strains, belonging to 530 different species. It started as a brewing collection and is still dominated by *S. cerevisiae*, but as part of the Institute of Food Research it's now also charged with looking more broadly at things such as food spoilage, human infections and yeasts with medicinal properties.

'Some of the yeasts here have been responsible for winning Nobel prizes,' says Chris. If Yvan de Baets at Brasserie de la Senne loved his one yeast as a favourite co-worker, Chris seems like a proud parent trying to raise a large family. His ambition is to collect at least two samples from every identified yeast species on the planet. The 530 he has so far probably account for a quarter of all those that have been categorised, and they in turn account for somewhere between 1 and 5 per cent of what's out in the world.

'Wherever you can find bacteria, you'll find a strain of yeast that thrives there,' says Steve. 'We could probably go out to the stand of trees outside that window and find thirty to forty new varieties. There are people in the Amazon basin, in Ecuador, collecting them now. Microbially, we're in the equivalent of the great age of research tours by people like Darwin on the *Beagle*. Take leafcutter ant colonies, for example. They're full of yeast! Why? What are they doing?'

The management of the collection is now turning its attention back to brewing yeasts, as craft brewers seek 'something different, something new'. There seem to be several avenues that brewers pursue here.

The first is the revival of yeast strains from long-gone breweries. 'If a brewery closes down or moves to a new yeast strain, we ask if we can keep the strain. Chris makes an active effort,' says Steve, looking over at his partner protectively. Chris nods thoughtfully. The pair are delighted that in recent years, Lacons, a brewery that existed in Great Yarmouth from 1760 until 1968, and Truman's, born in 1666 in London's Brick Lane, and closed in 1989, have both been revived by new owners. Thanks to deposits in the National Collection of Yeast Cultures, in each case the new owners were able to re-culture the original yeast, so they were able not only to brew a new beer based on the original recipe and badged with the old trademark, but actually brew the original beers once more.

Another route of exploration is to try to revive yeasts used for brewing long before this collection existed, before anyone even knew what yeast was. 'A friend of ours, Javier, thinks he's managed to revive yeast cells from ancient pottery shards and ferment with them,' says Steve. 'They can dry out. They can germinate, spore and then lie dormant for a long time. I have to say we've not managed to revive any yet, though. Javier's shards were buried in soil, which is rich in nutrients, so the yeast could have survived. But that would mean that he's now brewing with the descendants of the original yeast, rather than spores that have been dormant for thousands of years.'

But Javier's explorations have pushed him much further into the mysteries of ancient brewing.

'He found out about a kind of *chicha* that was brewed for rituals and contained faeces and menstrual blood, and brewed with a non-*Saccharomyces* yeast. He had a terrible hangover the next morning,' says Steve.

'That's horrible!' I say.

'I know!' says Chris vehemently. 'You've got to be incredibly careful brewing with non-*Saccharomyces* yeast!'

I wait for some indication that this is a joke. There is none.

'You can't just assume "yeast is yeast",' continues Chris. 'They're not interchangeable. In nature, when you're looking at yeasts you're looking at communities. Just like with human communities, different members play different roles. We had someone who wanted to isolate a yeast strain from a fungal infection and make bread with it. That is not a good idea!'

Even within the same species, there's huge variation. In 2014, the team here collaborated with White Labs, a similar facility in the United States, to research the flavour-giving properties of a selection of five British ale yeasts. Genetically they were the same, but when they were used for brewing the same beer in identical conditions, each varied widely in both the timing and quantity of flavour compounds it produced. This is why maintaining a collection like this is so important. It makes me realise once again that when we talk about wild and cultivated yeasts, we're being far too simplistic. Each brewery has a strain that's unique, and in many breweries that strain dates back to before Pasteur and Hansen. Microbiology may have helped clean up the strain and keep it more consistent, but yeast continues to evolve and adapt to the conditions in its local environment, so that even yeasts that are identical will eventually grow apart if they're homed in different breweries. The yeast at Carlsberg showed small differences over time from the one that was re-cultured for Re-Brew. Brewers were unwittingly cultivating and evolving these strains for centuries before we knew what they were. This realisation has led some to argue that before humans domesticated animals such as dogs, we'd already domesticated yeast, and it's the microbe that's really man's best friend.

After we finish our teas and coffees, I get to see the lab. The first thing Chris wants to show me is something called TY elements. These are bits of DNA that can jump around the genome. In each strain, the number of these varies, so like hops and their oils, each strain has a unique footprint. This means brewers can use TY elements to check the provenance of their strain. Chris shows me some readings from the test that does so. They look like stills from the special effects sequence at the end of *2001: A Space Odyssey*. Each is mostly like the last, but there are small differences here and there. With these readings, Chris can keep track of the collection and ensure everything is what it's supposed to be.

In one corner of the room is a glass cabinet full of Petri dishes. 'You don't want to stick your head in there!' warns Steve. This clearly annoys Chris, which is why Steve says it, but Chris insists it's fine and gestures for me to take a sniff. It smells like Marmite.

'Interesting,' I say.

'That's one word for it!' crows Steve.

'It smells better than an incubator full of *E. coli*,' says Chris, and I realise from his tone that he's saying this from experience.

The storage technique for preserving the National Collection of Yeast Cultures is a wonderful mix of the latest technology and old-fashioned improvisation. The container that houses each yeast sample is a length of drinking straw, or, more specifically, the red and white striped Sweetheart drinking straws that used to sit on every fish and chip shop and Wimpy counter when I was a kid. You don't see them around any more. The brand still exists, but the straws now look very different. I think Chris bought up the entire remaining stock when they stopped making them. 'They're the best kind,' he says simply.

Chris cuts the straws into one-inch lengths, and melts one end shut to form a tiny plastic test tube. He fills this test tube with freeze-dried yeast, then melts shut the other end to create a sealed packet. These little plastic packets survive storage in liquid nitrogen very well. There are small screw-top vials with a hundred little slots in each, and each slot can hold six straws.

We go next door to the storage room. In the corner of the room, behind a steel chain, sits something that looks about the size and shape of an industrial washing machine. Behold: the National Collection of Yeast Cultures. Inside this super deep freeze the boxes of yeast samples are stored in liquid nitrogen at minus 196 degrees Celsius (minus 321 degrees Fahrenheit). 'They're in suspended animation,' says Chris. 'As long as you keep the liquid nitrogen topped up, they should last forever.'

A litre of liquid nitrogen expands by a factor of 730 when it becomes gas. It can drive all the air out of a room, and can be fatal if the room is not well ventilated. 'Apart from the very real risk of asphyxiation, it's quite safe to deal with,' says Chris. 'If it hits the skin, it just boils off. The real problem is finding anything,' he adds, as clouds of icy smoke puther up from the deep freeze. When this smoke hits my skin it's still minus 80 degrees Celsius (minus 112 degrees Fahrenheit), but I feel nothing. Wearing long rubber gauntlets, Chris brings out samples to show me, and carefully puts them away again.

'This might sound stupid,' I say, 'but do you have a favourite yeast?'

'NCYC1026. She's a bit of a fave,' says Chris immediately, with a racy tone.

Steve is quite excited about Norwegian farmhouse yeast strains known as *kveik*. Brewer Lars Marius Garshol has been collecting them, and NCYC is working with him to separate two or three interrelated strains. 'He sent me a mixture, and I'll send them back to him individually, and he'll brew with each one in turn. Can you then recombine them? Will each one work on its own? We don't know yet!'

Steve also loves *S. paradoxus*, the closest wild relative to *S. cerevisiae*, which shows no sign of ever having been domesticated by humans. How can it be so close to *S. cerevisiae* but have such a different history?

Chris has disappeared. Steve calls his name and there's no answer. We look outside in the corridor. It's empty. 'Is he coming back?' ponders Steve. 'No, it doesn't look like it. Sorry, he does this.'

Steve and Chris are perpetually looking for new yeasts. 'That's the thing,' says Steve. 'You're being a detective. What's its identity? What does it do? Why does it do it? I've always enjoyed that. Did I tell you about the yeast that lives with the leafcutter ants? In the colony in Panama? Well, it's also been found in the sea off Portugal. What the . . .? How? Why? Where is it and what's it doing there?'

And now Chris is back, carrying a huge book. He opens it to a page he's keeping with his thumb, and shows me his beloved NCYC1026. It's a fast fermenter, suited to mid or high levels of alcohol, and it's unusual in that it's an ale yeast that falls to the bottom after fermentation, leaving none of ale's estery, fruity flavour, and no foamy head on the brew. Weird,

He also shows me a yeast that's triangular and looks like a crudely drawn fish. Another has what looks like a pitchfork coming out of its head. It doesn't have a head, of course. But it does have a pitchfork. It grows around nematodes – a type of roundworm – and uses this protrusion to hang on to them.

'Yeast is an incredibly complex culture,' says Steve, 'and words like that are not euphemisms. There's always variation. Certain conditions select for certain subsets of the population. What we're getting now is genome sequencing that helps us understand this more. But the data always supports – not proves – the story.'

The most ignorant people I've ever met are those who think they know everything. The cleverest are those who at least have some idea of how much they *don't* know. Throughout my journeys on this book, I've learned ten times more about beer than I knew before, and I thought I knew a lot before I started it. Here, towards the end of those journeys, I've realised I know far less about yeast than I thought. Between them, what Chris and Steve don't know about yeast is staggering, and the amount they don't know seems to be increasing with every scientific advance.

The most perplexing question thrown up by yeast research over the last decade is the puzzle of the origin of lager yeast. Advances in genetic analysis have shown us that ale yeasts are made up of varying strains of *S. cerevisiae*, but lager yeasts, with their different characteristics, are actually a hybrid of *S. cerevisiae* and another mystery parent. In 2011, the mystery was solved: researchers in Patagonia, doing the kind of work Steve and Chris and their colleagues do, discovered a yeast that feeds on fungus spores that grow on trees, which they named *S. eubayanus*. Its genetic profile had a 99 per cent match with the mystery parent of lager yeast, meaning it is without doubt the yeast that hybridised with *S. cerevisiae* to create bottom-fermenting yeast. There's just one problem: the offspring of this union appeared in Europe a hundred years before it could possibly have been transported across from South America by humans. So how did it get here?

S. eubayanus has possibly been found now in China and other parts of Asia, too, so this might explain it. But no one is yet sure.

And then, in mid-September 2016, when I've all but finished my first draft of this book, a group of scientists from the University of Leuven in

Belgium announce that they have sequenced the genomes of 150 different yeasts collected from over a hundred different breweries around the world. By analysing this collection – mostly brewers' yeasts, with some wine, sake, bread and biofuel-making yeasts thrown in – they've been able to create the first ever family tree of domesticated yeast varieties.

The first big surprise the family tree throws up is that by estimating the number and longevity of each generation of yeast, the scientists have calculated that humans only began domesticating yeast in the fifteenth or sixteenth century. We still didn't know what yeast was then, but this is probably the time around which the first commercial brewers started repitching yeast from one brew to the next, aiding the evolution of strains that liked the conditions in each particular brewery. This is later than most brewing historians would suggest, and means that before this date all beer was made with wild yeast. This date ties in with the earliest references to lambic beers. It makes a lot of sense that if the practice of repitching and cultivating yeast became widespread at a given moment in time, that's when some brewers would choose a different path of specialising in spontaneous fermentation.

Domestication meant that yeast lost its ability to reproduce sexually (the prize-winning work of Claes Gjermansen notwithstanding) and developed the ability to digest maltose, a form of sugar that, as the name suggests, is abundant in brewing. 'With this domestication, the yeasts started to look almost like a new species, much like how dogs don't look like wolves anymore,' says Kevin Verstrepen, a yeast biologist at the Flanders Institute for Biotechnology who led the research.

So why did this domestication happen so much later than we thought? 'For most of human history, beer making happened in homes and sporadically,' says Verstrepen. 'Because it keeps for a long time, you can imagine making beer only once a month or so. If you're making beer sporadically, your short-lived yeasts will have to survive in the wild for generations between batches. They'll interbreed and share genes with other wild yeasts and stay feral. This is one reason why wine yeasts – which are used just once per year – look almost identical to wild yeasts even today. But around the 1500s and 1600s in Europe, you start to see more commercial brewing, in towns and cities and monasteries.' With continuous, large-scale brewing, the transfer of yeast from one brew to the next became practical.

But even after all this, the Leuven scientists still don't yet have a definitive answer for the origin of lager yeast.

10. Tanks on the Lawn

'The Heineken A Yeast is just like my wife: extremely demanding, but absolutely worth it.'

This remark from the Heineken tour guide gets a mixed reaction around the room. We're in a stylish, modern bar, illuminated by green neon, in the heart of the Heineken museum – sorry, the Heineken *Experience*.

Many breweries have a visitors' centre. Some have a museum. The biggest global brands – Heineken and Guinness being the two that come to mind – have fame and stature that make their owners believe they need to go further. The Heineken Experience* is the brewing process and the brand's story rendered as theme park attraction. This is literally true near the end of the tour, where you stand on a hydraulic platform and are immersed in a 360 degree recreation of the beer being bottled and packaged, feeling every rumble and jolt as it goes along the production line.

And then you're in the bar.

It doesn't matter what kind of brewery tour you have. You can be funnelled through an immaculately choreographed machine that cost millions of euros, like the beer itself, or you can follow a slouching bearded guy around an industrial unit as he points at brewing vessels and drawls about hopbacks and heat exchangers. It makes no difference: by the end of the tour, you want to taste that brewery's beer, *real bad*.

I've always had less of a problem with Heineken than I do with some other global beer brands, certainly much less of a problem than other beer geeks I know. In my advertising days I used to work with Heineken, and from that experience I know they genuinely care about the quality and reputation of their beer. In fact sometimes they care too much: I once got

---

* In their press releases, Heineken's PR people are mandated to always write the brand name in capital letters, so if they were writing to me about this, they'd have to call it the HEINEKEN Experience, or maybe even the HEINEKEN EXPERIENCE, rather like a seven-year-old behaves when they first learn how to write their name.

into a very sticky situation with a senior Dutch marketing executive when I tried to explain to him that people in Britain really didn't share his view that the watery, 3.4 per cent version of Heineken we then had in the UK was genuinely the best beer in the world.*

I don't mind Heineken, the beer itself, either. On a layover in Dubai on my flight to Australia for the Galaxy hop harvest, I found a bar that only sold Heineken and enjoyed it a great deal, under the circumstances. But I don't drink much of it if I have a choice of something else. I like a well-made lager, and Heineken is a well-made lager, but its flavour profile is a little too sweet for me.

That sweetness derives from the aforementioned demanding A Yeast. In 1888, Dr Hartog Elion, a disciple of Pasteur, used Hansen's techniques, which Carlsberg had shared freely with Heineken, to isolate Heineken's own single strain bottom-fermenting yeast. Here in the Heineken Experience we're told that this yeast 'changed the future of beer forever'.

Now, that's just bad form. Heineken was one of the few breweries rich enough to take early advantage of Emil Hansen's breakthrough. To use Hansen's work to create your own single strain yeast is fine – that's what Carlsberg had intended. But to write Carlsberg and Hansen out of the story, to claim that this – copying Carlsberg's technology – is the yeast that changed the future of brewing, is just rude – especially when there's a letter in Copenhagen from Heineken thanking Carlsberg for the yeast samples and instructions on what to do. But when it comes to the detail on brewing and ingredients, big brewers seem to feel the truth is there to be twisted to suit marketing's purposes. So according to the Heineken Experience, the Heineken laboratory is responsible for 'isolating and growing the perfect yeast – the best, purest yeast ever – for every brewery, for now and forever'.†

---

* 'But why should they believe that it is?' I asked, wanting him to give me some tangible facts we could use in the ads. 'BECAUSE THEY WANT TO!' he bellowed, banging hard on the table between us and making the whole room rattle. For this and other Heineken-related reasons I've written about in previous books, my career switch to writing arrived just in time.

† On the same tour, we're told that Heineken only uses hop extract – which many brewers regard as cheaper than and inferior to cones or pellets, and which Josef Tolar insists provides bitterness and nothing else – because whole hops have a sour character. This is something I have never noticed, never heard discussed among beer geeks, and never been told by any other brewer.

What saddens me is they don't even need to lie like this. The truth is impressive enough. The Heineken here is smooth and creamy with just a touch of bitterness. The flavour imparted by the A Yeast is distinctive. And Heineken's laboratory set-up is clearly a good one. Heineken is not the biggest beer brand in the world, but it is sold in more countries than any other brand. The character and consistency of the A Yeast is surely responsible for a large part of that success. They should be able to celebrate that without claiming credit for the work of a rival brewery without whom they would never have been able to isolate and culture their famous yeast.

Bearing all this in mind, the main reason for my trip to Amsterdam seems impudent. *Carnivale Brettanomyces*, a festival of wild yeast and spontaneously fermenting beers, is in its fourth year. According to the organisers, this weekend-long beer festival at various venues across the city is 'an ode and platform to the less obvious and unknown fermenters', offering 'a broad spectrum of alternative fermented beers: lambic and Flemish Red, bone-dry pale ales and leathery stouts, *Gose* and *Berliner Weisse*'.

These beers are fermented by organisms that would strike terror into the heart of Hartog Elion and his descendants, and now Heineken's home city is flooded with them. The wild boys have their tanks parked on Heineken's lawn. This weekend, Amsterdam is a clash of beer cultures in both senses of the phrase. In the green corner: the control and consistency that brewers have been working towards for hundreds of years, the culmination of a process that gave us microbiology and modern beer brands. In the green, red, orange and purple corner: naturalness, wildness, spontaneity and danger. This is a fight for the soul of beer.

Like every big city, there are many more beers and beer bars in Amsterdam than there were last time I was here nine years ago. Before heading along to the festival venues I decide to have a quiet drink on my own to centre and collect myself, and walk into an 'American beer bar', narrow and gloomy, with bare wooden floorboards and walls papered in beer labels. Sitting at the first table I pass are Andreas Fält and Steve Holt, friends from the UK brewing industry. Andreas imports exotic craft beers, and he's here with an international group of sour beer fans enjoying a blood-orange *Berliner Weisse* beer from the Sahtipaja brewery in Sweden, and insists I join them.

'I've been trying to get some of the Sahtipaja beers into the UK for a while now, but I've failed, so I've come here to drink them instead,' he says.

'So you're a fan of sour beers then? I thought you were really into your IPAs.'

'I'm a sour *fanatic*,' says Andreas, 'and I missed the first three years of this event. It's great to see the sour beer community coming together. After massively hopped IPAs and big stouts, it's the next evolution in the beer market. It clears your palate and resets it. It has big potential.'

After my recent Cantillon conversion, I don't disagree. But for me, sour beer still has a touch of attitude about it. It feels as though people who were drinking hoppy IPAs ten years ago were happy then that their choice of beer said something cool about them: 'I love this beer but you probably won't like it because it's quite challenging. You see, my palate is so much more sophisticated than yours.' And then big IPAs became mainstream. If you're a craft beer snob, you're no longer special. So the snobs have retreated behind the wall of sour, climbed to its ramparts and said, 'Fine, have your IPAs. But let's see you try to mainstream *this*!'

But I'm guilty of my own bad habits and thinking, too. I fell in love with IPA in a big way. It became such an obsession that I undertook a three-month sea voyage to India with a barrel of IPA to recreate the conditioning the beer underwent in the nineteenth century. This had a near-catastrophic effect on my finances, my marriage and my sanity. On a day-to-day basis, New World hopped pale ale is all I drink, and I'm supposed to be a beer writer. Habitually I'm little different from the old blokes in the pub who will only ever drink Foster's Top. So I've come here with an open mind, to meet sour beer on a level field.

Andreas is thrilled to find some beers by Crooked Stave, a brewer in Denver, Colorado. Ten years ago, this style of beer was something you had to go to Belgium to find. Now, the first question anyone asks when a new beer is presented is 'Where's it from?'

'The UK, the Swedes, the Dutch, the Americans of course, even Spain – everyone is experimenting,' says Andreas. The *Carnivale Brettanomyces* programme lists brewers attending from the UK, Belgium, Denmark, Norway, Sweden and Italy, as well as fifteen based here in Holland, a country regarded by most as having only big lager brands.

The first Crooked Stave beer is Surette Provision Saison. Brewer Chad Yakobsen did his master's degree on *Brettanomyces* before setting up the Crooked Stave Artisan Beer Project to bring his findings to life. Surette

Provision is brewed with *Brettanomyces* yeast and aged in wooden barrels. It has a soft, perfumed aroma and a building, teasing sourness that makes your mouth water as you swallow. There's a creamy yeast sediment left in the bottom of the bottle, so you can try the beer with or without it. While many of us have an aversion to cloudy beer and most brewers work very hard to get their beer to 'drop bright', adding 'finings' to beer to give yeast something to coagulate onto and sink to the bottom, there's a tradition with the wheat beers of Belgium and Germany that you pour the beer without the sediment, have a taste, then swirl the bottle and pour the sediment in for the complete flavour. In some bars the yeast is even served in a shot glass on the side. Here, when I pour the sediment into my glass it swirls, milk-like, through the body of the beer. The aroma fills out, and floral notes bloom. It's softer and rounder, and builds to a higher peak of tartness.

Referring to a beer, or even a style, like this as 'sour' simply doesn't do it justice. In fact it's inaccurate. *Brettanomyces* can digest a wider range of sugars than *Saccharomyces* yeast, meaning more of the sugar has been turned to alcohol. (The souvenir T-shirt of the festival has a doodle of a goat and the slogan 'BRETT will eat everything.') *Brettanomyces* mostly gives beer a dry rather than a sour taste, or some combination of dry and sour. People describe these flavours as musky, horsey, or barnyard. There are teasing hints of cloves and other spices, and the supposed 'sourness' might come across as appley or citrus. Some have a spritzy acidity akin to a crisp white wine – which no self-respecting wine fan would describe as 'sour'.

Tasting Surette Provision makes me think about the spaces between flavours, the relationship between dryness and sourness. We know what 'sweet and sour' means in a food context. We understand a scale of sweetness to dryness in wine. In white wine, 'dry' means acidic. But in red wine, dryness is defined by tannins, the compounds that give an austere, sometimes arid effect in the mouth, as well as body and structure, something that's more about the way it *feels* rather than taste itself. What its fans enjoy about Brett is that it's characterfully dry rather than dryness just meaning 'not sweet'. Beers like this are all about sour and dry working together, an alternate continuum of flavour, a back way that we don't normally travel.

Next, we pay thirty euros for a 750ml bottle of Noyaux from Cascade Brewing in Portland, Oregon. This describes itself as a 'northwest style sour ale', aged in oak barrels for fourteen months, after which raspberries and apricot noyaux – an almond-flavoured crème liqueur made from apricot kernels – are added for a further seven months of ageing.

The idea of adding fruit to beer once filled me with deep suspicion, and still does if the brewer doing it is just looking for a new gimmick. But it's an important insight into the history of beer. Fragments of ancient pottery shards suggest dates, honey and other fruits were often added to a brew, and not just for flavouring. Yeasts live on the skins of fruit, and adding them to the mix could have been the trigger for fermentation, a tastier alternative to sorghum brewing sticks.

But beers like Noyaux still freak me out when I taste them. I guess they're the palate's equivalent of a roller coaster, scary and thrilling, too much for some, addictive to others.

Amid the machismo of the craft beer world, after the palate-numbing intensity of hops and the heavyweight bulk of imperial stouts, the conversation between Steve, Andreas and his friend Ana over this beer is all about its wildness and intensity. But, really, many of these beers balance complexity and delicacy. No, they're not for everyone, but they're not rough. In a way, they're not wild at all. They're sophisticated, because they're blended by someone who understands them, who understands flavour. And not everything here meets that description.

11. Gammon and Goat

There are two types of people who walk into a specialist beer bar.

The first walks up to the bar, makes eye contact with the server, then looks along the pumps, perhaps frowning critically, before ordering quickly. The second enters the bar and gets halfway across the room before they see the chalkboards on the wall and comes to a halt, gazing at the board, open-mouthed, sometimes for minutes at a time. In a festival situation, these are often the ones openly carrying programmes. In London, I'm very much in the first camp. In Arendsnest, my favourite bar in Amsterdam, I'm firmly in the second.

Katjelam Flemish Rye is rounded and rustic. Its character doesn't benefit from being broken down into base elements such as 'sour' and 'earthy' – the whole is more than any compartmentalised description can evoke.

Oedipus Zur Wilden Ria is a beer the sourheads tell me I must try. It's a mix of *Berliner Weisse*, Belgian old lambic and a rhubarb-flavoured pale ale. It smells of ripe feet, the sweetness of rot and decay rather than sourness. At first I just get torrid dryness, and then other flavours emerge like zombies. No, that's not right – at first there's tart, lemon meringue, then the dryness, followed by something that reminds me of *moules marinière*. No, wrong again: it's Parmesan cheese. No, gammon – definitely gammon.

I've come to Arendsnest to watch a live blending event, which sounds incredibly exciting. It takes me a while to find it – and this is a small bar. On one of the tables outside by the canal sits a small cask. With no announcement or fanfare, someone starts pouring beer in through the bunghole. Twenty people watch, buzzing with smartphones, and I run across, before slowing down as I approach the table and have a quiet word with myself.

We are watching, filming, photographing and making notes about a man pouring beer into a funnel.

Next in goes a two-litre carton of yoghurt. This is followed by a bottle of red wine, then more beer, with different geeks taking it in turns to pour, while everyone else films and photographs. As Michael Pollan notes, fermented flavours are invariably those most prized by a culture. But they are also the most culturally specific, the most likely to divide opinion around the world. The idea of eating whale meat that's been buried in the ground for months until it's rotten and stinking is instinctively repulsive to people who would readily eat soured, mouldy, rancid milk products, and vice versa. I remind myself of this as I leave the spontaneous blenders to their work.

Carnivale Brettanomyces was the idea of Jan Lemmens, a young man who encountered Belgian-style beers while working in Amsterdam's best bottle shop. He's still there, and organises this festival in his spare time, for no profit, purely out of dedication to and passion for a microscopic organism.

'The first time I tasted Brett, it changed the way I thought about beer,' he says as we sit down for a pint outside In De Wildeman, the hub of the festival. It's pretty close to what the British would call a pub. The Dutch would call it a brown bar. Its bare wood, simplicity and apparent age make it the perfect venue for a festival of wild beer, or indeed any other occasion for savouring beer.

At the bar a British brewery, Elgood's, is exhibiting their new range of specialist beers. Like many old breweries, Elgood's has a coolship similar to the one at Cantillon. Coolships aren't always intended to inoculate the beer with wild yeast – as the name suggests, they were originally designed to cool heated wort before it could be fermented. Elgood's coolship had been out of use for years before someone suggested they might use it to create beers with wild character, and age them in barrels with the 'British fungus'. There's an emerging rediscovery that the Brett character commonly associated with Belgian styles was originally a trait in British beers, and that it might be worth exploring how it manifests itself in those styles.

I sample a porter which has a nice, sour twist at the end from being barrel-aged with Brett. Elgood's believe this is how British beer would have tasted 200 years ago. I like it: the twist livens up a dark, dense beer.

'There are so many flavours to Brett,' says Jan. 'It's not just the one thing. I wanted to learn about the taxonomies, the characteristics of different strains within Brett. Beer is usually all about control and consistency. Brett changes and develops – it's different. People want complexity, and, after a while, IPA and hops don't really offer that.'

Jan is wearing a festival-branded T-shirt with a slogan about releasing the goat inside. I ask him about the symbol, which seems acutely relevant.

'Goats eat anything,' he says, 'and so does Brett.'

And I guess there's something about drinking everything, too, about pushing your horizons. The broader movement celebrating wild fermentation – its adherents refer to themselves as 'fermentos' – is about challenging our relationship with food and drink and the natural world that produces it, embracing rot and mould and questioning the sanitised culture that rejects them out of hand. Pasteur never intended his discoveries to be an all-out war on microbes, or that his name would be given to the process that attempts to obliterate them from our food chain.

12. Later . . .

The world is turning, but not on its axis. It's 1.30 a.m. and, finally drunk after pacing myself through a day of tasting extraordinary beers, I decide it's time to head back to my hotel. Most of the festival venues are in the north-west of the city, at the left-hand top of the concentric 'U's formed by Amsterdam's canals, and my hotel is just bottom right of the outside 'U'. I start walking south and east, criss-crossing streets that are still buzzing with possibility, and somehow end up outside In De Wildeman, which was north and west of the bar I started walking away from twenty minutes ago

The pub is the emptiest I've seen it all weekend, which shouldn't be surprising at this hour, but there are still around forty people in the small space, hunched over tables, drinking beer carefully.

I decide there is A Purpose for me being here. Before I can think what that might be, I've ordered a special, limited edition beer by Cantillon called Marmouche, which is made by soaking hand-picked elderflowers in two-year-old lambic. I'm nervous of it as the barman pours it into a glass and sets it before me and when I raise it to my mouth it's a bruiser, a storm-trooper that breaks down the door to the bedroom my palate is sleeping in and screams in its face:

– WAKE UP.

It looks like a lager, and tastes like everything but. Like a chainsaw, it slices through the accumulated fug of a day's beer drinking in a clean, efficient, almost surgical fashion. It bludgeons me into submission. It's nothing personal. This is good for me – a short, sharp shock to sort me out. It arrived announcing chaos, and leaves order.

– WANT TO TRY THAT AGAIN?

I take what I imagine to be a brave, lusty gulp, but there's still a surprising amount of beer left in the glass. It cannot, will not, be rushed.

It's now some time after 2 and In De Wildeman is finally closing up, or at least thinking about doing so, like a ham actor hoping for one more curtain call. Menus are collected lethargically. How long have they been sitting there in that precarious pile? Why are there only two empty chairs stacked on their tables? This is one of my favourite things about drinking in Europe, a long way from the aggressively precise chucking-out time that still characterises the British pub.

– I'M STILL FUCKING HERE.

Obediently, I take as full a draught as I dare. It goes beyond flavour: beer and fruit and holidays and bad 1970s sitcoms all seem to spill over my palate at once. Something dead and musty at the back (of my mouth? Of my mind?) warns me not to get too carried away. I said 'dead'. Do these flavours that I've been attempting to describe evoke life, or death? Is this what subconsciously attracts us to beers like this? Does the growing passion for wild beers indicate some kind of existential shift? I think of the broader

world of fermentation, the idea of controlled decay. Microflora, nature's
cleaners, composting and breaking down the dead to make way for the new
Bitterness and sourness are the two defining flavours of modern craft beer.
They're also the two flavours our palates are programmed not to like: the
taste of poison, and the taste of decay.

I think about Jan Lemmens and his goat. 'I'd love it if the goat could
become more than a local thing,' he said when we were chatting this afternoon. I think perhaps he doesn't realise that it already is, that he's tapping
into an expression of something deeper. In English, the term 'goatish' means
giving in to the appetites this city famously caters for. The goat inside is our
wildness, our lust for life.

As our lives become more tamed, more controlled by big brands and
global systems, media and work, we instinctively kick back to our wild roots.
We can see this in everything from the primal need to party that festivals
like this cater for, through to the desire brewers have to explore how things
were before we had chemistry, controlled breeding and genetics. Craft beer
has jumped on wild yeast because this whole scene stands directly against
brewers like HEINEKEN, rolling back the creeping suffocation of commercial homogeneity. Mainstream brewers are terrified by the thought of
a wild yeast even entering their brewery. Wild beer brewing isn't just about
taste – it's a political act. The goat is also a devilish symbol, threatening
corruption, seduction and abandon.

It's 2.15 a.m. I'm sitting in an empty pub, wondering if sour beer is trying to reveal to me the meaning of life and death. A pang of bitter lemon
calls from the back of my throat. I really should be in bed asleep as soon as
possible, even though there are still people on the streets outside, offering
the illusion that this could carry on forever, searching to feed the eternally
hungry goat inside. I finish my beer and set down the glass.

– GOOD BOY.

– SIX –

Reinheitsgebot

'We're here celebrating a law. A law! *When does that ever happen?'*

DR MARTIN ZARNKOW, Technical University
of Munich at Friesing-Weihenstephan

1. Introducing the *Reinheitsgebot*, #1

The *Reinheitsgebot* stands as a monolith in global beer culture: there's nothing else quite like it. For 500 years it has coughed politely in international conversations about beer and dropped strong hints that Germany takes beer more seriously than any other country in the world. No one else has passed a law stating that beer must only be made from its classic core ingredients: hops, barley and water (and later, once we understood it, yeast).

By implication, no one else cares quite as much about beer as Germany does. That's why, at least within the styles in which it specialises, Germany brews the best beer in the world.

Brewers in other countries that want to be taken seriously in brewing adopt this stringent, restrictive law voluntarily. If we brew using it, they argue, then we're really serious about quality. We're slamming the knife blade of our integrity an inch deep into the tabletop of the international brewing scene. We won't compromise. We won't cut corners. We mean it. We're straight-edge, hardcore.

Reinheitsgebot is a byword for brewing quality. There are new dangers in a world where one brewer – sorry, one 'Fast-Moving Consumer Goods marketing company' – controls more than a third of global beer production and sees the word 'investment' only as a sneaky euphemism for 'cost', and regards 'cost' in the same terms other, saner people view the word 'cancer'. We need a law – even a law that is no longer enforceable – to remind us of the essence of beer, to defend against the creep of cheaper adjuncts into recipes: to keep beer special.

2. Introducing the *Reinheitsgebot*, #2

The *Reinheitsgebot* is a sham. It's singularly responsible for holding back German brewing as the rest of the world enjoys a craft beer revolution that broadens the mind and the palate with a playful attitude towards technique, style and ingredients.

And you know what's worse? It never really existed anyway.

Somehow the *Reinheitsgebot* pulls off this great trick of not really being about beer purity at all, not being the first or oldest piece of food standards legislation in the world as is so often claimed, not being consistent in its approach, not outlawing as much as you think, and not even being an enforceable law. Until the nineteenth century it applied only to Bavaria. It was only formally adopted throughout Germany in 1919, and it was formally withdrawn in 1988 after the EU declared it a restraint of free trade.

Five hundred years my arse.

And yet, despite all that, it's *still* being used to stifle creativity in brewing! Widespread belief in the thing is suffocating German brewing, forcing one of the greatest brewing nations in the world to compete in the global craft brewing revolution with one arm tied behind its back.

3. The Loaded Smile

'Don't you put that fucking thing in your book. Don't you make me not buy your book. Don't make me not like you. OK?'

The famous German beer pundit smiles at me. It's a smile that says, 'I know that we've only ever spoken in the politest terms before now, and that this is probably the first time you've ever seen me display any kind of strong emotion because on the level that we usually speak, when we meet each other at various beer events around the world, we retain this veneer of professional courtesy, because even though we drink together, we've never really got totally wasted together, which is the shortcut to true friendship for people who don't get to spend hours and hours getting to know each other but are friends anyway, and I realise that on that basis my outburst might seem extreme and a little weird, so I'm smiling now to let you know that I was only joking, that it was only banter. But by not quite allowing the smile to reach my eyes, which are still full of warning, I'm letting you know that I fucking mean it, OK?'

You might think that's a lot of information to pack into one smile. Trust me, she managed it. Clearly, opinions on the *Reinheitsgebot* diverge, and feelings about it run high.

4. 500 Jahre

When I had the idea of writing a book about the four key ingredients of beer, it never occurred to me that the law which stated those were the only ingredients you're allowed to brew with was about to enjoy its 500th anniversary. On 23 April, 1516, during a meeting of the Bavarian Assembly of Estates, Duke Wilhelm IV issued a decree:

We hereby proclaim and decree, by Authority of our Province, that henceforth in the Duchy of Bavaria, in the country as well as in the cities and marketplaces, the following rules apply to the sale of beer:

From Michaelmas to Georgi [St George's Day], the price for one Maß [a Bavarian litre] or one Kopf [a bowl-shaped container not quite as large as a Maß] is not to exceed one Pfennig Munich value, and

From Georgi to Michaelmas, the Maß shall not be sold for more than two Pfennig of the same value, the Kopf not more than three Heller [half a Pfennig].

If this not be adhered to, the punishment stated below shall be administered.

Should any person brew, or otherwise have, other beer than March beer, it is not to be sold any higher than one Pfennig per Maß.

Furthermore, we wish to emphasise that in future in all cities, market and in the country, the only ingredients used for the brewing of beer must be Barley, Hops and Water. Whosoever knowingly disregards or transgresses upon this ordinance, shall be punished by the Court authorities confiscating such barrels of beer, without fail.

Should, however, an innkeeper in the country, city or market buy two or three pails of beer (containing 60 Maß) and sell it again to the common peasantry, he alone shall be permitted to charge one Heller more for the Maß or the Kopf, than mentioned above. Furthermore, should there arise a scarcity and subsequent price increase of the bar-

ley (also considering that the times of harvest differ, due to location),
We, the Bavarian Duchy, shall have the right to order curtailments
for the good of all concerned.

It's worth quoting at length because when you see it in context it's a piece of pricing regulation that mentions the ingredients of brewing only as an afterthought. Yet it's that stipulation that's remembered, centuries after the pricing regulations became irrelevant.

The law has changed – to say the least – over time. Yeast wasn't included in the original list of ingredients because it would be another 300 years before anyone knew that yeast existed, and longer than that before anyone knew it turned base ingredients into beer.

But here we are. Whatever twists and turns it's enjoyed and endured, wherever it has or hasn't applied, the *Reinheitsgebot* was passed 500 years ago this year, and Bavaria – which has always had a fierce local pride – is celebrating. Beer and *Reinheitsgebot* form one of the main focuses of German tourism this year, 2016, and there are events happening all through the year, all across Bavaria. It's a celebration of the purity and possibilities of barley, water, hops and yeast. In July there's a big beer festival in Munich to commemorate *Reinheitsgebot 500*. After years of travel and research exploring these ingredients, there's nowhere else I could possibly end my journey.

5. Searching for the Beer Fountain

The train journey from Munich to Ingolstadt takes you through farmland that undulates in giant, gentle waves of green and gold.

Twenty minutes outside Munich you're in the middle of barley fields that have turned golden by the third week in July. The ears are bent over, still with quite an arc in them, but in a couple of weeks they'll be ready to go. Someone will be inspecting them daily, ready to call when they're fit. The uneven weather means that it's sweltering now, meaning the barley may well have ripened early, but heavy thunderstorms are forecast over the next few days. If my livelihood depended on this crop, that would be giving me sleepless nights.

Twenty minutes further north the landscape rolls away in squares and stripes of spooky green corn, golden stubble that's already been harvested, stands of trees and, more than anything else, hop gardens. Low white villages with red roofs and tall church spires punctuate the fields. The hops stand in big, confident blocks. This is the heart of the Hallertau region, the centre of German hop growing and officially the largest continuous hop-planting region in the world. It's rivalled only by Yakima Valley in its importance to the global hop supply. Like all other hop-growing areas I've visited over the last few years, it's distractingly beautiful. A month after Midsummer's day, the bines have reached the wires and the plants are standing tall. But to my inexpert eye they seem a bit skinny, and should have more laterals and bigger flowers by now.

Ingolstadt is a pretty little town on the northern bank of the Danube. It's home to Audi, Dr Frankenstein and his monster,* and the *Illuminati* – the real group rather than the stuff of paranoid conspiracy theory.

It's also the former home of Duke Wilhelm IV, and the town where the *Reinheitsgebot* was signed.

Because it was initially concerned with controlling prices, the *Reinheitsgebot* wasn't referred to as a 'purity law' until much later. Beer was an important staple and its steady supply had to be assured. But it wasn't the only vital commodity: bread was also essential, and bread was made from wheat. At the start of the sixteenth century there were two main styles of beer brewed in Bavaria: brown beer and white beer. Brown beer was made from malted barley, and white beer was made with the inclusion of a significant quantity of wheat. The *Reinheitsgebot* outlawed one of the two dominant Bavarian beer styles at a stroke. In the context of a law that's mainly about regulating price and supply, the restriction of ingredients can be seen as part of a broader move to regulate affordable food supplies. The day of its signing was also significant in the context of quality control: St George's Day marked the end of the annual brewing season. Later than that, the high temperatures dramatically increased the likelihood of beer being infected and spoiled by microorganisms, and I'm reminded of Cantillon, where

---

* The popular image of the Gothic castle up in the mountains comes from somewhere else. In the book, the doctor creates his monster at Ingolstadt University.

even if you want wild yeast inoculation you can't brew beyond a certain date or you get the wrong kind of inoculation. In 1516, the new law was implemented on the last day of the old brewing season to allow the longest time possible for brewers to adapt by the start of the next season in October.

Less certain, but still probable, is the idea that the *Reinheitsgebot* was also motivated by concerns about quality. It outlawed the use of cheaper adjuncts, and there are commenters on it who also cite Stephen Buhner's case here as well that it outlawed the use of psychotropic plants in beer. Again, there's little evidence that this was a primary concern among the nobles. A more likely secondary motivation is that it helped build a sense of Bavarian identity among a group of powerful men who came together to shape a common law. Bavarian 'brown beer' at this time was what we now understand as lager, brewed with bottom-fermenting yeast and stored in caves before serving.* The beers of northern Germany more closely resembled those of Belgium, deep and rich and brewed with a variety of flavourings. The *Reinheitsgebot* established a fixed identity for Bavarian beer.

The *Neue Schloss* is the old castle where Wilhelm lived and did business, and the specific location of the signing of the *Reinheitsgebot*. It's an imposing building, all blocky towers and tall, sharp gables, and is the landmark that gives Ingolstadt its identity. I've come here to get a sense of what those true motivations were, and what the nobles were like. But there's no commemoration of the *Reinheitsgebot*. The *Schloss* is now a military museum, and there's not even a plaque to inform anyone about the famous Bavarian purity law. On one doorway I find an old carving of men with barrels standing either side of a giant bunch of grapes. But there's no hint of beer.

I started talking to the German and Munich tourism authorities the previous November about what was planned to commemorate the 500-year anniversary, but they've been frustratingly vague on details of any specific events. Eventually they told me the main celebrations were taking

---

* So here we are again at the question of malt, its colouring and how we describe it. This was lager, which, as soon as I say the word, you imagine as pale gold. Bavarian-style lagers were always a deeper brown than the pilsner style we know today, but in the sixteenth century they were 'brown' compared to the 'white' of wheat beer. If you think about it, wheat beer isn't 'white' at all – it's pale yellow. Similarly, 'brown' beer couldn't possibly have been deep brown because there would have been no fermentable extract if it was. Whatever colour they really were, 'white' and 'brown' were descriptors relative to each other rather than the most accurate description possible of what they were.

place on 23 April. That would have been really helpful – if they hadn't waited until 25 April to let me know.

On St George's Day in 2016, Angela Merkel came to Ingolstadt and drank a (non-alcoholic) beer to celebrate. The town also commissioned what they claim to be the first ever communal beer fountain, which now stands somewhere in the streets of Ingolstadt. But none of the articles mentioning this bother to say where it is, and it's not on any map. Despite a lot of research online, I'm reduced to wandering the streets of Ingoldstadt randomly, hoping to stumble across something *Reinheitsgebot*-ey.

There are banners across all the main streets bearing the legend *500 Jahre Reinheitsgebot Ingolstadt 1516–2016*, and they remind me of the conversations I've had with tourist offices when I've asked 'So what's happening for the five-hundred-year anniversary?'

'We're commemorating it across the whole year!'

'Yes, but what's actually happening? What form will those commemorations take?'

'Well . . . we're commemorating it!'

Finally I pass a tourist information office disguised as a box office for musicals across Bavaria, but betrayed by a small window display of commemorative *500 Jahre Reinheitsgebot* coins that you can buy and look at in their special commemorative cases. I enter and ask the lady behind the counter if she has any details of *Reinheitsgebot*-related events or attractions. She looks nonplussed, thinks for a few seconds, then hands me a seventy-six-page programme packed full of stuff, none of which is happening this weekend. I guess I could have planned this better. But the big celebration in Munich is this weekend. Sorry for assuming there would be some kind of coordination here.

I find the beer fountain quite by accident, on a wall next to the town hall. It looks great, with a big bronze plaque depicting the ancient townsfolk of Ingolstadt filling their tankards from the tap that protrudes from the centre, above a small basin designed to look like an old wooden bucket. But the tap now dispenses water instead of beer. I suppose that makes a lot of sense.

Around the next corner I find a building that boasts a 700-year history, a large beer garden and a museum of brewing. But on a Friday lunchtime at the height of summer, as the commemorative banners flutter across the streets outside, it's closed.

Occasionally, at times like this I resort to childish sniggering for comfort, and so when I see a building with the word *Hofpfisterei* beneath a mosaic of a rakish seventeenth-century gentleman hoisting a tankard, I feel a sense of relief that lasts until I get to the door and realise that whatever I'd misconstrued as hop fisting is actually a word for 'bakery', and the boozing rake has nothing to do with the sign. Exploring further, trying to figure out what he's up to, I find some offices and a wool shop.

I Google the best beer garden in town. It takes a ten-minute walk outside the comforting old town walls and across a vicious ring road to get there, and, when I do, I find a long, modern kiosk on a small lawn full of deserted tables and chairs, surrounded by a forty-foot-high wall. It looks like a visitors' café belonging to an entrepreneurial maximum-security prison.

Ingolstadt is a pretty town, but it's not exactly buzzing with *Reinheitsgebot* love. I get the sense that in 2016 Germany isn't quite sure how to commemorate its most famous law. Examine it too closely and its contradictions unravel its true meaning.

6. 'Lecture Hall 13'

The following day I board a local train.and head to the suburb of Freising, home to the Weihenstephan Monastery. This is an unexpected bonus. Weihenstephan is commonly recognised as being the oldest continuously operating brewery in the world. Benedictine monks built an abbey on top of a hill here in 725 CE, and the brewery has been in operation since 1040, making use of the hill to dig deep cellars to condition the beer.

Weihenstephan is most famous for its wheat beer. In the International Beer Challenge, one of the beer competitions I help judge each year, the beers are tasted blind and Weihenstephan frequently wins its category, and has been named best beer in the world overall.

The *Reinheitsgebot*'s ban on wheat beer was extremely unpopular, and in 1602 the Elector of Bavaria, Maximilian Wittelsbach, replaced the ban with a system of special licences that allowed the holder to brew wheat beer. This would probably have been a popular move if he hadn't then bought every one of these licences himself, giving his family a monopoly on wheat beer production for the next two centuries. German *Weissbier* still retains a more aristocratic air than other beers.

Wheat beer is naturally hazy thanks to the proteins from the wheat and because yeast is still suspended in the beer. It can be filtered, so there are two main types of Bavarian wheat beer: *Hefeweizen*, meaning 'yeast wheat', and *Kristalweizen*, the filtered version.* I don't need to tell you which is the favourite of the true wheat beer fan. *Hefeweizen* has more body, and is immediately identifiable on the nose from its rich aromas of banoffee pie or bubblegum, seasoned with cloves. For a long time I assumed this character came from the wheat, because wheat is the big difference in ingredients from other beers and these flavour notes are the big difference in character from other beers. But I was wrong – these aromas are produced by wheat beer yeasts, which are different from conventional brewing yeasts. The new research into the genetics of yeast published in autumn 2016 show that most brewing yeasts limit the production of a compound called 4-vinyl guaiacol (4-VG), which creates clove and smoke flavours that most people don't want in their beer. We have steadily bred this flavour out of our brewing yeasts over the centuries, but it crops up in *Hefeweizen* yeast.

One of the people at the forefront of discovery is Dr Martin Zarnkow, Head of Research and Development at the Technical University of Munich at Friesing-Weihenstephan, and also much more than that. We've arranged to meet in 'Lecture Hall 13', which I discover to be a lecture hall in the same way that the 'nineteenth hole' on a golf course is still part of the game. I sit outside in the beer garden nursing my *Hefeweizen*, and soon a tall, stout, bearded man sweeps up the drive on a beautiful vintage motorbike, extricates himself from his helmet and speaks for two hours across a range of subjects that cover every aspect of this book (which he didn't know I was writing until I explained when we met) and far more beyond it. I realise he knows more about beer than anyone else I've ever met.

The mutual friend who introduced us promised me that Martin would give me chapter and verse on the *Reinheitsgebot*, that no one knew it better

---

* It's interesting, and potentially confusing, that the German words for 'white' and 'wheat' are so similar and sound virtually identical when said aloud. *Weissbier* means 'white beer'. *Weizenbier* means 'wheat beer'. The two terms are often used interchangeably.

than he did. After about an hour on the origins of brewing and the nature of yeast, I finally spot a pause long enough to ask him about it.

'The main thing about the purity law is that it protected bottom fermentation,' he replies. 'Firstly, fermentation with cereals other than barley doesn't give you the same flavour. Take oats. When oats have been malted, you get a special bitterness. Now in Britain, you use some oats in some top-fermented beers, but oats really don't work in bottom-fermented beers.

'Secondly, it's about longevity. When the *Reinheitsgebot* was introduced there were three main styles of beer in Bavaria: feasting and medicine beers, that were stronger and full of spices, top-fermenting beers that had a shorter shelf life and were really mixed fermentation beers, and bottom-fermenting beers, which were more stable and so had a longer shelf life. So the specific aim of the *Reinheitsgebot* was to protect bottom fermentation with barley malt and lagering, to get a stable beer.'

But we don't need that to create stable beer now, I argue. Technology has moved on.

'Ah, but lager beers were not only the most stable, they were also the most drinkable beers. Think about it: why does beer have such drinkability when, say, Coca-Cola doesn't? You drink a great lager beer and when you finish it, you immediately want another. You don't drink that kind of volume with anything else because it is not just thirst or refreshment, or even the alcohol. Beer has something more, and bottom-fermenting beer is more drinkable than top- or mixed-fermentation beers. Bottom-fermenting yeast cannot survive at 37 degrees Celsius (98.6 degrees Fahrenheit) – the temperature of the human body. But top-fermenting yeast can, so it survives the action of the stomach and restarts in the intestine and . . .'

Martin gestures below the table. I'm expecting a joke about a different kind of bottom fermentation, but instead he just mimes some unpleasant experiences.

I ask how he feels about the charge that the *Reinheitsgebot* stifles innovation. Martin shifts in his seat, as if the question makes him as uncomfortable as the results of yeast fermenting away in the lower intestine.

'If you want a specific flavour or aroma in your beer, there are ways to get it within the *Reinheitsgebot* tradition. Let's say some craft brewer wants an apple character to his beer, so he wants to add apple juice, which is not allowed under the purity law. Well, there's a brewer in Poland who has made a beer with smoked wheat malt. By controlling yeast autolysis, they get a transfer of acids that produces apple-like aromas. For me, *that's* innovation! Not adding apple juice to beer!

'The *Reinheitsgebot* teaches you to be innovative. We have a hundred and ten different bottom-fermenting yeasts here, all with different characteristics. Why not use that? In our top-fermenting yeasts, we have Birmingham ale yeast and Coventry ale yeast. Those places are very close together, yes? But the yeasts are very different. Or why not experiment with a mixed-fermentation beer such as *Berlinerweisse*?

'I like the discussion about the *Reinheitsgebot* coming from the craft beer industry, OK? I like their beers. There are different styles of beer available now. I like that they make their IPAs. What I don't like is their dismissal of the most drinkable beer in the world. This law has protected the style of beer that has become the world's favourite, because it promotes drinkability.'

He shakes his head, and takes a drink from his zero-alcohol wheat beer, a trade-off between his twin passions of beer and vintage motorbikes.

'The *Reinheitsgebot* is a collective force of will, and it's an excellent bit of marketing that is more along the lines of wine rather than beer. We're here celebrating a law. *A law!* When does that ever happen?'

Between these observations on Germany's purity law, our conversation ranges over a great range of subjects, and yet only one.

Martin has visited Gobleki Tepe, site of the oldest known temple in the world, in south-eastern Turkey. This is where Einkorn wheat was first domesticated, and Martin has devoted years to trying to rediscover the birth of brewing, 'Malting isn't necessary, enzymes are necessary,' he says while telling me about the ancient Sumerian beer he brewed. He tells me one ancient beer he brewed turned out red, and how he worked out that this was due to the iso-alpha acids reacting in the beer and changing its colouring, suggesting some 'brown' beers could have been darker because of the hops, and could still have been brewed with pale malt. He suggests the Vikings were the first to use hops, that hop poles have been found in Viking settlements in northern Germany, and I wonder if this would explain the anomaly of the hops in the Graveney boat, discovered in Kent and dating back hundreds of years before hops were supposedly first used in British brewing. He shows me the results of experiments that prove you can still get fermentable extract from unmalted grains. Malting yields by far the most fermentable extract, but Martin brewed with raw grain, crushed grain, cooked grain, and crushed and cooked grain. Malted grain gave a beer of 6 per cent ABV, but the unmalted, crushed and cooked grain yielded a beer of 3 per cent ABV, and there were traces of fermentation in all brews. He suggests that brewing could pre-date the invention of pottery because you could have brewed in pits lined with clay. And he says he may have found evidence of *S. eubayanus*, the mysterious second parent of hybrid lager yeast, in old Bavarian cellars that may establish and explain its presence in Europe before ships could have brought it back from South America.

Every single one of these stories is a new avenue of research, a potential new chapter for me to explore. When I get back home I end up spending a lot of money buying technical brewing books and academic journals that Martin refers to, and a story I thought I had almost succeeded in telling spirals off into more possible new directions than I can count.

But the story that sticks with me the most is Martin's take on a recurring theme on my journey: the reason evolution favours many of the processes and attributes that end up making beer. 'When yeast ferments, it gives off flavour compounds. But why is nature producing "rubbish"? Why does the yeast use its energy to produce products that are just waste? It's the same with hops – why such an intensive aroma?

'In each case, it's a cry for help, a form of communication. With yeast, when the oxygen runs out and there's still sugar, the yeast changes from producing alcohol to detoxifying the product. By-products cry out for insects – come and pick me up! We have photos of the legs of insects with a lot of yeast cells clinging to their hairs. The yeast hopes that the insect will fly to the next fruit, which has both sugar and oxygen available. The only insect we've ever observed being able to cut the skin of a grape is the wasp. Their intestine allows hybridisation of yeast within it, and hybridisation happens many times. We're still at the beginning of this research, still searching the cellars.'

Wasp intestines are breeding grounds that allow new strains of yeast to emerge and may well be the origin of modern lager brewing yeast. Fine. Nothing surprises me about beer any more. Thinking of the insects being attracted to the flavour compounds produced by yeast for that purpose, I share Michael Pollan's point about the most prized flavours in any culture being the products of some kind of fermentation.

'We can monitor their reactions now,' he says, 'by using gas chromatographs and observing reactions. The brains of fruit flies go crazy in contact with the products that the yeast creates! Just like we do with fermented flavours.'

So there we have it. In the end, we're little different from fruit flies. We respond to the flavours yeast creates because it wants us to come and rescue it, to help it move around to the next available sugar source. We are nothing but slaves to microbes, and we don't even realise, because the microbes give us so much in return.

7. 'Would You Like Another Beer?'

The evening before I meet Martin, the significance of what these four ingredients create is made clear to me in a way I hope never to repeat.

After a hot, sweaty walk to the station in Ingolstadt, the journey back to Munich is muggy and sleepy. The hop gardens of Hallertau slide past once again. The lowering sun strobes through the trees. An attempt to write up my notes degenerates into a game of *Angry Birds*. My wife, Liz, slumbers beerily in the seat opposite.

When we get off the train, we decide to head straight for the *Reinheitsgebot 500* beer festival in the centre of town. Having missed the official celebrations in April, this was the next-best time in the calendar to come and celebrate the anniversary, and I'm looking forward to meeting the organisers, learning more about the significance of *Reinheitsgebot*, and, of course, drinking some of the beer it helped to create and preserve.

The streets are still hot and steamy. 'If we're going to go out, I need to buy some leggings and get these sweaty jeans off,' insists Liz. She directs me towards a street café, actually the terrace of a hotel bar, and orders me to wait there for her with a beer while she pops into the department store across the road.

With a nice, crisp Helles in front of me, I take out my laptop and start to write up my notes. As I'm Googling Hallertau to check that Ingolstadt is indeed one of the key towns in the world's biggest hop-growing region, my fingers somehow slip across my trackpad and bring up a breaking news story of shootings in a Munich shopping mall. I realise that there have been sirens blaring constantly in the background all the time I've been sitting here. I look at the big department store Liz has disappeared into. I call her:

her phone has died after the long day out. I Google the story and learn the incident is happening in a shopping mall about four miles away from where we are. I relax, post a Facebook message to tell our friends we're nowhere near the trouble, and carry on writing.

A few minutes later, a few drops of rain are falling on my screen and a waitress appears telling me the terrace is now closed. 'It's OK, I can sit under the umbrella,' I smile, but she insists the terrace is now closed, but that I can carry on drinking my beer inside.

I find a table inside and sit down. Soon Liz arrives and sits across from me, cooler in her new leggings. 'There's a shooting incident happening in the city,' I tell her. 'It's OK, it's a few miles away from here so we're fine, but you should know.'

Liz orders a glass of wine and asks to borrow my iPad so she can see the news. And then, outside, everyone starts running, very fast, away from the centre of town.

In Hollywood movies, when people run from terror there's a lot of screaming. Extras emote terror in any way they can, eyes wide, arms in the air, bellowing at the top of their lungs. When it happens for real, the strangest thing about it is how silent it is. Scores of people are running down the street now, silent apart from the pounding of their feet. Around one in ten of them sees the door to the bar and runs in here instead, an escape route from the main drag. Their movements are jerky with adrenaline, but apart from that they couldn't be more different from their silver screen counterparts. In reality, when you think you're running for your life, screaming is a waste of oxygen that could be powering your limbs that bit faster, the cigarette paper between life and death.

'Im Keller. Alles im Keller!'

The staff are calm, professional and completely in control as they hustle dinner guests, drinkers and people fleeing who knows what at this stage down a very eighties cocktail bar-style spiral staircase into a small cellar space with doors leading off to the toilets, kitchens and storerooms. They stand at the top of the staircase, preventing anyone from leaving and, I guess, anyone else from entering.

There are around forty of us in the cellar. The mood is calm. Most are on smartphones, telling people they're OK and trying to find out what happened. There are eyewitness reports and then, later, definite confirmation of a second shooting incident in Marienplatz, just a few hundred yards away from the street we're in. The stampede down the street was from that direction. It seems we're closer to the trouble than we thought. Next, Munich's main train station, from which Liz and I just came, is quickly evacuated. We're caught between the two.

I go to the toilet and find a woman hiding by the urinals, behind her two sons. She looks embarrassed when I walk in and makes to leave, but I go to a cubicle and close the door. Back out in the cellar, a couple of other women are trying to get into a storeroom, but the door is locked and the staff try to explain that we're perfectly safe where we are. One teenage girl is crying and huddling into her mother's embrace. Under the spiral staircase lies the top half of a broken bar stool. The bit that connects to the base and allows it to swivel is missing the base it fits into, leaving a long metal spike. One man keeps picking up the chair by its arms, hefting it in front of him with the spike facing outwards, weighing up its potential. But the overwhelming feeling is not terror or panic, nor even anger, though that is stronger than I expected. It's confusion – the realisation that as events like this are unfolding, no one has any idea what's going on. All the breaking news reports online are half an hour at best behind what's happening here. Twitter might have up-to-date news from people on the ground, but a search for 'Munich' brings up lots of people expressing their distress and sending their hopes and prayers, and a few vile idiots already drawing conclusions that suit their hate-filled paranoia. None of it is of any practical use. I guess a search for 'München' would have produced better results, and I curse myself, not for the first time, for flunking German at school.

After about half an hour, a waiter brings out bottles of water. Without realising, Liz and I picked up our drinks glasses when we fled into the cellar, which I'm suddenly and emotionally very proud of, but they have long been emptied. The waiter jokes about pouring us some inferior wine and beer to what we had before. I point to my glass of water and say *'Englische bier'*, and he pretends to laugh.

Half an hour after that, we're allowed back upstairs. The police are telling everyone to stay off the streets, but everything seems calm. We decide to stay for a while, answering concerned texts and tweets, reassuring everyone we're fine.

My plan to finish this book with a celebration of the *Reinheitsgebot* is in ruins. The whole beer festival has been cancelled and the organisers, understandably, no longer want to do the interviews we had scheduled. This is obviously the least important factor of the tragedy that unfolded in Munich tonight, but it's the reason I'm here, and I don't know what to do now.

And then our waiter reappears at our table.

'Would you like another beer?' he asks.

In normal life, the whole meme of 'Keep calm and carry on' has been utterly debased. It used to be quite funny and charming, but has now become a mined-out cliché with no more value than a fake British bobby's helmet. But in Anna's Bar, and in the rest of Munich, those of us who are lucky enough not to have been caught in the storm are doing just that. I can't get the words out of my head, because watching the sentiment played out in real time is a fucking miracle. Right now, no one knows how many gunmen there are, or where they are, or if they're still at large. When our waiter asks us if we'd like another drink, this most ordinary interaction feels impossibly defiant. Never in my life, not even the first time I was able to buy alcohol legally, have I felt so empowered saying, 'Yes, a beer would be great, thanks.' Someone might come through the door firing in a minute. They probably won't. They almost certainly won't.* So what's the appropriate thing to do?

Keep calm and have another beer. That's how this journey ends. It may seem flippant, even nihilistic, but the only alternative to that is terror, and I don't think anyone in this particular bar is ready to give them that. After years spent researching how special beer is, suddenly its normality, its mundaneness even, seems like its biggest miracle of all.

8. The Best Pale Ale in the World

Months earlier:

'Mate, what's up with the British craft brewing scene?' asked Ross.

---

* A day later, it emerged that the teenage Munich mass-murderer killed nine people before turning the gun on himself. He acted alone. He had no obvious links to any Islamic terrorist organisation. He was bullied at school, seemingly targeted children in his shooting spree, and was obsessed with American high school killings and the atrocity committed by the fascist Anders Breivik in Norway in 2011. The 'three gunmen' didn't exist. The 'confirmed second shooting' in Marienplatz never happened. All the time we were cowering in the cellar, the lone gunman was already lying dead in an alleyway.

I was about to get defensive and reply, 'Nothing, why?' when I realised that this question, asked with this particular inflection, means something quite different to an Australian than it does to a Brit. We've adopted quite a lot of Australian idioms in Britain over the last few decades, but we've adapted them to our own uses. We put the word 'mate' at the front of a sentence when we want to have a quiet word with someone about something that's concerning us about their behaviour.

'Mate, why were you so mean to Emma last night?'

'Mate, don't you think you should maybe take it easy on the sauce for a while?'

We use it to show – or to pretend at least – that we're asking out of concern rather than trying to be hostile. If you do want to be hostile, of course, you just move the word to the end of the sentence, where it adds menace to a phrase that could otherwise be construed as concern.

'I'd be careful if I were you, mate.'

Ross didn't know this. Everything is so much more straightforward in Australia. He was using 'mate' in the way Australians do, almost as punctuation. When he asked me what was up with the British craft beer scene, he was saying, 'Hi, friend, how's all this exciting stuff in beer going your end?'

I worked this out just in time.

'It's amazing,' I smiled.

Ross Jursich and I were sitting in the Beach Hotel in Byron Bay. Referred to by Byron residents as the Beachie, it's a tropical paradise. It sits on the beach front, the link that joins Byron's two long, golden beaches that sweep away to either side, next to a small car park full of VW camper vans carrying surfboards.

The pub is essentially a huge, semi-covered courtyard. It has two big bars that are sheltered by little roofs and offer a degree of shade to barflies. Many of the beer fonts are encased in ice. It gets so busy here at peak season that the main entrance from the street below has separate doors for people entering and leaving.

Byron is home to surfers, dreamers and burnt-out hippies, and the Beachie is its slow-beating heart. The Stone & Wood guys saw this bar as their spiritual home – if not for them, then certainly for their beer. Pacific Ale was the first beer they brewed. With it, they wanted to capture the feeling of coming up from surfing or swimming, sand between your toes and salty water drying on your legs, and ordering a cold schooner at one of these two bars. They wanted Pacific Ale to be both the perfect beer for anyone drinking here, and a distillation of the atmosphere and the feeling of ordering that beer here for everyone drinking it anywhere else, a taste of Byron that could be sampled anywhere in the world.

In all my travels around the world exploring the nature of beer, that lager in a terrorised bar in Munich is the one I will always remember most keenly. But there are other beers, and other occasions that stand out now I'm at the end of my journey: the sophisticated blend of hops at Bale Breaker after a parched day in the hop fields; the intense reverence surrounding that first sip of Carlsberg's Re-Brew; the surprising delight of Schlenkerla Marzen in that ancient Bamberg brewpub. But I think the beer I enjoyed the most was the schooner of Pacific Ale I ordered to watch the sunset after Ross finished telling me the story of Stone & Wood and went home to his family.

When you drink in the Beachie, you soon realise the sense of drinking by the schooner. On my first day in Byron I insisted on pints, and by the time I reached the final third of the beer it was always warm and dull. Even with a schooner, the heat and humidity meant that within minutes the condensation on my glass would create a sizeable puddle on the tabletop.

Would I be pushing things too much if I said the beer was the colour of sunlight? Probably, but it did have a distinctive look to it. Unpasteurised and unfiltered, it was a golden haze in the glass that certainly evoked summer.

On the nose there was the unmistakable passion fruit aroma of the precious Galaxy hop, chased by a hint of mango. It smelled clean, fruity and fresh. In the mouth, it had a touch of resiny bitterness, but it was smooth and creamy, the fruit blooming, quenching and generous, just like the place and the people who live and work there.

Like all the great beers I've tasted, Stone & Wood's Pacific Ale is the product of a sophisticated understanding of how the alpha acids in hops behave, of water chemistry, barley malting and yeast husbandry. But that knowledge alone doesn't guarantee good beer. You also need inspiration, creativity and vision. These aren't separate from scientific knowledge – they're symbiotic with it.

At university I did a business studies course that was available as both an arts and a science degree. Some modules were classed as science, others as arts, and, depending on how many of each you did, you came out with either an MA or an MSc.

The business finance course was science, and the one about organisational theory and behaviour was art. In each, one of the topics was the theory of the firm. As with any academic course, the first thing you did was learn the definition of the term. In the finance course, the definition of the firm was $F = (P, K)$, where P is labour and K is capital – the equation means the firm is a non-specific function of the interaction of both. In organisational theory, the firm was defined as something along the lines of 'a complex organisation of people with different skills and agendas, negotiating to make decisions to achieve a variety of different outcomes'. One definition was trying to be far too simplistic, the other as wide-ranging and woolly as it could possibly get. One was trying to shut down debate, the other to open it up. Both were correct in the eyes of the university's examining board, but if I'd mixed them up and put the finance definition in my organisational theory paper and vice versa, both would have been marked wrong.

Art and science – and craft, whatever that means – are not real, they're not objective: they're categories created by humans as ways to clarify and classify the world. They're different ways of looking at the same things. Trying to understand beer by looking only at one or the other is like trying to look at a pint glass with one eye closed: you can see it, but you miss its depth, perspective and roundedness.

When I think now about the science of understanding water chemistry, the incredible and ancient technology of malting, the magic of hops and the fact that, ultimately, we're being controlled by microscopic fungi we still don't really understand, I realise the idea of 'raw materials' in beer is a fallacy. There's nothing raw about them. Each is incredibly sophisticated, each refined by centuries of scientific endeavour and discovery. After 10,000 years of brewing, we're still at the beginning of finding out what these four ingredients can do. And after all the work that's gone into understanding each ingredient so far, if the scientists, the maltsters, farmers and hop growers and, of course, the brewers who bring them all together, were to all get what they truly deserve for their efforts, and if the price of beer was an accurate reflection of its real worth, beer should be costing £10 a pint. As a drinker, I'm very glad it doesn't. But the fact that the most complex, varied, beautiful and difficult to make alcoholic beverage in the world is also usually its cheapest and most taken for granted, is something of a cosmic joke.

We settled down and built civilisations because modifying grain to give yeast access to its sugars took more equipment than simply picking grapes and crushing them, which was perfectly compatible with a nomadic lifestyle. Our beer styles evolved to suit local water sources, because we'd rather drink beer than the water itself. And hops? Hops stand apart as the one ingredient in beer that isn't strictly necessary, but is the only one most of us know. Hops are not practical in any way – difficult to grow, painful to harvest, and decaying and losing their essence from the second we start handling them. But we adore them still, for what Meantime's Alastair Hook calls their 'prettiness', the way the look, smell and taste of them makes us feel.

We apply the best thinking science can offer in order to increase our aesthetic pleasure. We pursue rigour and excellence in our pursuit of hedonism. And that's why beer represents, for me, at the end of this journey, the very best of everything we are.

ACKNOWLEDGEMENTS (AND DISCLOSURE)

I was lucky enough to be able to travel around the world to write this book. None of the money raised by pledges from supporters who helped crowd-fund the cost of the original British publication went towards this travel: it was only possible because of the generous support of brewers and their associated suppliers. It's common practice for journalists to be offered press trips by the organisations they write about, but some people regard this practice with suspicion, as if it might taint or bias the copy resulting from that trip. I know that the support I received for this book didn't sway what I wrote – usually these are companies I admired anyway, and at no point did any of them ask that I write about a given subject, or write about it in a cer-tain way, or ask to see copy before it was published here. I would therefore like to thank the following companies for their support, and also declare to the reader that I received support in the form of flight/ground transport and/or accommodation from: Budweiser Budvar, Carlsberg, Greene King, Guinness, Charles Faram, Hop Products Australia, Meantime Brewing, Shepherd Neame and Stone & Wood. Thank you for your generosity and kindness. This book would not have succeeded without you.

A great many more brewers, maltsters, farmers, hop growers and yeast scien-tists were generous with their time, records and occasionally the odd sandwich or glass of beer. Thank you so much for indulging me: Bale Breaker Brewing, Brasserie de la Senne, Crisp Maltings, Hogs Back Brewing, Hampton Estate Farms, Hop Growers of America, Molson Coors, the National Collection of Yeast Cultures, Puterbaugh Farms, Roy Farms, Scotney Castle hop farm, Warminster Maltings, Weyermann Maltings and Westerham Brewery.

A great many individuals, some within those companies, others associ-ated with them, were generous with their time and knowledge, and also worked hard to make visits and meetings happen on my behalf. Many are mentioned in the book but some were more behind the scenes, so thank you Robin Appel, Yvan de Baets, Roger Banham, John Bexon, Chris Bond, Frances Brace, Richard and Ali Capper, Roger Coe, Eibhlin Colgan, Jamie Cook, Paul Corbett, James Cuthbertson, Peter Darby, Jerry Dyson, Beate Fersti, Chris Garratt, Simon George, Claes Gjermansen, Charlie Gorham, Dave Griggs, Peter Haydon, Feodora Heavey, Alastair Hook, John Humphreys, Steve James, Ross Jursich, Jo Kreckler, Jan Lemmens, Tim Lord, Aisling McCarthy, Rob Moody, Rolf Munding, Kimberley Owen, Bob Pease, Lotte Peplow, Rupert Ponsonby, John Porter, Brad Rogers, Christina Schöenberger, Josef Tolar, Martin Kec, Sylvia Kopp, Tony Redsell, Paul Rudge, Ross Ryan, Ros Shiel, Ian Strang, Genevieve Upton, Caolan Vaughan, Robert Wicks and Martin Zarnkow.

For encouragement, contacts, feedback, ideas, moral support, calming words and all kinds of other help, thank you to Stephen Beaumont, Richard Boon, Emma Cole, Travis Elborough, Andreas Fält, Chris Gittner, Mike Hill, Steve Holt, Matt Kirkegaard, Kate Manning, Ben Metcalf, Dusty Miller, Wendy and Julian Pienaar, Dan Saladino, Evan Rail, The Seattle Twelve, Joe Stange, Adrian Tierney-Jones, Al Wall and Tim Webb. Thank you to Rod Jones and Ed Wray for forensic technical advice and proof reading: any remaining mistakes in the text are entirely my own. And special thanks to Jay Brooks, who, having had the idea to write a book very similar to this one, decided not to go ahead when he found out I was writing it. Jay, if you'd raced me, you would probably have won.

I'd like to thank Jason Cooper twice over: first, for being the editor who pressed the green light on my writing career back in 2002 and going on to edit my first two books, and second, for getting the band back together as soon as he arrived at Unbound in late 2014, seeking me out and urging me to write my first book about beer in eight years. Thanks also to Mathew Clayton, Richard Collins, Anna Simpson and all at Unbound for making it work and bringing this book to life, and to Neil Gower for yet another amazing cover.

Thank you to Michael Metivier and all at Chelsea Green Publishing in Vermont for taking on the international version of this book, understanding exactly what I was hoping to do with it, and giving me the opportunity to publish it in North America.

Finally, thank you as always to Liz Vater, for putting up with me, believing in me, and giving me a really hard time over boring, impenetrable, badly written first drafts.

BIBLIOGRAPHY

General

Bamforth, Charles, *Beer: Tap into the Art and Science of Brewing*, Plenum, New York, 1998

Barnard, Alfred, *The Noted Breweries of Great Britain and Ireland*, Joseph Causton & Sons, London, 1889–91

Brown, Pete, *Man Walks into a Pub: A Sociable History of Beer*, Pan Macmillan, London, 2003

Brown, Pete, *Three Sheets to the Wind: One Man's Quest for the Meaning of Beer*, Pan Macmillan, London, 2006

Brown, Pete, *Hops and Glory: One Man's Search for the Beer that Built the British Empire*, Pan Macmillan, London, 2009

Buckland, Khadija, *Marstons: A Brewer of Pedigree*, M. W. F. Hurdle, Nottingham, 1999

Buhner, Steve, *Sacred and Herbal Healing Beers*, Siris Books, Boulder, Colorado, 1998

Cornell, Martyn, *Beer: The Story of the Pint*, Headline, London, 2003

Eßlinger, Hans Michael (ed.), *Handbook of Brewing: Processes, Technologies, Markets*, Wiley-VCH, Germany, 2009

Gourvish, T. R., & Wilson, R. G., *The British Brewing Industry 1830–1980*, Cambridge University Press, London, 1994

Hornsey, Ian, *A History of Beer and Brewing*, RSC Paperbacks, Cambridge, 2003

McGovern, Patrick, *Uncorking the Past: The Quest for Wine, Beer and Other Alcoholic Beverages*, University of California Press, 2009

Mathias, Peter, *The Brewing Industry in England 1700–1830*, Cambridge University Press, London, 1959

Oliver, Garrett (ed.), *The Oxford Companion to Beer*, Oxford University Press, New York, 2010

Owen, C. C. 'The History of Brewing in Burton upon Trent', in *Journal of the Institute of Brewing*, Vol.93, no. 1, Jan–Feb 1987, pgs 37–41.

Pollan, Michael, *In Defence of Food: An Eater's Manifesto*, Penguin, London, 2009

Pollan, Michael, *Cooked: A Natural History of Transformation*, Penguin, London, 2013

Rogers, Adam, *Proof: The Science of Booze*, Houghton Mifflin Harcourt, New York, 2014

Schiefenhövel, Wulf, & Macbeth, Helen (eds.), *Liquid Bread: Beer and Brewing in Cross-Cultural Perspective*, Berghahn, New York, 2011

Sethi, Simran, *Bread, Wine, Chocolate: The Slow Loss of the Foods We Love*, HarperCollins, New York, 2015

Siegel, Ronald, *Intoxication: The Universal Drive for Mind-Altering Substances*, Part St Press, Rochester, Vermont, 2005

Malt

Anon, *The London and Country Brewer*, Messrs Fox, London, 1736

Appel, Robin, *The Malt-Stars of Warminster: The Remarkable Survival of Britain's Oldest Working Maltings*, Warminster Maltings Ltd, 2010

Beaven, E. S., *Barley: Fifty Years of Observation and Experiment*, Duckworth, London, 1945

Brooker, Peter, 'Barley Breeding and Development in the UK, an Historical Perspective', in *Brewery History*, Vol. 121, pgs 25–39, The Brewery History Society, 2005

Clark, Christine, *The British Malting Industry Since 1830*, Hambledon Press, London, 1998

Hyams, Edward, *Plants in the Service of Man: 10,000 Years of Domestication*, J. M. Dent and Sons, London, 1971

Katz, Solomon, and Voigt, Mary, 'Bread and Beer: The Early Use of Cereals in the Human Diet', in *Expeditions*, Vol. 28, no. 2, 1986, pgs 23–34

Mallett, John, *Malt: A Practical Guide from Field to Brewhouse*, Brewers Publications, Boulder, Colorado, 2014

Water

Chevallier, Jim, 'The Great Medieval Water Myth', blog post at http://leslefts.blogspot.co.uk, 16 November 2013

Cornell, Martyn, 'A Short History of Water', blog post at http://zythophile.co.uk, 7 December 2011

Cornell, Martyn, 'Was Water Really Regarded as Dangerous to Drink in the Middle Ages?', blog post at http://zythophile.co.uk, 4 March 2014

Hajn, Ivo, *Budweiser Budvar in the New Millennium*, Budweiser Budvar N.C., Czech Republic, 2002

Lynch, Patrick, & Vaizey, John, *Guinness's Brewery in the Irish Economy, 1759–1876*, Cambridge University Press, London, 1960

Palmer, John, & Kaminski, Colin, *Water: A Comprehensive Guide for Brewers*, Brewers Publications, Boulder, Colorado, 2013

Pilkington, James, *A View of the Present State of Derbyshire, including The Natural History of the Medicinal Waters of Buxton and Matlock by Erasmus Darwin*, William Marriott, Derbyshire, 2nd Edition, 1803.

Watkins, George, *The Compleat Brewer; or, the Art and Mystery of Brewing Explained*, J. Coote, 1760

Webb, T. J. B., 'Water at St. James's Gate Brewery', February 1967, paper written for Guinness and accessed at the Guinness archive, St James's Gate, Dublin

Hops

Bickerdyke, John, *The Curiosities of Ale and Beer: An Entertaining History*, Field & Tuer, London, 1889

Bignell, Alan, *Hopping Down in Kent*, Robert Hale, London, 1977

Calagione, Sam, *Brewing up a Business: Adventures in Entrepreneurship from the Founder of Dogfish Head Craft Brewery*, Wiley & Sons, New York, 2005

Cordle, Celia, *Out of the Hay and into the Hops: Hop Cultivation in Wealden Kent and Hop Marketing in Southwark, 1744–2000*, University of Hertfordshire Press, Hatfield, Hertfordshire, 2011

Corran, H. S., *Notes on St. James's Brewery*, Guinness Brewery, 1964

Darby, Peter, 'The History of Hop Breeding and Development', *Brewery History*, Vol. 121, Brewery History Society, 2005, pgs 94–112

Bibliography

Doel, Fran & Geoff, *The Hop Bin: An Anthology of Hop Picking in Kent and East Sussex*, The
History Press, Stroud, Gloucestershire, 2014

Hieronymous, Stan, *For the Love of Hops: The Practical Guide to Aroma, Bitterness, and the
Culture of Hops*, Brewers Publications, Boulder, Colorado, 2012

Hop Research Institute, 'Zatecky Chmel', accessed at the Institute's website,
http://www.chizatec.cz/en

Lawrence, Margaret, *The Encircling Hop: A History of Hops and Brewing*, SAWD
Publications, Sittingbourne, Kent, 1990

Maugham, Somerset, *Of Human Bondage*, George H. Doran, New York, 1915

Orwell, George, 'Hop Picking', in *New Statesman & Nation*, 17 October 1931

Orwell, George, *A Clergyman's Daughter*, Victor Gollancz, London, 1935

Parker, Hubert, *The Hop Industry*, P. S. King & Son, London, 1934

Sackville-West, V., *Country Notes*, Michael Joseph, London, 1939

Simmonds, Peter Lund, *Hops: Their Cultivation, Commerce, and Uses in Various Countries*,
E. & F. N. Spon., London, 1877

Woodske, Dan, *Hop Variety Handbook*, Self-Published, 2012

Yeast

Agence France-Presse, 'Climate Change Blamed for Putting Belgium Beer Business at
Risk', *Guardian*, 4 November 1015

Bayley, Paul, 'An evaluation of the number and distribution of Burton unions', *Brewery
History,* No. 129, Brewery History Society, 2008, pgs 36–73

Callaway, Ewen, 'Ale genomics: how humans tamed beer yeast', in *Nature*,
8 September 2016

Connif, Richard, 'Discovering the Wild Side of Yeast', on http://www.takepart.com,
19 January 2016

Glamann, Kristof, *Jacobsen of Carlsberg: Brewer and Philanthropist*, Gyldendal,
Copenhagen, 1991

Glamann, Kristof and Kirsten, *The Story of Emil Christian Hansen*, The Carlsberg
Foundation, Denmark, 2009

Jackson, Michael, *Great Beers of Belgium*, 5th Edition, Lannoo Publishers, Belgium, 2006

Katz, Sandor Ellix, *The Art of Fermentation: An In-Depth Exploration of Essential Concepts
and Processes from around the World*, Chelsea Green Publishing, Vermont, 2012

Markowski, Phil, *Farmhouse Ales: Culture and Craftsmanship in the Belgian Tradition*,
Brewers Publications, Boulder, Colorado, 2004

Parker, N., James, S., Dicks, J., Bond, C., Nueno-Palop, C., White, C. and Roberts, I.,
'Investigating flavour characteristics of British ale yeasts: techniques, resources and
opportunities for innovation', in *Yeast*, Vol. 32, No. 1, pgs 281–7

Smit, Barbara, *The Heineken Story: The 'Lager' than Life Tale of the World's Bestselling Beer*,
Profile Books, London, 2014

Sparrow, Jeff, *Wild Brews: Beer Beyond the Influence of Brewer's Yeast*, Brewers Publications,
Boulder, Colorado, 2005

Turner, B. E., & Apponi, A. J., 'Microwave Detection of Interstellar Vinyl Alcohol,
CH_2=CHOH', *The Astrophysical Journal*, Vol. 561, No. 2, 18 October, 2001

Von Wettstein, D., 'Emil Christian Hansen Centennial Lecture: From Pure Yeast Culture to Genetic Engineering of Brewing Yeast', Lecture given to the European Brewing Convention, 1983

Walther, Andrea, Hesselbart, Ana, & Wendland, Jurgen, 'Genome Sequence of *Saccharomyces carlsbergensis*, the World's First Pure Culture Lager Yeast', in *G3 Genes Genomes Genetics*, Vol. 4, No. 5, May 2014, pgs 783–93

Wendland, Jürgen, 'Lager Yeast Comes of Age', in *Eukaryotic Cell*, Vol. 13, No. 10, October 2014, pgs 1256–65

White, Chris & Zainasheff, Jamil, *Yeast: The Practical Guide to Beer Fermentation*, Brewers Publications, Boulder, Colorado, 2010

Yakobsen, Chad, '*Brettanomyces* Dissertation', accessed at http://brettanomycesproject.com/dissertation

Rheinheitsgebot

Alworth, Jeff, 'Attempting to understand the Reinheitsgebot: 500 Years of Brewing Law', in *All About Beer Magazine*, Vol. 37, No. 1, 11 March, 2016

Klawitter, Nils, 'The Twilight of Germany's Reinheitsegbot', at *Spiegel Online*, http://www.speigel.de, 21 April, 2016

INDEX

Index

Index

Index

Index

Index

ABOUT THE AUTHOR

©FACEphotography

Pete Brown is a British author, journalist, blogger and broadcaster specialising in food and drink, especially the fun parts like beer and cider. His broad, fresh approach takes in social history, cultural commentary, travel writing, personal discovery and natural history, and his words are always delivered with the warmth and wit you'd expect from a great night down the pub. He writes for newspapers and magazines around the world and is a regular contributor to BBC Radio 4's *Food Programme*. He was named British Beer Writer of the Year in 2009, 2012 and 2016, and Fortnum & Mason's Online Drink Writer in 2015. He lives in London.

petebrown.net
@petebrownbeer